Secret State, Silent Press

If truth is the first casualty of war, could war ever become the first casualty of truth? Implicit in Keeble's analysis of the Gulf 'War' – and the quotes here are appropriate – is the enlightening thought that had the British people known the facts they would never have sanctioned the West's bloody invasion of Iraq. Explicit, however, is the dark and disturbing story of myth-making media engaged in an unquestioning mission to support a dubious military adventure. It is uncomfortable for the journalists involved, like me, to read. But only by understanding how easily we were lured into accepting the word of the political and military élite can we hope not to repeat the exercise.

Roy Greenslade

Secret State, Silent Press

New militarism, the Gulf and the modern image of warfare

Richard Keeble

UNIVERSITY
UP *of* **JL**
LUTON PRESS

British Library Cataloguing in Publication Data

A catalogue record for this book is available from the British Library

ISBN: 1 86020 539 9

Published by
John Libbey Media
Faculty of Humanities
University of Luton
75 Castle Street
Luton
Bedfordshire LU1 3AJ
United Kingdom

Tel: +44 (0)1582 743297; Fax: +44 (0)1582 743298
e-mail: ulp@luton.ac.uk

Cover Design by Simon Walker
Typeset in Arial and Sabon
Printed in Great Britain by Bookcraft (Bath) Ltd, Midsomer Norton

Contents

Introduction

Most writing about the media and war fails to problematise adequately the nature of warfare or place the media within a wider, historically contextualised, social, economic and political setting. In contrast, this book seeks to problematise radically the Gulf war of 1991 arguing, controversially, that there was no war at all. At its heart lie these crucial questions: What kind of state systems were operating in the UK and US, the countries under review? What kinds of warfare do those states conduct? And most significantly, what roles does the press play in relation to these states and societies, and how does the press represent the wars they engage in?

I have been able to provide some tentative answers to these questions only through synthesising an eclectic range of theoretical and analytical perspectives. Thus theories are, for example, drawn from media and cultural studies, the sociology of militarism, various historical studies (for example, of the Middle East, of the US and UK domestic and foreign policies; of the secret services of the US, UK and Israel; of military technology); military strategic studies; propaganda studies; media content analysis and discourse analysis. Central to my argument is the notion of 'myth' which is used throughout in the sense of manufactured story/constructed illusion. The story carries considerable potency and credibility because it is not a complete fantasy. The mythical fantasy is, in fact, based on widely held assumptions, beliefs and ideologies. There is no massive conspiracy to con the public. Rather, the construction of the myth emerges out of profound political, historical, cultural, ideological forces which this work seeks to identify. Because the analysis of the construction of the myth forms the central theme to the book, the Middle East conflict of January-February 1991 will be referred to throughout either as the Gulf 'war' or the Gulf massacres.

The study sample takes in, from the UK: the *Sun*; the *Star*; the *Mirror*; the *Mail*; the *Express*; the *Guardian*; the *Independent*; the *Times*; the *Telegraph*; the *News of the World*; the *People*; the *Sunday Mirror*; the *Observer*; the *Mail on Sunday*; the *Sunday Telegraph*; the *Sunday Express*; the *Sunday Times* and the *Independent on Sunday*.

From the US, I focus primarily on the *Washington Post*; the *New York Times* and the *Los Angeles Times*.

The range of sources used to illuminate the text is very broad. They include:

- Academic journals – such as *Media Development*; *International Affairs*; *Race and Class*; *Media, Culture and Society*; *British Journalism Review*; *Security Studies*; *The World Today*; *Survival*; *Columbia Journalism Review*; *Journal of Communication Inquiry*; *Theory, Culture and Society*; *Journal of Communication*; *Journalism Quarterly*; *Current Research on Peace and Violence*; *Screen*; *Orbis*.

- Mainstream magazines – such as *UK Press Gazette*; *Journalist's Week*; *Newspaper Focus*; the *Listener*; *Atlantic Monthly*; *New York Review of Books*; *Harpers Magazine*; *Commentary*, *Le Monde Diplomatique*.

- Alternative/non-mainstream magazines and newspapers (particularly important since they provided information and insights into alternative, critical perspectives marginalised or silenced in the mainstrean newspapers and usually ignored in academic studies) – in the UK these include: *New Statesman and Society*; *Bulletin* of Article 19; *Index on Censorship*; *Khamsin*; *Socialist Action*; *Stop Press*; *Despatches*; *Media Workers Against the War Newsletter*; the *Journalist*; *Lobster*; *City Limits*; *Open Eye*; *New Left Review*; *Socialist Review*; *Middle East International*; the *Pacifist*; *New Internationalist*; *Journalist's Handbook*; *Living Marxism*; *Granta*. In the US they include: *Middle East Report*; *Monthly Review*; *Open Magazine*; *Covert Action Information Bulletin*; *Tikkum*; *Lies of our Time*; *Z Magazine*; *International Socialist Review*. And in France: *Mediapouvoirs*.

- Studies of the 'war': for instance, by Martin Yant (1991); Dilip Hiro (1992); Mohamed Heikal (1992); Norman Friedman (1991); Lawrence Freedman and Efraim Karsh (1993); edited by Victoria Brittain (1992); edited by Phyllis Bennis and Michel Moushabeck (1992); edited by John Gittings (1991); by the Commission of Inquiry for the International War Crimes Tribunal (1992)

- Studies of media coverage of the 'war': for instance, by John Macarthur (1993); Philip Taylor (1992); Douglas Kellner (1992); the Gannett Foundation (1991); Glasgow University Media Group (1991); Richard Steeden (1992); Martin Shaw (1996); edited by Robert Denton (1993); edited by Hedrick Smith (1992); edited by Hamid Mowlana, George Gerbner and Herbert Schiller (1992)

- Published speeches: for instance, by Godfrey Hodgson (1991); Martin Shaw and Roy Carr-Hill (1991); Tom Bower (1992)

- Biographies: for instance, by Richard Pyle (1991); Roger Cohen and Claudio Gotti (1991); David Yallop (1994) Tom Bower (1995)

- Autobiographies: for instance, by Harold Wilson (1974); Miles Copeland (1989); 'Andy McNab' (1993); Sandy Gall (1984; 1994)

- Journalistic accounts of the 'war': for instance, by John Simpson, of the BBC (1992); US freelance Rick Atkinson (1994); John Bulloch and Harvey Morris, of the *Independent* (1991); edited by Brian MacArthur (1991); as collected by the IPI (1991); by Ben Brown and David Shukman, of the BBC (1991); by Alex Thomson, of ITN (1992); by Christopher Bellamy, of the *Independent* (1993); by Richard Kay, of the *Mail* (1992); by Michael Kelly, US freelance (1993); by Stephen Sakur, of the BBC (1991); Peter Arnett of CNN (1994); Martin Bell (1995)

- Accounts of the 'war' by military leaders: for instance, General Norman Schwarzkopf; Sir Peter de la Billière; Gen Khaled Bin Sultan, Saudi Arabian Joint Forces Commander; Gen Colin Powell

- Analyses of the 'war' by military experts: for instance, Paul Rogers (1991); Edward Luttwak (1991); Christopher Lee; R.A. Mason (1991); Stephen Badsey (1992)

- Interviews with journalists:

  London-based: Roy Greenslade, then editor of the *Mirror*; Harvey Morris, Gulf desk editor at the *Independent*; Godfrey Hodgson, of the *Independent* (for background); Peter Almond, of the *Telegraph*; Mark Dowdney, of the *Mirror* (for background); Michael Evans, of *The Times*

  Middle East specialists: Martin Woollacott of the *Guardian*; John Bulloch of the *Independent*, Colin Bickler, Reuters war correspondent

  Front-line correspondents: Edie Lederer, of AP, based with US Air Force; Don McKay, of the *Mirror*, based at Muharaq air base, Bahrain; Keith Dovkants, of the London *Evening Standard*.

  Riyadh-based: David Fairhall, of the *Guardian*, and Fuad Nahdi, of the *Los Angeles Times*.

- In addition the views of other journalists from secondary sources are incorporated into the text. They include Gilbert Adair; James Adams; Kate Adie; Philip Agee; Gordon Airs; Steve Anderson; John Balzar; Barry Bearak; David Beresford; Ian Black; William Boot; Jeremy Bowen; Ben Bradlee; John M. Broder; Chris Buckland; Julie Burchill; Louise Cainkar; Alexander and Leslie Cockburn; Adel Darwish; Ray Ellen; Ben Fenton; Robert Fisk; Sandy Gall; Robert Harris; Max Hastings; Simon Henderson; Seymour Hersh; Brian Hitchen; Jim Hoagland; Robert Jensen; Peter Kellner; Saeed Khanum; Robert Kilroy-Silk; Phillip Knightley; William Kovach; Perry Kretz; Mark Laity; Jim Lederman; Nan Levinson; Richard Littlejohn; Andrew Lorenz; Andrew Lycett; Brian MacArthur; Paul Majendie; James Meek; Christopher Morris; Kate Muir; John Naughton; Dean Nelson; David Northmore; Richard Norton-Taylor; Maggie O'Kane; George Parker; Steve Peak; John Pilger; Rodney Pinder; Peter Preston; Peter Pringle; Alex Renton; Mort Rosenblum; William Schaap; Patrick Sloyan; Joan Smith; Ramsay Smith; Ron Spark; Martha Teichner; Bernard Toth; Patrick Tyler; Ralph

Vartabedian; Christopher Walker; Colin Wills; Bob Woodward; Peregrine Worsthorne; Woodrow Wyatt

Thanks to Professor Hugh Stephenson; Wynford Hicks; Bob Jones; Bruce Hanlin and Colin Bickler; George Gantzias, Professor Douglas Kellner; Waltraud Boxall; Elli Collis; Richard Steeden; Giovanni Ulleri. Special thanks to Maryline and Gabi – to whom this book is dedicated.

Richard Keeble
Great Abington, Cambridgeshire
May 1997

1 New militarism and the media: an overview

There was no Gulf war of 1991. In the way in which the term is generally used and understood, what took place in the Persian Gulf in January-February 1991 was not a war at all. It was nothing less than a series of massacres. This is not a mere semantic quibble. The distinction (and the accompanying notion of the 'war' myth) has profound theoretical and analytical implications for any study of the press coverage.

There was no credible enemy. The Iraqi army was constantly represented in the UK and US press in the run-up to the conflict as 1 million-strong, the fourth largest in the world, battle-hardened after the eight-year war with Iran; lead by monster madman Saddam Hussein. When in January and February 1991, Iraqi soldiers were deserting in droves and succumbing to one slaughter after another, Fleet Street still predicted the largest ground battle since the Second World war. Images of enormous Iraqi defensive structures with massive berms and a highly sophisticated system of underground trenches filled the media. In the end there was nothing more than a walkover, a rout. A barbaric slaughter buried beneath the fiction of heroic warfare.

The nature and significance of the 'war' were rather created in the realms of myth, rhetoric and media spectacle. Focusing on the conflict as a construction in this way can draw attention to the broad political and economic factors, the nature of the militarism of the states involved and the propaganda role of the mainstream media within those states.[1] Major, high profile wars are no longer fought as merely military events. People are slaughtered, children and soldiers are traumatised, buildings, hospitals, radio stations, tanks are destroyed. But major wars are now fought as media spectacles for largely

---

1   See Chomsky, Noam and Hermann Edward (1994): *Manufacturing consent*; Vintage; London. For a discussion of the propaganda model see Lester, Elli (1992): 'Manufactured silence and the politics of media research: a consideration of the propaganda model', *Journal of Communication Inquiry*; Iowa, University of Iowa; Vol 16. 1, Winter pp 45-55 and Rai, Milan (1995): *Chomsky's politics*; Verso; London.

non-strategic purposes. The Gulf 'war' had little to do with getting Iraqi soldiers out of Kuwait. It had little to do with protecting Saudi Arabia from an Iraqi invasion. It had little to do with protecting the oil supplies. The conflict had little to do with getting rid of Saddam Hussein. He was supported by the international elites of the East and West in the decade leading up to August 1990, he was supported by the CIA even after August 1990 and no doubt a powerful faction in the allied elite still supports his regime.[2]

It is impossible, in fact, to consider the origins of the conflict and the press construction of the Gulf war myth without reference to the integrated media, political, economic, military system. By the late 1970s a significantly new form of militarism was evolving in Britain and the United States from a system established since the Second World War. To a large extent, the Gulf war was manufactured to resolve some of the contradictions within this 'new militarism'. Paradoxically, the invention of the Gulf war also served the interests of the Iraqi elite in resolving some of the contradictions of old-style, classical militarism.

From militarism to new militarism

Resolving the democratic contradictions of militarism: in the UK

Traditional militarism of the Second World War, in which the mass of the population participated in the war effort, either as soldiers or civilians, threw up some serious democratic dilemmas for the Western elites. Throughout the West, the old elites were discredited by appeasement and collaboration with the Nazis. Progressive movements and trade union militancy flourished in Britain. (Harris 1984: 66) In 1944, the number of official strikes recorded was 2,194 – up to then the highest ever.[3] And mass employment encouraged the further emancipation of women. On the continent, a 'transnational revolutionary mood' emerged between 1943 and 1947. (Kaldor 1990: 86; Gunn 1989: 7-8)

A new liberal tone was even in evidence in the mass-selling newspapers in Britain. (Curran and Seaton 1991: 81-82; Lewis 1984: 221-225) The new liberal consensus backing widespread social reform and state intervention in the economy was to find expression in the Beveridge Report and the 1944 Education Act. (Giddens 1985: 242) Winston Churchill was used for rhetorical, ideological purposes by Margaret Thatcher when she was Prime Minister (1979-1990) to symbolise the greatness of Britain under a Conservative leader. (Barnet 1982) But Churchill, despite his virulent racist and anti-communist views,[4] had angered many on the right by introducing

---

2 Graham, Helga (1996): 'How America saved Saddam', *New Statesman and Society*; London, 20 September pp 24-26 and Keeble, Richard (1997): 'How the West pulls punches against its favourite demon'; Gemini News Service; London; 14 January.

3 Dabb, Tony (1995): 'Official secrets', *Socialist Review*; London; April pp 20-21.

4 See Ponting, Clive (1994): *Churchill*; Sinclair Stevenson; London.

Labour ministers into the national wartime government. (Morgan 1990: 6-8) Then, in 1945 a Labour government was returned with a massive, unprecedented majority.

Since 1945, the democratic problems posed by mass conscription have been resolved in a number of ways. In the UK, wars involving mass conscription have been eliminated from military strategies. The emphasis has shifted to nuclear 'deterrence' following the secret launch of the UK nuclear weapons programme in the late 1940s. Military strategy emphasises low-intensity operations away from the media glare. National service was ended, in the 1960s the War Department was renamed the Ministry of Defence and the nuclearised army became the professional, massively resourced institution of committed volunteers constantly prepared for action and denied any trade union rights. (Dockrill 1988; Wallace 1970)

New militarism is inherently anti-democratic. Shaw argues (1987: 153): 'The state would dispense with the people in a future nuclear war, it had largely dispensed with the pretence of involving them in preparing for war too. The secret, capital-intensive part of the state's military power was to be developed: the people were not expected to discuss or decide but merely to give their passive consent.' And to a certain extent, new militarism embraces the contradictory processes of militarisation and demilitarisation. According to Shaw, (1991: 14) 'Militarisation at one level has been accompanied by demilitarisation at others; for example, militarisation of elite politics or economic strategy has gone hand in hand with demilitarisation of mass employment, life and politics.' Moreover, new militarism does not constitute a complete break with traditional militarism since some of the elements of militarism (such as the emphasis on air power or the propaganda role of the media) continue in significantly modified form into the new era.

Resolving the democratic contradictions of militarism: in the US

The United States also witnessed some significant democratic advances during the Second World War. Unions gained in strength and workers struggled for higher wages. But these gains were quickly demolished. Hellinger and Judd (1991: 156-160) argue that the press's near unanimous opposition to the 1948 presidential campaign of the short-lived Progressive Party presaged its collaboration in the hunt for internal subversives in the 1950s.

Significantly, mass conscription during the Vietnam war (though not a total war for the US) was also accompanied by substantial social dislocation – with the emergence of student radicalism, black radicalism and urban riots. Since then, the emphasis has been on avoiding Vietnam-type confrontations. Technological development has been the army's top priority. The 1970s saw the shift to an all-volunteer army. Men have increasingly given way on the battle front to the (computerised) machine. As in the UK, military strategy also shifted to stress low-intensity conflict and the deployment of relatively small, elite forces often in secret missions. Short, manufactured, spectacular, new militarist wars have evolved from the early 1980s to reinforce the power of the political and economic elites and the marginalisation of the mass of the public. The shift has occurred – from militarism to new militarism.

New militarism and mediacentrism: warfare as fiction

Military strategy becomes essentially a media event: an entertainment, a spectacle. Warfare, moreover, is transmuted into a symbolic assertion of US and to a lesser degree UK global media (and military) power. Media manipulation becomes a central military strategy. This 'mediacentrism'[5] is a pivotal element of new militarist societies. Significantly, James Combs identifies the emergence of a distinctly new kind of warfare with the UK's Falklands campaign of 1982 and the US invasion of Grenada of the following year. He argues (1993: 277): 'It is a new kind of war, war as performance. It is a war in which the attention of its *auteurs* is not only the conduct of the war but also the communication of the war. With their political and military power to command, coerce and co-opt the mass media the national security elite can make the military event go according to script, omit bad scenes and discouraging words and bring about a military performance that is both spectacular and satisfying.'

The shift to volunteer forces and the nuclear 'deterrent' signalled in both the US and UK a growing separation of the state and military establishment from the public. The populist press, closely allied to the state, served to create the illusion of participatory citizenship. Moreover, the media play other crucial roles in new militarist societies by engaging the public in a form of glamorised, substitute warfare. Instead of mass active participation in militarist wars, people are mobilised through their consumption of heavily censored media (much of the censorship being self-imposed by journalists) whose job is to manufacture the spectacle of warfare. People respond to the propaganda offensive with a mixture of enthusiasm, contempt, apathy and scepticism. Yet most crucially, media consumption and public opinion polling provide the illusion of participation just as satellite technology provides the illusion of 'real live' coverage of the conflict.

MacKenzie (1984) has described the 'spectacular theatre' of 19th century British militarism when press representations of heroic imperialist adventures in distant colonies had a considerable entertainment element. Featherstone, too, (1993; 1993a) has identified the way in which the Victorian 'small' wars of imperial expansion in Africa and India were glorified for a doting public by correspondents such as William Russell, G A Henty, Archibald Forbes and H M Stanley.

But Victorian newspapers and magazines did not have the social penetration of the mass media of today. And Victorian militarism was reinforced through

---

5   This definition of 'mediacentrism' differs from that promoted by Schlesinger, Philip and Tumber, Howard (1994): *Reporting crime: The media politics of criminal justice*; Clarendon; Oxford. They apply it to studies of the media which focus on media content and journalists' relationships with sources. For this approach they substitute a 'source-media analysis' model.

a wide range of institutions and social activities: the Salvation Army, Church Army and uniformed youth organisations, rifle clubs, ceremonial and drill units in factories. 'In all these ways, a very large proportion of the population came to have some connection with military and paramilitary organisations.' (MacKenzie op cit: 5-6) By the 1970s this institutional and social militarism had given way to a new mediacentric, consumerist, entertainment militarism in which the mass media, ideologically aligned to a strong and increasingly secretive state, had assumed a dominant ideological role.

Within this media-saturated environment, Luckham (1984: 5) has identified the potency of the 'fetishism of the weapon' within what he describes as 'the armament culture' (though he avoids adopting the notion of militarism). During the new militarist wars media consumers were encouraged to identify with weapons of mass destruction, which, in turn, were constantly described as having human attributes. Moreover, Luckham argues that the modern, high-technology weapons of extraordinarily destructive firepower have transmuted warfare into a form of fiction. He says: 'The limitless possibilities opened up by nuclear physics, space technology, genetic engineering and artificial intelligence have been the staple themes of science fiction. Materialised in the form of nuclear missiles, laser beams, chemical weapons, germ warfare and computers they transmute war into a new and elaborate genre of fiction.' (ibid: 11)

During the Second World War, weapons technology and its use, culminating in the nuclear bombing of Hiroshima and Nagasaki, bore little relation to any strategic rationale. Military strategy had become profoundly irrational and had entered the realm of fiction. As Reynolds (1989: 151) argues, there is no evidence to suggest that control over weapons produced a consistent and rational relationship between the means of violence and the ends sought by its use. Since 1945 this 'fictionalisation' of military strategy has intensified with the development of weapons systems of ever-increasing firepower. Fred Halliday (1983: 545) has argued against this position suggesting that the Cold War was essentially a rational process. '...it was not irrational in that it reflected responses by conscious political agents in the United States to what they saw as a challenge to capitalist power.' But during the 1991 massacres, there was, in fact, little relationship between the massive firepower used by the US-led coalition forces and the threat posed. Militarism and, in particular, new militarism have sought at the level of media-directed rhetoric to legitimise and rationalise the profound irrationality and illegitimacy of the nuclear-based, high technology military system.

Since new militarist warfare is essentially a media spectacle, the military's main concerns are to control and manipulate the image. Unlike the militarist wars which lasted years, new militarist wars are over quickly. As Benjamin Bradlee, former executive editor of the *Washington Post*, commented bluntly of the events of January-February 1991: 'The trouble with this war was it was so fucking fast.' (Macarthur 1993: 147) But the Gulf 'war', which lasted 42 days, in new militarist terms was a long 'war'. The military become, then, the primary definers of the fast-moving event while journalists, kept far from any action, are in no position to challenge their inventions.

Moreover, the strategic imperatives of new militarism mean that wars become inherently difficult to report and 'fictionalisation' is further encouraged. They are fought by planes (to which journalists normally have no access) and in space and often at night. New weapons incinerate their victims making calculations of casualties even more difficult. The emphasis on computer games in military planning means that the distinction between 'real' and Nintendo-style wars becomes blurred. In these new wars, civilians don't die (except in 'accidents'), weapons are clean and precise, and the soldiers are all at heart pacifists. This is unreal warfare. As Phillip Knightley (1991: 5) commented: 'The Gulf war is an important one in the history of censorship. It marks a deliberate attempt by the authorities to alter public perception of the nature of war itself, particularly the fact that civilians die in war.' Yet the Gulf conflict, in fact, was not so much a unique event but the culmination of a process that began with the Falklands 'war' of 1982 and moved through the US attacks on Grenada (1983), Libya (1986) and Panama (1989).

According to the post-modernist French theorist Jean Baudrillard (1976; 1988), the contemporary post-modern culture is one of hyper-reality, of reproduction and simulation rather than production. Indeed, the mediacentric culture of new militarism is founded on imitation – with the nostalgic reinvention/reproduction of the rhetoric of classical militarism ('Hitler' Hussein, 'allies', 'heroism', 'liberation', 'Maginot Line'), of Hollywood or of sport dominating media and military discourse. Mann talks of 'spectator sport militarism'. He writes (1988: 185): '...wars like the Falklands or the Grenadan invasion are not qualitatively different from the Olympic games. Because life and death are involved the emotions stirred up are deeper and stronger. But they are not emotions backed up by committing personal resources. They do not involve real or potential sacrifice, except by professional troops. The nuclear and mass conventional confrontation involves at most 10 per cent of GNP – a tithe paid to our modern "church", the nation. The symbolic strength of the nation can sustain popular support for adventures and arms spending.'

New militarist wars end up as hyped-up media events with no more lasting effects than a popular TV series or sporting contest. Since the wars are manufactured they fail to articulate real threats, problems or conflicts that deeply affect the public and so are quickly forgotten – as in the cases of the US interventions in the Lebanon, Grenada, Libya, Panama and even the Gulf.

The threat posed by the 'enemy' is grossly exaggerated. The 'enemy' is globalised and in the process fictionalised. This process was rooted in the Cold War when the Soviet threat, it has been argued, was largely imaginary – serving to legitimise the West's (and in particular the US's) military-industrial complex, global ambitions and military adventures. (Kaldor 1991: 35; see also Halliday op cit: 549) Throughout the Cold War, Western intelligence services constantly exaggerated the strength of Warsaw Pact forces. (Adams 1994: 255) When the Soviet Union failed to intervene in Poland in 1981 following the emergence of the Solidarity movement, its military impotence could no longer be concealed. New enemies were needed if the consensus was to remain firm in the post-Cold War, new militarist era. This invention of enemies became increasingly desperate with the collapse of the Soviet Union. The manufacture of Saddam Hussein as the global threat culminated this process of enemy invention in the 1980s.

The manufacture of war – in the US and UK

Moreover, the causes of the conflicts lie more in the (unspoken) dynamics of US/UK domestic and foreign politics than in any credible external threats. These threats are largely manufactured, it can be argued, to hide the reality of unnecessary offensive action.

In the case of the US and the UK

- The appearance of a major 'war' was needed so that the US elite could eradicate the trauma of the Vietnam defeat from their collective memory. The first words President Bush proclaimed after the massacres were: 'By God, we've kicked the Vietnam syndrome once and for all.'[6]

A survey by the Gannett Foundation found that, in the coverage of the crisis and massacres in the major US press, the word most commonly used was Vietnam.[7] Vietnam was a war that 'got out of control'. Desert Storm in the Gulf, in contrast, was the US military's attempt to wage the perfect 'war': to control it and give it a contrived, happy ending.

- A major 'war' could serve to bring some sense of unity to deeply fractured societies (of mass poverty, racial and gender injustice, unemployment, recession and endemic crime) and legitimise the media/military/civilian elites in the eyes of the public.

- A major 'war' was needed by the US (backed up by the UK and its other allies) to assert its primacy in the 'New World Order' as proclaimed by President Bush after the Iraqi invasion of Kuwait. The US's position, basically underpinned by military power and massively burdened by debt and recession, was increasingly coming under threat from the more civilian-oriented economies of Germany and Japan. War could then be seen as a symbolic assertion (though essentially defensive) of US military and media power in the Third World.

- Even a mythical 'war' could serve to destroy the social/economic

---

6 *New York Times* 2 March 1991.

7 Gannett Foundation (1991): *The media at war: The press and the Persian Gulf conflict*; New York City. A database search over the period 1 August 1990 to 28 February 1991 of mainstream US newspapers found 6,314 mentions of Vietnam (and just 985 mentions on TV). The next most common words were 'human shields' (2,002 print mentions; 586 TV mentions), allied dead/casualties (1,492 print mentions; 517 TV mentions). Mentions of Iraqi casualties did not feature at all in the overview. p 42.

infrastructure of Iraq which, while posing no threat to the West, was seen as a threat by the Israeli elite. A 'war' could serve as a lesson to future Middle Eastern governments who considered challenging the Western right of access to the oil reserves.

- Following the enormous expenditure on the military in the US and UK in the 1980s and the decline of the Soviet threat, armies faced a terrible problem. If they had no major enemy, how were they going to test their weapons? The Gulf 'war' provided the ideal testing ground. Afterwards, arms dealers could proudly display on their weapons 'As used in the Gulf' stickers. The massacres can then be seen as an obscenely macabre arms equipment exhibition with humans and a society's infrastructure as targets. The flights of the British Tornados, it could be argued, were not for strictly military purposes (how could they be since there was no fighting enemy?) but to prove their value to potential buyers – in particular, Saudi Arabia.

The manufacture of war – in Iraq

For the Iraqi regime, too, a mythical war could also serve a number of purposes:

- It would prove the strength of the Iraqi people in facing the onslaught of a mighty, global enemy. The army didn't need to fight the 'war'. Martyrdom, in any case, was noble.

- Thus, the longer the 'war' continued the greater, more credible the 'victory' could be made to appear. In reality, one massacre followed another.

- The 'war' could help solve some of the problems of the highly militaristic Iraqi society. Since the ceasefire in the Iran-Iraq war of 1988 thousands of men were returning to cities from the front, ending up dissatisfied and jobless. (Karsh and Rautsi 1991: 18-30) Many of them were engaged in revolts against the oppressive regime, especially the Kurds and Shi'as. (Pilger 1991) A war could eliminate large groups of them. There was no record kept of them. There would be no figures of casualties. They didn't really matter. The UK/US press attached little importance to them. The elites of both sides could view the Iraqi conscripts as mere non-people, animals, cannon-fodder. The brutalism of one side, it could be argued, was mirrored by the brutalism of the other.

- The Iraqi elite during the 1980s amassed a formidable arsenal.[8] But as usual with Third World militaristic states it was primarily not for use against any major foreign enemy. Instead, it was for internal security crushing domestic opposition and revolts and serving as a symbol of the power of the elite. (Thee 1980: 23) This was the real significance of

---

8   SIPRI (Stockholm International Peace Research Institute annual report) 1991 shows that Iraq bought more than $431 billion worth of arms between 1970 and 1989. Supplying countries included all five permanent members of the UN Security Council. USSR $19.2 billion (61 per cent of total); France $5.5 billion (18 per cent); China $1.6 billion (5 per cent); Brazil $1.1 billion (4 per cent); Egypt $1.1 billion (4 per cent). Others $2.8 billion (8 per cent).

Saddam Hussein's 'Mother of Battles' rhetoric. The 'war' the Iraqi elite fought in 1991 was not against the US-led coalition – it was against the Kurds and the Shi'as. As Faleh Abd al-Jubbar comments (1992: 13): 'The rout relieved Saddam of the most troublesome part of his army and preserved the most loyal divisions.'

Moreover, much of Iraq's security strategy was determined by the regime's fear of a military coup. Since the regime knew it was particularly vulnerable to air attack, the air force's capabilities were deliberately held back. As Norman Friedman comments (1991: 27): 'Military strategy tended toward static tactics because more mobile ones required forward commanders with greater initiative and because such men could easily turn on the regime.' Such a strategy must have been known to allied commanders before the Gulf 'war' of 1991. It totally contradicts the image that dominated the press of a ruthlessly expansionist Iraqi military.

This is why the 'war' was a kind of fictional, shadow contest. Neither side was really fighting the 'enemy' defined by the rhetoric. Each was rather fighting more their domestic opposition.

- The Iraqi state, supported by significant sections of the elites of East and West for over a decade before August 1990 was brutally authoritarian. It did not suddenly change its character with the invasion of Kuwait. National security was only maintained through the repression of all dissent, by enforced militarism, by the activities of a massive security/intelligence force. A 'war' could help alter that. Then the terror would be inflicted by the 'enemy' (until recently an ally). And that terror would be exploited to help unite the people behind the leadership.

- Iraq's claim to Kuwait dated back to the imperial carve-up after the First World War and was guaranteed to tap some considerable nationalistic fervour. Similarly the attack on the Kuwaiti ruling family had powerful symbolic significance. It highlighted the massive wealth of the Western-backed ruling elites in the Middle East, their subservience to Western financial, geostrategic interests and the exploitation and injustices on which the oil wealth was based.

- The 'war' could be used to tap the Islamic revival and help further legitimise the ruling elite. Significantly, just before the war, Saddam Hussein ordered his Ba'ath Party to change its slogan from 'The Ba'athists stride forward' to 'The Believers stride forward' and changed the flag to read 'Allahu akbar' (God is great). As the conflict continued, uprisings were seen throughout the Islamic world – in Turkey, Jordan and the Yemen in the Middle East, Algeria and Egypt in Africa and in Pakistan and Indonesia in Asia. (Vaux 1992: 79)

New militarism, mediacentrism and the myth of the vulnerable state

The notion of vulnerability is a central element of new militarist state's dominant ideology. This is paradoxical since many theorists argue that the state in the US and UK in the 1980s became increasingly centralised, authoritarian and 'strong'. (Held 1984: 349-352; Gamble 1988) As Peters (1985: 105) argues: 'In an age of vast state strength, ability to mobilize resources and possession of virtually infinite means of coercion, much of state policy has been based on the concept of extreme vulnerability to enemies, external or internal.'

The state's power grew both internally (with the increase in police powers, surveillance techniques and control of political and industrial dissent) and externally (with the global reach of its imperial, military ambitions). Yet, during the Cold War, the state was represented in the press as constantly vulnerable to attack from communist missiles or massed soldiers moving westwards over Europe. As the direct challenge from the Soviet Union began to wane at the beginning of the 1980s, the threat from international terrorism (still generally linked to the 'Red menace' and left-wing 'extremism') was highlighted.

Following the Iranian revolution of 1979 which deposed the Shah and installed the Ayatollah Khomeini, Islamic 'fundamentalism' rapidly became the new 'global threat' to Western civilisation. According to Adam Tarock (1996: 162), 'Iran's revolution, which brought with it the revival of Islam as a political ideology, fostered in the West a siege mentality which the nationalism of the previous decades had created.' Furthermore, a series of enemies were largely manufactured during the 1980s (the 'Argies', 'mad dog' Gadaffi of Libya, 'evil, drug-running, criminal' Noriega of Panama, culminating with the 'new Hilter' Hussein, of Iraq)) to legitimise intervention in the Third World by the US and UK.

On the home front, the state was represented as vulnerable to attack by peace campaigners (secretly working alongside their Kremlin backers), criminals (hence the emphasis on law and order), IRA terrorists and trade unionists. Significantly, Mrs Thatcher described the striking miners (of 1984-85) as 'the enemy within' which had to be destroyed.

Moreover, the new militarist state is often represented as critically vulnerable to attack by the media – either internal or external. This is paradoxical given the enormous powers of the state to manipulate the media, to intimidate journalists (through legislation, regulations and censorship), to spread disinformation and control access. It is also paradoxical given the primary role of the press in promoting and reflecting the interests (often contradictory and competing) of the dominant elites. Yet, following the Vietnam debacle, major elements of the US civilian and military elites argued that the press had played a crucial role in fermenting opposition to the war. Since then the press has been accused, in times of alleged 'crisis' in the UK and US, of threatening the security of the state.

Such accusations, it can be argued, follow on from the mediacentrism of the political culture and are part of a subtle, multi-pronged propaganda strategy to reinforce moves by the state to constrain further the media and domestic opposition and cement the dominant consensus.

For instance, following the Falklands 'war', it was argued that satellite technology beyond the control of the nation state, would allow journalists editorial freedom to challenge the state. Government control of the press in the Falklands, it was claimed, was a unique event (given the remote geographical situation of the islands) never likely to be repeated. In this way, the state was seen as vulnerable to threats from technological advances within the media. (In the event, the US invasions of the 1980s culminating in the attack on Iraq showed that the new media technologies were, in fact, highly vulnerable to manipulation by the state.) And most significantly, the representation of Saddam Hussein as a cunning, evil propagandist was central to the manufacture of the 'credible enemy' and the Gulf 'war' myth.

Secret wars of new militarism and the media myth of defence

The dominant view reproduced in the mainstream media represents the state as having fought defensively only in exceptional cases since 1945. The Gulf 'war', accordingly, was represented as the consequence of a legitimate defensive response to an unprovoked attack by Saddam Hussein on innocent, vulnerable, tiny Kuwait (and, by implication, on vulnerable Western civilisation). But such an interpretation grossly over-simplifies a complex reality and most significantly obscures the offensive elements of the UK and US state systems and military strategies.

In fact, since 1945 the UK – and the US – have deployed troops somewhere in the globe at least once every year, usually away from the media glare.[9] As Steve Peak points out, the Falklands 'war' was the 88th deployment of British troops since 1945.[10] These deployments have taken place in 51 countries and nearly all of them in Africa, the Middle East, South-East Asia, the Far East and around the Caribbean. Newsinger (1989) describes British intervention in Indonesia as 'a forgotten war'. Britain's longest running

---

9 Wilson, Harold (1974): *The Labour Government 1964-79*; Penguin; London records how troops together with a number of Metropolitan policemen were sent to the Caribbean island of Anguilla in 1969 to put down a minor rebellion – in total secrecy. But 'the operation leaked – there was no doubt some elements in the police detachment talked freely'. pp 787-788.

10 Peak, Steve (1982) 'Britain's military adventures', the *Pacifist*; London; Vol 20. 10. Lists 1945 Java and Sumatra; 1945-48 India and Pakistan; 1945-47 Greece; 1945-54 Trieste; 1945-1948 Palestine; 1945 Vietnam; 1946-54 Egypt; 1947 Aden; 1947-48 Northern Ireland; 1948 Gold Coast; 1948 Yangtze incident; 1948-60 Malaya; 1948-52 Eritrea; 1949-51 Somaliland; 1949 Aqaba; 1950-53 Korea; 1950 Singapore; 1951 Aqaba; 1952-56 Northern Ireland; 1952-1956 Kenya; 1953 British Guyana; 1953-55 Persian Gulf; 1954-59 Cyprus; 1954-58 Aden; 1955-56 Singapore; 1955 Seizure of Rockall; 1956 Hong Kong; 1956-57 Bahrain; 1956 Suez; 1957-59 Muscat and Oman; 1957 Belize; 1957 Togoland; 1958 Nassau; 1958 Aden; 1958 Jordan and Lebanon; 1958 Bahamas; 1959 Gan; 1960 Cameroons; 1960 Jamaica; 1961 Kuwait, Bahamas, Zanzibar; 1962 Belize, British Guyana, Hong Kong; 1962-66 Borneo; 1963-66 Malaysia; 1963-66 Swaziland; 1963 Zanzibar; 1963 Cyprus; 1963 British Guyana; 1964 Zanzibar, Tanganyika, Uganda, Kenya; 1964-67 Aden; 1965 Mauritius, Beira blockade, Bechuanaland; 1965-77 Oman; 1966 Hong Kong, Seychelles, British Honduras; 1966-67 Libya; 1967 Hong Kong; 1968 Bermuda, Mauritius; 1969 to date Northern Ireland; 1969-71 Anguilla; 1969 Bermuda; 1969-76 Dhofar/Oman; 1972 QE2, British Honduras; 1973 QE2; 1974 Cyprus; 1976-77 British Honduras (Belize); 1977 Bermuda; 1980 New Hebrides; 1982 Falklands.

post-1945 campaign (leaving aside Northern Ireland) was in Malaya from 1948 to 1960. But this was never described as a 'war'. It was rather known as the Malayan 'emergency'. Other major campaigns have been those in Java and Sumatra and Palestine in the 1940s, Kenya 1952-1956, Cyprus 1954-1959 and again in the 1960s; Borneo 1962-1966 and Northern Ireland from 1969. Rose (1986) argues that British troops have been involved in more wars in more places across the globe than any other country since 1945.

In the case of the US, the investment in warfare and offensive military strategy is still greater than that of the UK. Cecil Currey (1991: 72-73) argues that since 1950, America has used either force or its threat about 500 times, mostly in Third World countries. Former CIA agent John Stockwell (1991: 70-73) suggests that the agency has been involved in 3,000 major operations and 10,000 minor operations which have led to the deaths of 6m people worldwide mainly in Korea, Vietnam, Cambodia, Africa and Central and South America. It has overthrown functioning democracies in more than 20 countries and manipulated dozens of elections.

Pentagon adviser John M. Collins, in his seminal analysis of strategy in these largely secret wars, known as Low Intensity Conflicts (LICs), isolates just 60 examples this century.[11] He points out: 'All LICs normally are contingencies and technically transpire in peacetime because none have yet been declared wars.' (Collins 1991: 4) Similarly Asaf Hussain (1988: 45) identifies the US's deep commitment to LIC involving both military and non-military (political, economic, cultural and social) forms of conflict. 'It means being prepared to engage in protracted struggle against various non-Western states with a minimum of US combat involvement and mobilization of indigenous forces.'

The dominant media view fails to acknowledge the inherent aggression of state representing the short, sharp attacks (or defensive actions as argued by the administrations of the day) of the US on Grenada, Libya and Panama in the 1980s as the typical form of warfare. In fact, the reverse is nearer the truth. Some 57 per cent of Collins's sample lasted fewer than five years but 33 per cent exceeded 10 years. For instance, he points out that the LIC against Libya has being going on since 1970. The 11-minute attack on Libyan targets in April 1986 was just a tiny feature of this multi-pronged conflict.

---

11 Collins, John M. (1991): *America's small wars*; Brassey's (US); Washington/London. His 60 LICs are Philippines 1899-1913; China 1900; Columbia, Panama 1901-14; Morocco 1904; Cuba 1906-9; China 1912-41; Mexico 1914-17; Haiti 1915-34; Dominican Republic 1916-24; Nicaragua 1926-33; Philippines 1942-45; Burma 1942-45; France 1944; China 1945-49; Greece 1946-49; Philippines 1946-55; Indochina 1946-54; USSR 1946-; Iran 1951-53; China 1953-79; North Korea 1953-; Guatemala 1953-54; Vietnam 1955-65; Laos 1955-65; Lebanon 1958; Cuba 1970-73; Iraq 1972-75; Opec 1974-75; Cyprus 1974-78; Mayaguez 1975; Cambodia 1978; Nicaragua 1978-79; Iran 1979-; Syria 1979-; El Savaldor 1979-; Bolivia 1980-86; Afghanistan 1980-; Nicaragua 1981-90; Falklands Islands 1982; Lebanon 1982-84; Grenada 1983; Philippines 1984; Philippines 1984-85; Haiti 1985-86; Angola 1986-; Narco conflict 1986; Persian Gulf 1987-88; Panama 1987-90 p 16.

See also Hussain, Asaf (1988): *Political terrorism and the state in the Middle East*; Mansell Publishing; London/New York. He identifies 46 US interventions since 1945. pp 30-31.

Why secret wars?

Given the democratic problems posed by overt, mass participatory warfare, most warfare of new militarist societies avoids traditional mass army battle confrontations such as occurred in the Gulf in 1991. Instead permanent warfare is conducted through special force interventions, the support of proxy forces and leaders, through diplomatic, trade and other economic sanctions, through secret service destabilisation. Many other factors influenced the development of LIC doctrine. A feature of American strategy since the beginning of the century, it developed still further as an offshoot of the nuclear stand-off between East and West during the Cold War and in response to the US defeat in Vietnam. As Halliday (1989: 72) says: 'LIC theorists insisted that the US combat forces should not be involved in the long-run, Vietnam style operations. The "lesson" drawn here from Vietnam was that the US effort failed because it was too direct and too large.' Significantly Collins's sample showed LICs mounting substantially in the post-Vietnam, new militarist era.

In addition, LIC strategy was developed in response to the perceived threats to vulnerable US strategic interests. (Miles 1987) The US Defense Secretary reported in 1987: 'Today there seems to be no shortage of adversaries who seek to undermine our security by persistently nibbling away at our interests through these shadow wars carried out by guerrillas, assassins, terrorists and subversives in the hope that they have found a weak point in our defenses.' (Klare and Kornbluh 1989: 93) LIC strategies were aimed at fighting most appropriately and effectively those 'shadow wars'. During the 1980s, LIC strategists 'came out' in the US and numerous conferences were held and strategy documents compiled exploring the concepts. But the LIC debate was largely ignored by the mainstream media.

Special forces, such as the UK's SAS and the American Navy Seals, which are so crucial to LIC strategies, reportedly played important roles in the build-up to the massacres and during them. They attached homing devices at or near bombing targets in Iraq, hunted for Scud launchers and collected intelligence. They were the subject of a series of 'inordinately flattering' features in the US and UK media. (Ray and Schaap 1991: 11) Yet accounts of their daring deeds of 'superhuman' courage and endurance, since they were shrouded in almost total secrecy, amount to a form of fiction. (de la Billiere 1995: 319-338; Brown and Shukman 1991: 81-104; Hunter 1995: 169-175; Kemp 1994: 191-197)

After the massacres, the SAS provided one of the dominant symbols of British heroism. Accounts of the fate of the lost SAS patrol – by 'Andy McNab' (1994) and 'Chris Ryan' (1995) – became best-sellers. As Newsinger comments (1995: 36): '...the image we are left with is of a lone British soldier, hungry and cold, being hunted across the most difficult terrain by hundreds of Iraqis and yet still making good his escape....These are tales of the underdog, of British masculinity triumphing against all the odds, over the lesser masculinity of a brutal enemy. In this way is the myth of the "soldier hero", the myth of the SAS sustained.' In the end, the SAS role in the Gulf massacres was probably only minor. LIC strategy was hardly relevant against an enemy that largely refused to fight. The 1991 Gulf conflict, it could be argued, rather saw the application of LIC-type secrecy (deliberately developed during a series of invasions in the 1980s) to a spectacular, manufactured 'war' which was, in reality, a 42-day secret massacre hidden behind the media construct of heroic warfare.

The permanent warfare of new militarism: missing from the media

The arms trade, largely hidden from the gaze of the media, is the archetypal 'substitute, permanent warfare' of new militarist societies. Wars are not fought directly; instead the means of waging wars are sold. Moreover, arms sales to dictatorships (such as Iraq) reinforce oppressive systems and increase regional and global tensions. Following the oil price rises of 1973 and 1979, much of the revenue accumulated by Middle Eastern governments and a large proportion of the credit distributed to Third World countries was used to buy arms. In fact, during the 1980s in the lead up to the Gulf 'war', it has been argued the global arms trade was exploding 'out of control'. (Campaign Against the Arms Trade 1989: 21)

Of the six leading importers of major weapons systems between 1983 and 1987, five (Iraq, Egypt, Saudi Arabia, Israel and Syria in that order) were in the Middle East. Only India imported more. (Stockholm International Peace Research Institute 1988) The very secrecy surrounding the arms trade serves to intensify it. As a seminal work on the impact of the arms trade on the Third World argues: 'Since there is no international register of arms transfers and very few reliable published details of individual countries' arms purchases, governments can never be sure what kind or quantity of arms its rivals may be purchasing. This causes suspicion and paranoia which often sets the tone for a regional arms race.' (Campaign Against the Arms Trade op cit: 27)

The UK's promotion of its arms sales (particularly to Iraq) intensified during the 1980s spurred on by vigorous support from the Thatcher government. (CAAT: 1991) A £20 billion deal with Saudi Arabia in 1988 amounted to Britain's biggest overseas order ever. (Harkins 1995: 54-59) But secrecy surrounds the activities of the Defence Export Services Organisation (launched in 1966 by the then-Labour government as the Defence Sales Organisation). Officially sanctioned leaks of sales appear in newspapers (where the political, social and moral implications of the arms trade are rarely examined) and specialist military magazines and occasionally statements are made in parliament. Otherwise, not even MPs are told of arms sales for reasons of 'commercial confidentiality'.

The ideological consensus of the national security state

This served in part to undermine further the democratic dynamic accompanying mass conscription as the Cold War intensified after 1945. The security of the state was perceived to be under constant threat from communist enemies both abroad and at home. Progressive forces could easily be smeared in the press as 'communist' and physically intimidated by the state's forces. Vast areas of debate in the UK (republicanism, militarism, imperialism, Irish unity, the power of the City, state terrorism) became no-go areas.

Noam Chomsky (1991: 28) comments: '...for the USSR the Cold War has been primarily a war against its satellites, and for the US a war against the Third World. For each it has served to entrench a system of domestic privilege and coercion. The politics pursued within the Cold War framework have been unattractive to the general population, which accepts them only under duress. Throughout history, the standard device to mobilise a reluctant population has been the fear of an evil enemy, dedicated to its destruction. The superpower conflict served the purpose admirably.' The ideological consensus which emerged around new militarism and was reproduced faithfully in all the mainstream media during the Gulf crisis sprang logically from the Cold War consensus. Such a consensus, it should be stressed, was not always monolithic. It incorporated debate and dissent – within clearly identified limits.

Joan Smith (1985: 78-102) has identified the way in which the mainstream press welcomed in rapturous, positive terms the British government's acquisition and testing of nuclear weapons during the 1950s. At the same time, the press indulged in crude smear tactics against the government's opponents. Smith also highlights how in the five years between the testing of the A Bomb at Monte Bello in 1952 and the first H Bomb tests, the government became 'much more sophisticated in its handling of the press'. She comments: 'It even offered facility trips to the trials to journalists, a tactic which brought with it three major benefits. First, the sense of excitement engendered in reporters who were privileged to act as witnesses to an exciting event was not conducive to critical or investigative journalism...Second, it ensured pages of newspaper coverage of a scientific development in which Britain was once again well behind the two superpowers. And third, it offered reporters plenty of human interest angles to report on – interviews with servicemen whose families were waiting breathlessly at home were good for newspaper sales.' (ibid: 83)

Except during short, rare periods (in the early 1960s and in the early 1980s) when the Labour Party, somewhat uncomfortably, adopted unilateralism (thus marking a temporary breakdown of the consensus), the nationalistic, patriotic ideologies that underpinned the Cold War stalemate won the committed support of all the major political parties and mainstream media.

As Mary Kaldor comments (1990: 4-5), Cold War ideology both expressed and legitimised the dominant power relationships in modern society. The elite was divided over the disastrous Suez adventure of 1956 and this division was reflected in the media – most of the press coming out against the French, UK, Israeli attacks. (Thomas 1967: 32-33) Following the nationalisation of the Suez canal by Egypt all the papers with the exception of the *Guardian* had called for the use of force. But then, following the attacks, the consensus suddenly shifted and nearly all the press, including the *Daily Telegraph* and *Mail*, came out in opposition. Only the *Express* and *Sketch* remained the 'real newspaper friends' of the Prime Minister, Anthony Eden.

Otherwise the Cold War consensus held firm in both the media and the elite. It broke on only two occasions. In 1960 supporters of the Campaign for Nuclear Disarmament won a surprise victory at the Labour conference (Taylor 1970) and in the early 1980s massive opposition to the Thatcherite and Reaganite armaments programme and Cold War rhetoric drove thousands of peace campaigners on to the streets of Britain and the Labour Party reluctantly into the arms of the unilateralists. But unilateralism was never endorsed by any Fleet Street newspaper. (Aubrey (ed) 1982; Keeble 1986; McNair 1988: 176; Glasgow University Media Group 1985)

In the United States too, the Cold War confrontation served to reinforce the militarist consensus in the dominant economic and political elites and in the mainstream media. As Hellinger and Judd (op cit: 206) argue: 'For more than forty years there has been a remarkable degree of consensus among US elites that the nation should preserve a high level of readiness to go to war. Presidential candidates of the two major parties have tried to outdo one another in advocating military preparedness...For voters, the choices have been conducted within extraordinarily narrow limits. From 1945 until 1989, when the Soviet Premier Mikhail Gorbachev declared his policy of perestroika and the Eastern Bloc governments began to fall, no Democratic or Republican presidential candidate questioned the premises of the Cold War – that the national defense must be constantly strengthened to deter the Communists.'

Secret state: silent press

Though the dominant political ideology, reproduced in the mainstream media, stresses the myths of democratic involvement, plurality and openness, the principal characteristic of the modern state, as identified by John Keane, is 'armed secrecy'. (Keane 1991: 101-103) The mainstream media are tied closely to this secret state through shared economic and political interests. The secret state provides the essential political, social and cultural foundation for the manufacture of the Gulf war myth.

Significantly, Guy Debord (1991: 3) locates his concept of the society of the spectacle in the culture of secrecy. He writes: 'The society whose modernisation has reached the stage of integrated spectacle is characterised by the combined effect of five principal features: incessant technological renewal, integration of state and economy, generalised secrecy, unanswerable lies; an eternal present.' The activities of the secret state are largely repellent, illegal, extremely costly, often in support of deeply obnoxious dictatorships – and difficult to justify in public. Hence the need of the state to maintain constant vigilance and secrecy. Yet titbits of information are supplied to friendly media; carefully orchestrated leaks, denials, lies feed the public's curiosity about the secret service, double agents and the like. (Lott 1990; Kerr 1990)

As Debord remarks, the state has developed a sophisticated system of allowing people to believe they are 'actually in on the secrets'. (*op cit*: 16) Spy sagas (le Carré, James Bond, Graham Greene etc) are an ever-present feature of the entertainment industry. Yet the real political impact of the secret state has never disturbed the dominant ideologies of the 'democratic' state. Spying, in many respects, has been transmuted from being an often reprehensible activity (dirty tricks) into a 'depoliticised' entertainment spectacle. Two state systems operate in most advanced capitalist, new militarist states. There is the state of the democratic facade (elections, public opinion polls, the free press) and there is the secret and perhaps far more powerful state. The secret states of the UK and US operate on a global scale, as during the Gulf crisis of 1990-1991, in collusion with the secret states of more overtly authoritarian, militaristic societies.[12]

Secret state and the media: in the UK

The extent of official secrecy is the missing element from most histories of modern UK or US.[13] The study is certainly fraught with complexities. Damning allegations of 'conspiracy theory' inevitably accompany any attempt at such an analysis. Simply because a lot of the evidence is highly sensitive, checking for accuracy becomes extremely difficult.[14]

Yet many serious researchers have identified the UK as one of the most secretive of states. David Northmore (1990) describes the UK as 'the most secretive state in the so-called developed world' with well over 100 laws prohibiting the disclosure of information. Philip Schlesinger (1991: 33) has outlined in detail the significant features of the new, authoritarian, secret state in the UK. And Edward Thompson (1980: 151) has argued: 'The operators of the British security services are some of the most secretive and arrogant to be found in modern bureaucratic states.' He continues (ibid: 156-157): 'It remains true that the growth of an unrepresentative and unaccountable state within a state has been the product of the twentieth century. Its growth was, paradoxically, actually aided by the unpopularity of securi-

---

12 Heikal, Mohamed (1992): *Illusions of triumph*; Harper Collins; London says on the Gulf states: 'By 1974 every state had its secret service whose chiefs, together with the rulers, confidants and senior officials, formed an inner administrative alliance. Beyond them was an outer circle containing four elements: representatives of foreign intelligence services, confidants of sheiks and kinds, oil company representatives and arms salesmen.' p 45.

13 Significantly Paxman, Jeremy (1990): *Friends in high places: Who runs Britain?* Michael Joseph; London makes no mention at all of the secret services.

14 Bale, Jeffrey M. (1995: 16-22): 'Conspiracy theories and clandestine politics', *Lobster*; Hull; June. A fascinating exploration of the elements of conspiracy theories. He writes: '...serious research into genuine conspiratorial networks has at worst been suppressed, as a rule been discouraged, and at best looked upon with condescension by the academic community. An entire dimension of political history and contemporary politics has thus been consistently neglected.' p. 16.

ty and policing agencies; forced by this into the lowest possible invisibility, they learned to develop techniques of invisible influence and power.'

Similarly Clive Ponting (1990: 16) has argued: 'Current or recent operations of all secret services and intelligence agencies are naturally surrounded by secrecy, but in Britain a policy of maintaining total secrecy about virtually every aspect of their work was adopted at an early stage and is still taken to extraordinary lengths today...The experience of other Western democracies demonstrates that a doctrine of total secrecy is neither inevitable nor indispensable for the successful operation of intelligence agencies in peacetime. In Britain, however, absolute secrecy has been the policy of all post-war governments.'

Significantly, Britain was the first to set up a secret service – in 1909 (followed by Germany in 1913, Russia 1917, France 1935). The US came relatively late in the game – in 1947. Alongside the growth of the secret services has been the growth of the mass media globally. It could be argued that this process has been complementary. Every government since 1945 has reserved its most vital decisions relating to national security to a small group of ministers, usually without even consulting the whole cabinet. (Ponting 1989: 177) Yet, under Thatcher, the growth of secret government intensified. The institutional links between the security services and the media have, in general since 1945, been close.[15] Bloch and Fitzgerald report the 'editor of one of Britain's most distinguished journals' as believing that more than half its

---

15 Thompson, Edward (1980): 'A state of blackmail', *Writing by candlelight*; Merlin Press; London. pp 113-134. Largely a review of Chapman Pincher's *Inside story* and a critique of the process by which his high-level informants constantly break the Official Secrets Act in leaking to him (for various political reasons) secret information. He comments: 'The columns of the *Express* may be seen as a kind of official urinal in which, side by side, high officials of MI5 and MI6, Sea Lords, Permanent Under Secretaries, Lord George-Brown, Chiefs of the Air Staff, nuclear scientists, Lord Wigg and others stand patiently leaking in the public interest. One can only admire their resolute attention to these distasteful duties.' p 116.

The intimate links between top journalists and the secret services are highlighted by Gall, Sandy (1994) in his autobiographical *News from the frontline: A television reporter's life*; William Heinemann; London. He reports without any qualms how, after returning from one of his reporting assignments to Afghanistan, he was asked to lunch by the head of MI6. 'It was very informal, the cook was off so we had cold meat and salad with plenty of wine. He wanted to hear what I had to say about the war in Afghanistan. I was flattered, of course, and anxious to pass on what I could in terms of first hand knowledge.' p 158

Following the resignation from the *Guardian* of Richard Gott, its literary editor, in December 1994, in the wake of allegations that he was a 'paid agent' of the KGB, the role of journalists as spies came under the media spotlight. According to *The Times* editorial of 16 December 1994: 'Many British journalists benefited from CIA or MI6 largess during the Cold War.' British intelligence services invited the journalist Jon Snow to work for them; he rejected their offer. ('Bylines, spylines and a bidden agenda', the *Guardian* 30 December 1994) A large MI6-financed secret organisation, the Information Research Department, involved 300 officials in spreading anti-communist propaganda to the national press, BBC and British embassies from 1948 until it was wound up by Foreign Secretary David Owen in 1977. Information about some of its activities became officially known after Public Record Office documents were released on 17 August 1995. See Norton-Taylor, Richard and Milne, Seumas (1995): 'Labour's role in secret anti-communist plan revealed', the *Guardian*; 18 August. Dorril, Stephen: 'The puppet masters' (in the same edition of the *Guardian*) claimed that some elements of the IRD 'lingered on'.

foreign correspondents were on the MI6 payroll. (Bloch and Fitzgerald 1983: 134-141) Following the passing of the 1989 Security Service Act links between the media and MI5 and MI6 grew still closer, according to James Adams. (op cit: 94-98; see also Urban 1996: 54)

David Leigh has highlighted the extent to which secret services penetrated the media and destabilised the Labour governments of Harold Wilson and ultimately forced his resignation. Similar pressures, he suggests, were exerted by the security services on Willy Brandt in West Germany and Gough Whitlam in Australia forcing similar resignations. (Leigh 1988: 220-232; 232-233).

Moreover, in their analysis of the contemporary secret state, Dorril and Ramsay give the media a crucial role. The heart of the secret state they identify as the security services, the cabinet office and upper echelons of Home and Foreign and Commonwealth offices, the armed forces and Ministry of Defence, the nuclear power industry and its satellite ministries together with the network of very senior civil servants. In addition, as 'satellites' of the secret state their list includes 'agents of influence in the media, ranging from actual agents of the security services, conduits of official leaks, to senior journalists merely lusting after official praise and, perhaps, a knighthood at the end of their career'. (Dorril and Ramsay 1991: x-xi) And according to Roy Greenslade, editor of the *Mirror* at the time of the Gulf crisis: 'Most tabloid newspapers – or even newspapers in general – are playthings of MI5. You are the recipients of the sting.' [16] Journalists' collusion in the secret state was a significant factor behind the manufacturing of the Gulf 'war' myth.

Secret state and the media: in the US

It is not without significance that of the two US presidents of the 1980s, one was a former Hollywood actor – the archetypal product of the culture of the spectacle. The other was a former director of the CIA, engaged in covert activities for the agency since the early 1960s under the cloak of his oil business activities. Bush's elevation to the presidency represented the actual takeover of the 'democratic' state by the secret state.

By the 1980s, the growth of the power of the executive office of the president based around the National Security Council and the CIA (together with many other covert organisations) had created a secret state within the state. As Hellinger and Judd argue: 'There now exists a recognisable pattern of hidden powers, a covert presidency, that rests on centralising presidential direction of personel, budgets and information; on the manipulation of the media and on the expanding use of national security to control the political agenda.' (op cit: 190)

Armed secrecy remained a permanent feature of both militarist and new militarist states. Yet it could be argued that by the 1980s secrecy was 'getting out of control' thus providing one of the crucial elements of new militarism.

---

16 Quoted in Milne, Seamus (1994): *The enemy within: The secret war against the miners*; Verso; London; reprinted by Pan, London in 1995 p 262.

According to Alan Friedman (1993: xix): 'The truth is that the 1980s were a decade of deceit both at the White House and Downing Street, a period during which accountability to Congress or Parliament was almost completely ignored and the abuse of power became the rule rather than the exception.'

The roots of new militarism in the media-military-industrial complex

The military-industrial complex

A number of sociologists, state theorists and arms analysts have identified the social and political significance of the military-industrial complex. (Wright Mills 1956; Chomsky 1991; Barnaby 1984; Thompson 1982; Edmunds 1988; Berghahn 1981) Shaw (1987: 150) sums up when he says: 'The military function of the state enters society through the military-economic sector, its role is determining the balance in state spending (warfare/welfare), its absorption into the political framework, its centrality to the ideological formation of the citizen.' But he adds, appropriately: 'To say that militarism has become a core, defining reality of societies in peace as well as war does not, of course, mean that peace is the same as war.' Within this context, the many secret wars of the secret state, as well as the overt wars of the new militarist states culminating in the 1991 Gulf 'war', can be seen as logical (though not inevitable) products of political cultures dominated by the military-industrial complex. In contrast, the dominant ideology articulated in the mainstream media is silent on this. It represents the state as being inherently peaceful though vulnerable to aggression from abnormal states outside and irrational, uncivilised enemies within.

On the military-industrial complex in the UK, Smith and Smith (1983: 29) comment: 'The proportion of national income spent [in the 1970s] on the military was higher than both the typical peacetime level before 1939 and the proportion devoted to the military [down from 60 per cent during the Second World 'war' to 5 per cent] by other Western European states.' Defence spending rose by 28 per cent between 1978 and 1986 accounting for 13.2 per cent of total government expenditure. Defence was the second largest area of expenditure, after social security. (Derbyshire, J. Denis and Derbyshire, Ian 1988: 176) By the 1990s, the military-industrial complex had grown so enormous that the defence industry accounted for 11 per cent of industrial production, defence exports were worth up to £33 billion a year (the country being the third largest arms exporter after the US and Russia) and defence-related jobs amounted to 600,000. In 1989, the Ministry of Defence was the third largest landowner in the country, the largest customer for British industry and the largest employer of bureaucrats. (Paxman 1990: 237)

The post-war industrial growth of the US was, to a large extent, built on the militarisation of the economy. The policy basis for the massive military expansion appeared in National Security Council memorandum 68 of 7 April, 1950. The secret memo written by Paul Nitze with Secretary of State

Dean Acheson 'looking over his shoulder' was only released in 1975 in error. (Henwood 1992; Agee 1991: 20) It suggested a massive increase in military spending to counter the Soviet Union and to support US foreign policy; a mass propaganda campaign to build and maintain confidence and sow 'mass defections' on the Soviet side; covert economic, political and psychological warfare; tighter internal security and beefed-up intelligence.

Rearmament desperately needed an international emergency – and it came with the Korean war. Acheson was to say later: 'Korea came along and saved us.' (McCormick 1989: 98) Warfare, indeed, helped boost the global economy – and the US military budget. In 1950 it stood at $13 billion. Then, with the outbreak of the Korean war, an extra $16.8 billion was added to the bill, while US military forces doubled to 3.6 million. As Philip Agee (op cit: 20) comments: 'The permanent war economy became a reality and we have lived with it for forty years.' And Giovanni Arrighi argues (1994: 297) that massive rearmament during and after the Korean war solved 'once and for all' the liquidity problems of the post-war world economy and inaugurated the most sustained and profitable period in the history of global capitalism. (1950-73)

The boom in military spending continued relentlessly during the years of the Cold War. Michael T. Klare (1980: 37) identified the process in the US where the creation of large-scale military enterprises resulted in the formation of a 'self-perpetuating industrial combine' prepared to take independent measures (propaganda and 'scare' campaigns designed to create a perpetual crisis atmosphere, lobbying efforts, bribery and intrigue) to ensure a continuing demand for its products. By 1990, more than 30,000 US companies were engaged in military production while roughly 3,275,000 jobs were in the defence industries. Gore Vidal (1991: 177-178) goes so far as to argue that by the early 1990s 90 per cent of the federal budget was directed towards defence. And 70 per cent of all money spent on research and development was spent on defence work. (Drucker 1993: 126) As the economy fell into recession, profits for arms suppliers, in contrast, soared. Singer, IBM, Goodyear Tire, AT and T and Westinghouse all turned to military production. And, as Hellinger and Judd argue: '...the militarisation of the economy has created a complex system of dependence on military spending that will not easily be broken'. (op cit: 209)

It can be argued, then, that the Gulf 'war' of 1991 was manufactured in an attempt to reinforce the power of the military-industrial complex globally (yet, in particular in the US and UK) at a critical moment when the demise of the Soviet 'enemy' seriously threatened their *raison d'être*.

The media-military-industrial complex

Analyses stressing the social/political significance of the military-industrial complex often underestimate the ideological and political significance of the media. For instance, in his study of the roots of the Second Cold War (1979-1982), Fred Halliday (1986: 12) highlights the 'iron triangle' which, he argues, binds 'Congress, the Pentagon and the arms industry together in an unchallenged process of military expansion'. A similar analysis of the UK would stress the links between Parliament, the Ministry of Defence and the arms industry. Significantly Halliday talks of the 'barrage of political propaganda: promoting the idea of Soviet superiority, of declining US capabilities, of gaps in missiles, civil defence or naval strength' and thus could have gone on to mention the crucial role of the compliant media in promoting this propaganda.

Indeed, given the integration of the media industries' interests with those of the military-industrial complex and the importance of the media's role in supporting and celebrating the state's militarism it is worth identifying the media-military-industrial complex as a factor behind the manufacture of the Gulf 'war' myth. Yet the sophisticated ideological/media/propaganda system operating in both the US and UK means that these developments (and the broader political and environmental threats they posed) rarely if ever feature in the dominant political debates.

2 Creation of the new militarist media consensus in the UK

W hen the Iraqi army invaded Kuwait on 2 August 1990, the bulk of Fleet Street immediately called for a military response. After the deadline for Iraq's withdrawal from its self-proclaimed 19th province passed on 15 January 1991 all of Fleet Street backed the allied attacks.

Thatcher and the journalism of deference

Building on the inherent weaknesses of Labourism (Hutton 1996 orig. 1995: 30), Thatcherism can in retrospect be seen to be part of a wider European and indeed global shift to the right. (Gunn 1989: 7-8) In the face of the post-1973 global recession and the extraordinary spate of 14 Third World revolutions over the decade (including Angola, Mozambique, Benin, Nicaragua, Grenada and Iran), the Western capitalist elites from 1980 began an equally extraordinary counter attack.

Mediacentrism and the Iranian embassy siege 1980

New militarism – glorified as a media spectacle – lay at the root of the Thatcher offensive. In 1980 the Special Air Service Regiment (SAS), the archetypal covert paramilitary group (with the full connivance of dominant sections of the British media), set the 'no-compromise' strong state tone of the decade with their assault on the Iranian embassy to rescue hostages. (Geraghty 1980: 237-243; Kemp 1995: 149-154) This represented the first time the SAS was officially deployed on the British mainland – and they became instant media heroes. As the *Sunday Times* investigative 'Insight' team commented: 'Having shunned publicity for the force for the better part of thirty years, the Government seems now to have decided that the best way of making their deployment within Britain acceptable is to turn them into real-life James Bonds – objects of hero-worship. And it has to be said that the strategy has proved singularly successful.' ('Insight' 1980: 109)

The secret complicity of the BBC in the state's strategy of eliminating the hostage-takers was also a significant feature of the drama. (Schlesinger 1991: 29–59) Schlesinger shows that while the impression given to the public was of 'live' transmission of the SAS storming the building, in fact, ITN's report began four-and-a-half minutes afterwards and the BBC's eight minutes later. (ibid: 30) The event came at the end of a period of significant collusion between the state and the media. During two gun seiges in 1975 – at the Spaghetti House in Knightsbridge, London, and at Balcombe Street – and then later in the year during the kidnapping of a Greek Cypriot girl, Aloi Kaloghirou, the police won the support of the media in their strategies to deal with the crises. Yet the state's handling of the Iranian embassy siege and the media's response were to set important precedents for the decade – not least in that they showed how crucial secrecy could be maintained (enhanced even) under the glare of television cameras.

Mediacentrism and the Falklands new militarist manufactured war

Just before the Falklands adventure Thatcher was being polled as the least popular post-war prime minister. (Dillon 1989: 120) On 14 April 1982, *The Times* featured a Gallup poll which indicated the public thought Thatcher was the worst prime minister in British history. The victory in a manufactured, new militarist 'war' was to change all that. Just as there is considerable evidence that the American administration, through satellite, diplomatic and personal intelligence, knew full well of Iraq's ambitions towards Kuwait in the build-up to August 1990, and probably encouraged it, so too it has been argued that Britain expected Argentine's invasion of the islands – but saw the opportunities for a quick and successful new militarist adventure. (Morley 1991, see also Greaves 1991)

The invasion by the 'Argies' was perfect for propaganda purposes. Britain, the vulnerable state, could represent itself as the victim of an unprovoked aggression. Very few people before the war exploded had ever heard of the islands. A map, produced by the Foreign Office, just months earlier, had even omitted them! Argentina at the time was closely allied to the West, deeply embroiled in supporting the Contras for the Reagan administration in Nicaragua. (Woodward 1987: 172-77, 187–89, 212; Andrew 1995: 465)

A secret document from the National Security Council files in Washington, released in March 1992, revealed that the US sought to persuade the UK into a ceasefire before Port Stanley on the Falklands was taken. President Reagan viewed the military junta led by General Galtieri as more acceptable than any leftist Peronist who might take over.[1] A massive propaganda campaign was,

---

1   See Boseley, Sarah (1992): 'How Margaret handbagged Ron's Falklands' truce call', the *Guardian*; 9 March.

therefore, required to demonise the sudden new 'enemy' and glorify the heroic response of the British government.

The Falklands was to set a hugely significant precedent repeated in Grenada, Libya, Panama and the Gulf (1990–1991). Here was a First World country with a considerable military tradition behind it taking on a Third World country almost entirely dependent on First World countries for supplying its army. (Indeed, Argentine's most deadly weapons had been supplied either by Britain or its allies.) Crucially, Argentine was a militarist state, run by a corrupt military dictatorship and relying on a conscript army, where morale and discipline was known by British intelligence to be low. (Bramley 1991; Witherow 1989) Britain, on the other hand, relied on a small, nuclearised professional army strongly committed to fighting to win. (Rogers 1994: 4–6)

Britain's national security was hardly at stake in this little adventure for control of an unknown group of islands populated largely by penguins. (Belgrano Action Group: 1988) Reginald and Elliot (1985: 5) describe it as a 'bizarre litle war'. The conflict solved nothing. Neither side ever admitted they were at war. Nuclear weapons were secretly carried by British ships (and one was actually lost in the South Atlantic). (Rogers op cit: 4–5) But the conflict was tightly limited by both sides. Though the Argentinian army withdrew from the islands, no formal ceasefire was signed (war never having been declared) and conflict over the rights to the sovereignty over the Falklands remains to this day.

But the logic of a permanent war economy is to fight wars. And this the British military were all set to do. Involvement in the escapade for the British public could be realised only through their consumption of the heavily censored, patriotic media. Dillon (1987: 123) is sceptical about the impact of the media. He writes: 'There is no denying that media manipulation by the government and news manipulation by the media were features of the conflict – as they are in all conflicts. But it is difficult to determine precisely what contribution they made to public reactions already excited by Argentina's attack beyond that of conferring and reaffirming the sentiments involved.' But, in fact, the Falklands 'war' demonstrated the centrality of the media in new militarist societies – just as later during the 1991 massacres. As Shaw comments: 'While Britain in the Second World War can be seen as the archetype "citizen war" of total war through democratic mobilisation, the Falklands are the vindication of small professional armed forces, acting on behalf of the nation but needing no real mass participation to carry out their tasks. For the vast majority involvement was limited to the utterly passive, vicarious consumption of exceptionally closely filtered news and the expression of support in opinion polls.' (Shaw 1987: 154)

In 1977, a secret Ministry of Defence paper on 'Public relations planning in emergency operations' stated that 'for planning purposes it is anticipated that 12 places should be available to the media, divided equally between

ITN, the BBC and the press ... The press should be asked to give an undertaking that copy and photographs should be pooled'. (Harris 1983: 149) But following the intervention of Mrs Thatcher's press secretary, Bernard Ingham, the Falklands reporting pool was increased from 12 to just 29 (all-male) British journalists.[2] And they, in the end, came to identify closely with the military. (Morrison and Tumber 1988; Hooper 1982) The patriotic imperative so deeply rooted in the dominant political and media culture, together with journalistic self-censorship and the hyper-jingoism and crude 'enemy' baiting of the pops, all served to transform new militarism into spectator sport with the war consumed as a form of entertainment. (Luckham 1983: 18)

Contrived delays in the transmission of television images meant that this was a largely bloodless war. (Greenberg and Smith 1982; McNair 1995: 176) Harris reported (op cit: 59): 'In an age of supposedly instant communication, what were perhaps the most eagerly awaited television pictures in the world travelled homewards at a steady 25 knots.' For satellite facilities were denied the media; film was stored on the next ship heading back from the Ascension Island military base. Taylor (1992: 14) records how the Task Force sailed in April without any facilities for transmitting black-and-white photographs. Six weeks later, the two press photographers had returned just two batches of pictures to London. In all, just 202 photographs were transmitted.

But not all the censorship was imposed by the state; journalists also indulged in self censorship. There were pictures of dead bodies in the Press Association library which had been released by the Ministry, but newspaper editors decided not to use them. (ibid: 15) The press were exploited not only as 'transmitters of a symbolic demonstration of military power' but also as propagandists to confuse and 'disinform' the enemy. When landings on the Falklands were being planned, disinformation was leaked to the media and, inevitably, to the Argentinians. (Harris op cit: 92)

The consensus support for the war in the three major parties meant that any opposition, however faint, could be condemned as traitorous. The BBC, following a 'Panorama' programme which dared to feature some war doubters and sceptics, was publicly attacked by Ministers and Conservative MPs. The Glasgow University Media Group (1985: 127–129), in their study of television coverage, show that the controversial 'Panorama' programme, 'Can we avoid war?' of 10 May 1982, in fact, contained more statements in support of Government policy than against. A study by McNair (op cit: 177) found that coverage, in general, was deferential to and supportive of dubious official claims of military success. The war was sanitised for television views

---

2 Ingham, Bernard (1991): *Kill the messenger*; HarperCollins; London. Margaret Thatcher's press secretary and former *Guardian* journalist claims that he persuaded the navy to allow 29 journalists to travel with the task force. Originally they had wanted none. Ingham reports: 'Max Hastings, then on the *Evening Standard*, seemed near to tears at the thought of being prevented from covering a war.' p 285.

and the non-military possibilities of a resolution to the conflict marginalised. (Indeed, a similar process was to operate during the 1991 Gulf conflict.)

But the media 'enemy within', threatening the vulnerable state, had to be attacked. Even so there was an element of theatre here. The Conservative government was responding to the demands and prejudices of its increasingly confident right-wing. The BBC could present itself as independent of the state and the defender of journalistic freedom and integrity. As Chomsky argues (1989: 48) such conflict has a 'system-re-inforcing character'. He writes: 'Controversy may rage so long as it adheres to the presuppositions that define the consensus of elites and it should, furthermore, be encouraged within these bounds, thus helping to establish these doctrines as the very condition of thinkable thought while reinforcing the belief that freedom reigns.'

Military and political leaders of new militarist societies know well that long overt wars are both costly and unpopular. The Falklands seemed to prove that a short war against a relatively weak Third World country (though its strength is generally exaggerated since victories are dependent on the existence of a credible enemy fighting force) was achievable. At the same time covert activity still remains the dominant strategy. After the Falklands six official inquiries were held into various aspects of government-media relations. Certainly the clumsy bureaucracy and inter-personal rivalries within the Ministry of Defence showed that 'cock-ups' (a concept much favoured in the journalists' culture since it seems to embrace a healthy scepticism towards the powerful – and, more significantly, marginalise the importance of more profound institutional and ideological factors) can co-exist with historically conditioned, long-term factors. But journalists criticised the Ministry of Defence (MoD) not because they opposed the absurdities and wastefulness of the imperialistic new militarist adventure but because various manifestations of bureaucratic incompetence prevented them from getting their story.

Post-Falklands new militarist mythologies

An intriguing mythology emerged from the conflict – most clearly articulated by Derrik Mercer, in *Fog of War*, the result of a detailed study of the reporting conducted by the Centre for Journalism Studies, University College, Cardiff, and commissioned by the MoD. (Mercer 1987: 2) While the leading media in advanced capitalist societies are best viewed as subtle propagandists for the dominant ideology, with important steering and management functions, the conflicts which emerged between journalists and government helped promote the myth of the adversary relationship. Mercer writes: 'The clash of interests between media and government has always been fundamental and frequently acrimonious. In a democracy this is inevitable and many would say desirable.' (op cit: 3)

Accompanying the myth of the adversarial press is the myth of the unideological press concerned with theoretically unproblematic 'practicalities', 'facts' and events. (Chibnall 1977: 23) Thus Mercer goes on: 'The media play essential roles in any democracy as channels for information, vehicles for dissent and watchdogs over authority although it should be said that journalism is more often concerned with the practicalities.' (ibid: 14–15)

But a significant new myth emerged following the Falklands adventure. This might be labelled the 'myth of the technological threat'. According to Mercer, the Falklands was a unique event (the same was to be said about the 1991 massacres in the Gulf); control of journalists was possible because of the peculiar, out-of-the-way situation of the theatre of war. Such control was seen as unlikely in the future – particularly given the possibilities for instant, uncensored reporting by the new satellite technology. Robert Harris came to a similar conclusion. He wrote: 'The Falklands conflict may well prove to be the last war in which the armed forces are completely able to control the movements and communications of the journalists covering it. Technology has already overtaken the traditional concepts of war reporting.' (op cit: 150)

Ideologically this myth is a crucial element of new militarist ideology representing the strong state as, in fact, vulnerable in the face of technological advance (which, in reality, it is able to exploit to extend its power) and historical contingency. Yet the Mercer/Harris scenario completely ignores the ideological constraints of the political consensus and the patriotic imperative of the professional culture that weigh so heavily on journalists in time of war and promote the journalism of deference and conformism. Moreover, it ignores the extent to which new militarist societies have demonstrated their ability to 'create enemies' and media-blitzed conflicts against relatively weak Third World adversaries. As McNail argues: 'The success of the Thatcher government in controlling media images of the Falklands war was not an anachronism, but the beginning of a trend.' (op cit: 179) The Falklands, Grenada, Libya, Panama and Gulf attacks were all essentially 'chosen' by the major powers. Donald A. Wells, in his seminal analysis of militarism, (1967: 105) comments pointedly: 'Military men choose their wars and governments choose the conflicts in which they propose to be involved.' But the myth of technological vulnerability was to surface powerfully during the Gulf crisis and serve to legitimise the censorship regime there.

Myth of the media 'enemy within': the Libyan new militarist mission

Mrs Thatcher was hoping for an action-replay of the Falklands factor when she gave the US permission to fly F111 attack jets from bases in East Anglia to bomb Libyan targets in 1986. It was an archetypal move of the secret state: only a select few of her cabinet were involved in the decision. (Young 1989: 476) Yet the attack appeared to win little support from the public. (Worcester 1991: 143) Harris, Gallup and MORI all showed substantial majorities opposed. Much of the press, however, responded with jingoistic jubilation. The *Sun*'s front page screamed: 'Thrilled to blitz: Bombing Gadaffi was my greatest day, says US airman.' The *Mirror* concluded: 'What was the alternative? In what other way was Colonel Gadaffi to be forced to understand that he had a price to pay for his terrorism'; *The Times*: 'The greatest threat to western freedoms may be the Soviet Union but that does not make the USSR the only threat. The growth of terrorist states must be curbed while it can still be curbed. The risks of extension of the conflict must be minimised. And in this case it would appear that it has been.' The *Express* headlined its editorial: 'A blow for freedom'. The *Star*'s front page proclaimed: 'Reagan was right'.

But there was an intriguing mediacentric dimension to the mission as the BBC, transformed into the 'enemy within' of the vulnerable state, was to come under some considerable attack from the Conservative government over its coverage of the attacks. An election was somewhere in the near future and the Thatcher government hoped a reinforcement of the Falklands factor with a Libyan factor would help her gain her hat-trick of victories. Though most of the mainstream press responded ecstatically to Britain's role in the bombing (the F111s flew from British bases) all their contrived jingoism could not hide the fact that the raid failed to capture the imagination of important elements of the elite. Opposition even came from Cabinet members.

The BBC became the perfect scapegoat. Kate Adie's on-the-spot reports could not fail to mention the casualties. (Sebba 1994: 266-267) Many of the main targets were missed. Four 2,000lb bombs fell on the suburb of Bin Ghashir, causing far more devastation than any 'terrorist' bomb could ever achieve. Even so, Norman Tebbit, chairman of the Conservative Party, engaged in a highly personalised attack on Adie. Yet there was an air of theatre about the whole event. Adie is one of the most trusted BBC correspondents. But both government and BBC could benefit from the Libyan theatre. The Tory right, on the ascendancy at the time, and ever hasty to criticise the BBC it so desperately wanted privatised as the 'enemy within', was satisfied; and the BBC, who stuck by their star reporter throughout the attacks, could appear to be courageously defending press freedom. Amidst the many contradictions and complexities of current politics, mediacentric elements are put to many diverse uses by the ruling elites.

New militarism: the home front

Thatcherism saw a narrowing of the consensus in British politics – and the new militarist adventure in the South Atlantic along with the rhetoric of the Cold War were used as ideological weapons to promote this. Scott has shown how recruitment to the ruling class in the UK has narrowed since 1945 thus accompanying the narrowing of the political consensus. (Scott 1991) Indeed, new militarism is accompanied by the emergence of a strong state and the breakdown of ideological contest in the political arena. As Brian McNair (1995: 24), in examining the breakdown of democratic pluralism, comments: 'Even in Britain, where the Labour and Conservative parties have traditionally been distinct ideologically, the late 1980s and early 1990s saw a coming together of agendas and policies on many social, economic and foreign policy matters.'

The strong state

Government opponents could easily be marginalised. When opposition did surface – as in the Campaign for Nuclear Disarmament (CND), the Greater London Council under 'Red Ken' Livingstone, the miners and other trade unionists, among students, travellers, blacks, and poll tax refusniks (Hollingsworth 1986; Gordon and Rosenberg 1989; Searle 1989) – they were dealt with heavily. As Bonefeld argues (1993: 197): 'The government's trade union policy contributed to the tightening up of the hierarchical composition of political domination. The form of the state that developed through the class conflict of the late 1970s and early 1980s was no longer characterised by institutional forms of class collaboration. The reassertion of the Right to political domination constituted the state as an agenda setting force that defined, through legal means, the role trade unions were allowed to play.'

A special unit of state (called the Defence Secretariat 19) was set up to deal with the CND 'threat', while Special Branch and MI5 began a systematic intimidation of CND supporters and other 'subversives'.[3] Richard Norton-Taylor reported in the *Guardian* that MI5 kept records on up to 1m people.[4] And former secret agent James Rusbridger reported on a secret service 'out of control' compiling dossiers on a wide range of 'suspects'. These could include anyone who belonged to a protest group, homosexuals and lesbians, owners of cars parked near selected political meetings and demonstrations, anyone who made a complaint against the police, anyone who wrote controversial letters in newspapers criticising government policy on sensitive issues such as nuclear weapons, anyone who wrote to newspapers criticising the secret services, anyone who made inquiries about civil defence. He cited the case of Mrs Madeline Haigh, of Sutton Coldfield, who was intimidated by Special Branch and MI5 after writing to her local paper protesting against the arrival of cruise missiles in Britain. (Rusbridger 1989: 165)

In 1989, the secret state was further strengthened with a new Official Secrets Act (OSA). The 1911 OSA had proved notorious, particularly after civil servant Sarah Tisdall was jailed in 1983 for leaking to the *Guardian* government plans for the timing of the arrival of cruise missiles in England. National security hardly seemed threatened by the disclosure. Then came the acquittal of top civil servant Clive Ponting charged under Section 2 (1) of the Act after he leaked information showing the government had misled the House of Commons over the sinking of the Argentinian ship, the Belgrano, during the Falklands conflict.

3 Campbell, Duncan and Connor, Steve (1986): *On the record: Surveillance, computers and privacy – the inside story*; Michael Joseph; London. They report: 'Ordinary civil servants protested that the DS19 proposal was against their rules of not engaging in party politics. But they were told to "put up or get out" by junior minister Peter Blaker. DS19 demanded enhanced MI5 surveillance of CND. Information about leading members of CND was turned to political ends before the 1983 general election, when Defence Secretary Michael Heseltine used selected information from the MI5 report in a letter to Conservative election candidates.' p 283.

4 'MI5 keeps records on one million'; the *Guardian*; 21 May 1992.

34

The new OSA covers five main areas: law enforcement, information supplied in confidence by foreign governments, international relations, defence and security, and intelligence. The publishing of leaks on any of these subjects is banned. Journalists are denied a public interest defence. Nor can they claim in defence no harm had resulted to national security through their disclosures. (Thomas, Rosamund 1991; Keeble 1994: 40) During the Thatcher years, police activities were also increasingly politicised. Not only were considerable constraints put on the right to demonstrate but brutal police action at a number of demonstrations – by miners, students and poll-tax refuseniks, for instance – suggested that the state wanted to intimidate people from attending marches simply for fear of the consequences.

Along with the growth of the secret, authoritarian state emerged an increasingly centralised system of government. As Anthony Sampson (1992) commented: 'The most pervasive change [in 13 years of Conservative rule] has been the centralisation of political and financial power. Ironically the prime minister who promised to reduce "big government" achieved unprecedented concentrations of power which appeared to overwhelm the traditional counterweights. Since the Seventies, the national cast of public characters has narrowed strikingly. The earlier drama included a range of major speaking parts, including trade unionists, local councillors, vice-chancellors, scientists, regional leaders and maverick politicians. Now the story line and supporting characters have been pared down to the central plot, revolving around money, the Treasury and – above all – Downing Street.'

The press and the strong state

The growing monopolisation and commercialism in the media during the Thatcher years was part of a general European media (European Research Group 1992) if not also global economic process.[5] But it encouraged the narrowing of the consensus – and the growing mediacentrism of society. Curran and Sparks (1991: 227) commented: 'In Britain, the erosion of popular organisations and the concentration of political life into forms related directly to the media have contributed to an increasing drying up of ideological wells of resistance. The mass media are not only one of the major sources of information about society but also one of the key sources or interpretative frames, too.'

During the 1980s. Rupert Murdoch's empire mushroomed and Robert Maxwell's manic media games kept his name constantly in the headlines. Yet it is wrong to exaggerate the role of individual media moguls. (Hanlin 1992; Tunstall and Palmer 1991) Both journalists and the moguls themselves have an interest in perpetuating a myth of media baron power. It satisfies the egos of the barons and to some extent excuses the journalists for some of the crude,

---

5   John Vidal in 'A world shackled by economic chains' (the *Guardian*; 8 May 1992) quotes
     Richard Tapper of the World Wide Fund for Nature: 'The top 50 companies of the world
     now control about 70 per cent of world trade, 80 per cent of foreign investment and 30 per
     cent of world GDP (about $3000 billion a year).'

unethical, activities they engage in. But in reality the power of the individual is but one amongst a host of many deeper and more significant ones.

Richard Norton-Taylor (1991: 13) sees the root of the media's deference and conformism in the heart of the journalists' culture. He writes: 'Self censorship is practised to varying degrees in every country where censorship is not otherwise imposed. It takes a particular form in Britain where it is bound up in a deep-seated culture of deference...The British press has traditionally aligned itself with the concept of the "national interest" or, in the phrase so frequently adopted by ministers "the public interest" by which they mean the governmental interests or the interest of the state.' In a similar vein, Tom Bower (1988), biographer of Robert Maxwell, has spoken of the 'journalism of inaction'. He said: 'The only conclusion which one can draw is that it was not the costs which deterred some newspapers from publishing investigations. The deterrent was more fundamental: namely the compromised status of the media in Britain today which results from the same conditions, the culture of inactivity which, as I have described, allowed Maxwell to flourish in the first place.' (Bower 1992: 14)

The introduction of new technology in newspapers during the late 1980s was accompanied by the deliberate destruction of formerly powerful print unions, (Foot 1991) In addition, there has been the growing centralisation of news organisations (thus reducing the role of the maverick – see Hodgson 1991); and mounting joblessness amongst newspaper journalists. This has led to a fall in journalistic morale and, it could be argued, encouraged still further conformism. Moreover, the growth of personal contracts for journalists has left them them less united and more dependent on management. Roy Greenslade, editor of the *Mirror* during the Middle East crisis of 1990-1991, has spoken of how 'modern newspaper staffs are frightened into not questioning authority'. (Greenslade 1995) He said it never once occurred to him to stand outside Fleet Street's pro-war consensus. It is only within this context of an increasingly centralised state and a highly conformist journalists' culture that media consensus over the 1991 Gulf massacres can be understood. At the same time, Thatcherism was identified with a series of attacks on the media which clearly reinforced this consensus but served a number of other purposes.

The media in the face of government 'flak'

With the rise of the New Right committed to the belief in the threat of the 'independent media' as a potential 'enemy within' there was need for the Thatcher government to respond. The intimidation of the BBC in January 1987 over Duncan Campbell's revelations about the Zircon spy satellite (then unknown to parliament) and a radio programme on the security services 'My country right or wrong', the intimidation of Thames Television over its screening of 'Death on the Rock' about the shooting dead of three unarmed IRA members by the SAS on Gibralter on 6 March 1988 (Bolton 1990), and the introduction of a series of laws restraining journalists (Police and Criminal Evidence Act, and the new Official Secrets Act) all issued from the strong state. Even the Prevention of Terrorism Act was used to coerce journalists into revealing sources. (Article 19 1989; *Index on Censorship* 1988)

A Human Rights Watch report of October 1991 expressed concern over the expansion of police powers to control and prevent public assembly, government interference in television interviews and documentaries, political vetting of community organisations in Northern Ireland, the Prevention of Terrorism Act and the anti-gay Section 28 of the Local Government Act.[6] But in certain instances it seemed as if the state's populist authoritarianism was 'out of control' – moving not so much into theatre as farce. The Irish broadcasting ban, launched in 1988, was an attempt to deny the 'terrorists' the oxygen of publicity, but it was so riddled with loopholes and absurdities (which left actors mouthing the exact words of IRA spokesmen) that it attracted the contempt even of prominent members of the elite.

These manifestations of the state security apparatus 'out of control' might be labelled hyper-statism. In the early 1980s, the historian and political commentator Edward Thompson (1982) developed the notion of exterminism to describe the process of military technogical advance which appeared to have a momentum of its own as it was driven by the Cold War arms race. With the collapse of the Soviet Union, exterminism was forced to shift its focus and together with the dynamic of hyper-statism in Britain (and in the States) was a significant factor behind the creation of the Middle East massacres of 1991.

---

6   Human Rights Watch (1991): *Restricted subject*; London, October.

3 Creation of US new militarist consensus

J ust as in Britain, in the United States during the 1980s media power became concentrated in fewer and fewer hands and the dominant consensus narrowed. The rise of the Republican New Right was accompanied by the emergence of pseudo politics, personality dominated and mediacentric. A series of new militarist adventures in the Third World were intended to cement this narrowing of the ideological consensus and contributed to the creation of a media culture of deference and conformism. Thus from the time of the Iraqi invasion of Kuwait, through the ensuing crisis and the massacres, the American media largely united behind the banner of the Bush administration. Because of the elite split over Gulf policy there was more debate aired than in the British press, but on the whole the consensus held firm.

The origins of this new militarist consensus can be traced to America's involvement in the Second World War. Some revisionist historians now suggest that Japanese plans for the attack on Pearl Harbour were well known to US intelligence and administration. (Farago 1967; Prange 1991; Rusbridger and Nove 1991) Certainly the attack provided the opportunity for the US's fledgling permanent war economy state to join the fight against the Nazis (now that the more serious enemy, the Soviet communists, had managed to survive the German onslaught).

The 'vulnerable state' (as represented by the elite) was responding as the innocent victim of an unprovoked attack. War was waged. And journalists faced a regime of 'total censorship'. As Gary C. Woodward comments: 'Everything written, photographed or broadcast was scrutinised by censors. Anything that did not meet the High Command's considerations of security was deleted. In the Pacific theatre, for example, Americans were not told initially of the heavy damage to the US Navy inflicted by the Japanese at Pearl Harbour.' (Woodward, Gary C 1993: 6) With the nuclear bombings of Hiroshima and Nagasaki of August 1945, the first warning to the Soviet Union in the new Cold War was delivered.

Growth of secret state and covert presidency

Alongside the development of the Cold War ideological hegemony and the permanent war state was the growth of the power of the executive office of the president based around the National Security Council and the CIA (together with many other covert organisations as a state within the state). (Moyers 1988) Secrecy and the development of a centralised, nuclear state were to become the dominant features of the domestic political scene, so covert LIC strategies, away from the glare of newspaper headlines, were favoured abroad.

Despite the enormous industrial and economic power of the American empire since 1945 (based on a massively expanding, state-backed arms economy), its overt military adventures have been disastrous. Korea ended in stalemate, the Bay of Pigs invasion plan for Cuba in 1961 was a humiliating disaster. (Cirino 1971: 282-284) So, too, was Vietnam. The attempt to rescue the hostages, held in the US embassy in Tehran, in 1980 crashed again – this time in a humiliating disaster in the desert. (Adams 1994: 149-154)

In the 1980s a series of military adventures proved equally disastrous. Lebanon (1982-83), Grenada, Libya, Panama and Iraq were all failures from a strictly military perspective – though massive propaganda campaigns were launched to portray the last four as military successes. The first followed the humilitation of Lebanon. The last three significantly followed the failures of covert action (assassination) to eliminate the heads of the 'enemy' states. It is, therefore, wrong to see the 1980s and early 90s as a period of American supremacy. Its new militarist adventures were all based on failures rather than successes.

Secret warfare: away from a probing press

But since 1945 America's main war-fighting activity was in the shady covert area – and here (through a series of managed media leaks) a number of 'successes' in the pro-insurgency field were claimed. The CIA's clandestine support for military coups against revolutionary or reforming regimes ranked up a number of significant victories: Syria 1949, Iran 1953, Guatemala 1954, Congo 1960, Iraq 1963 and 1968, Brazil 1964, Indonesia 1965, Chile 1973. (Ranelagh 1992) As Halliday points out, these successes were dependent on the relative vulnerability of the armed forces in the target country. He adds: 'When the CIA went into action against the revolutions of the 1970s this option was not available precisely because the revolutionaries had destroyed the old state machine, including its army, and replaced it with their own revolutionary armed forces. As in the case of Cuba during the period 1959-61, the CIA was thrown back on a surrogate form of covert action – aid to right-wing guerrillas.' (Halliday 1989: 74-75)

The global economic recession precipitated by the oil price increases of 1973 and 1979 completely overturned the global balance of power. (Baker 1991: 3-8) Initially the Third World made extraordinary gains and 14 revolutions shook the imperial powers.[1] In response, the imperial powers, led by the United States, completely altered their economic orientation to the Third World. From being suppliers of $50 billion a year of capital to the Third World in the two decades leading up to the mid-1970s, the imperial powers moved to drawing $100 billion a year from the Third World by the 1990s. This $150 billion shift was equivalent to the entire balance of payments of the United States, 15 times the annual investment of Iraq or Egypt. The result has been a massive rise of global poverty and Third World instability.

With the advent of the Reagan administration, the US elite was determined to roll back the revolutionary successes of the previous decade. The offensive was typically multi-pronged. Under the direction of William C. Casey (1981-86) the CIA ran a massive LIC offensive strategy – totally contradicting the media myth of defence. Counter revolutionary movements in Cambodia, Afghanistan, Angola,[2] Suriname and Nicaragua were backed from 1981 to 1988. And at enormous expense. In 1986 alone the Afghanistan operation received an estimated $470 million and more than $2 billion over the whole period.

Bob Woodward's (1987: 310-311) history of the CIA's covert wars of the 1980s details a complex web of clandestine activity. He also reports (ibid: 456) Ben Bradlee, *Washington Post* editor, as saying of the CIA in the 1980s: 'It's really out of control, isn't it?' At least 12 operations of security and intelligence support included those to President Hissen Habré of Chad, to Pakistan President Zia, to Liberia's leader Samuel Doe, to Philippine President Marcos, to Sudanese President Numeiri, to Lebanese President Amir Gemayel and to President Duarte of El Salvador (all of these ranking as dictators with appalling human rights records). Both Prades (1986: 383) and Treverton (1987: 14) suggest that by the mid-1980s the CIA was engaged in at least 40 major covert operations – but they were largely ignored by the media.

As Richard Barnet argues (1988: 218): 'The whole idea of low intensity warfare is to avoid "disturbing" – a euphemism for informing – public opinion in the United States (in the battle zone the intensity can be high indeed). The strategy depends on secrecy.' At their heart lies media propaganda through omission and mystification. Col Oliver North, during his July 1987 testimony to the Iran-Contra select congressional committee, argued that US national security justified covert paramilitary operations and the calculated dissemination of false and misleading information to the press by (and to) US

---

1   Halliday, Fred (1986): *The making of the Second Cold War*; Verso; London lists: Ethiopia 1974, Cambodia 1975, Vietnam 1975, Laos 1975, Guinea Bissau 1974, Mozambique 1975, Cape Verde 1975, Sao Tome 1975, Angola 1975, Afghanistan 1978, Iran 1979, Grenada 1979, Nicaragua 1979, Zimbabwe 1979 p. 92.

2   The *Guardian* reported (8 May 1992) a US Senate Intelligence Committee report that Jonas Savimbi, the Angolan rebel leader, received $250m in covert US aid during the 1980s. See also Wright, George (1992): 'The US and Angola'; *Z magazine*; Boston MA; May/June. pp 16-26 Also Stockwell, John (1978): *In search of enemies: A CIA story*; Andre Deutsch; London. Revelations by dissident, former CIA chief of the Angola Task Force.

officials operating on behalf of the secret state. 'There is a great deception practised in the conduct of covert operations. They are in essence a lie,' he told the committee with graphic frankness.

The Great Vietnam media myth

At the heart of LIC strategy and the Reaganite response to the Third World revolutions were American perceptions of the 'Vietnam syndrome'. For the American elite the defeat in Vietnam against a far less technologically sophisticated enemy – accompanied by assassinations, race and student upheavals at home – was a trauma of unprecedented proportions. A scapegoat was needed and the most obvious one was the messenger of the bad tidings – the media. Vietnam has been described as the 'first living-room war'. Long after the end of the war, it is argued, television images still dominate our perceptions of it – a US Marine Zippo lighting a Vietnamese village, the execution of a Vietcong suspect in a Saigon street, a Vietnamese girl running naked and terrified down a street after a napalm attack. Images such as these along with press criticism of the conduct of the war are said to have eroded public support.

Studies have shown this conventional wisdom to be a myth.[3] Surveys showed that media consumption, in fact, promoted support for the war. (Williams 1993: 305-328) The American military, after considerable deliberations on the issue since the Korean War, opted for an entirely voluntary censorship scheme for journalists – in the main because they did not have total control over access to the front line (unlike during the Gulf crisis of 1990-1991 when the military enjoyed total control). War censorship, it was also felt at the time, could not be introduced since no war had been declared.

Journalists were allowed remarkable access to the frontline. Sandy Gall comments in his autobiography (1984: 230-231): 'You could go anywhere at any time to cover almost any story. If there was a battle being fought in any part of Vietnam involving American troops or South Vietnamese or both the Press could go there simply by climbing aboard a helicopter or fixed-wing aircraft.' But this in no way resulted in journalists flagrantly ignoring the guidelines which outlined 15 categories of information reportable only with authorisation. Between August 1964 and the end of 1968, for example, around 2,000 news media representatives reported from Vietnam – yet only six committed violations so severe to warrant the military revoking their credentials. (Gannett 1991: 14-15)

Virtually every Vietnam reporter backed the war effort. As the Gannett Foundation report comments: 'Throughout the war, in fact, journalists who criticised the military's performance did so out of a sense of frustration that military strategy and tactics were failing to accomplish the goal of decisive-

---

3   Badsey, Dr Stephen (1995): 'Twenty things you thought you knew about the media', *Despatches* (journal of the Territorial Army Pool of Public Information Officers); London; Spring. pp 55-61. Argues, significantly: 'Historians have gone into media-military relations in Vietnam extremely thoroughly since 1975 and even the army's own official history, *The military and the media 1962-1968*, concludes that the American media was 'remarkably professional in its coverage of Vietnam.' p. 58.

ly defeating the North Vietnamese forces.' (op cit: 15) Veteran war corre-spondent Peter Arnett (1994: 88) commented: 'The consensus of the American high command was that their efforts were paying off in Vietnam, but that winning would take longer than anticipated. The reporters general-ly concurred in that view and I heard none voice doubts that the war was worth fighting.' In 1966, he said, he was entirely caught up in the war's momentum. 'I never asked myself whether it was right or wrong and the question did not come up in conversation, not with soldiers or my colleagues because we were all of us too close to the action. Too many of our friends had died; we were unwilling to write off that sacrifice.' (ibid: 193)

Most commentators have seen a shift to more critical 'advocacy' reporting following the Vietcong Tet offensive of 1968. But such a shift occurred among the American elite with significant sections beginning to question the costs, effectiveness and overall moral/political justification for the war. The media followed the shift in the elite consensus rather than created it. (Hallin 1986: 21; Williams 1987: 250-254; Cummings 1992: 84) Also after 1968 many in the US military were concerned to show the difficulties and daily frustrations of the war to the American public and welcomed the press as potential allies in conveying this message. (Woodward, Gary C op cit: 8)

With the massive costs and casualties, the American military learnt the dan-gers of overt warfare. (Williams, Reece 1987: 7-8) The secret war waged on Cambodia, for 14 months completely hidden from the media through a com-bination of lies and misinformation, showed the US government shifting back to LIC strategy. Nixon's policy of Vietnamisation, of 'peace with hon-our', essentially confirmed this move. By turning over the burden of the ground campaign to the Vietnamese the US army cut casualties from more than 14,000 in 1968 to just 300 in 1972. By 1974 there were only 35 per-manent correspondents left in Saigan. LIC fighting strategy predictably attracted LIC media coverage. Arnett comments (op cit: 284): 'Saigon bureaus were closed or reduced. The Vietnam story moved from the top of the network nightly news into the back pages of the papers alongside Dear Abby columns. The few reporters who remained in Saigon had to appreciate the comment made by a sardonic copy desk editor: "Gooks killing gooks don't make a story."'

But, in fact, the secret air war was intensified. One year after the Paris peace conference of 1973 the US Senate Refugee Committee reported that 818,700 refugees had been created in Vietnam and on average 141 people were being killed every day. As John Pilger (1986: 259) comments: 'But this did not qualify as a big story.'

Reagan and the journalism of deference

The advent of Ronald Reagan to the White House saw a massive new invest-ment in security operations and covert action – at both home and abroad. Phillip Knightley argues (1986: 342-343) that the CIA was running so much out of control that by the time Stansfield Turner became CIA director under

43

Carter in 1977 and tried to give orders to restrain covert operations he was simply ignored. Yet accompanying the growth of the secret state was the emergence of a supine, Reaganite media. As Kellner (1990: 227) argues: 'A combination of ignorance, servility and cowardice explains why the mainstream media have failed to fully develop, or even investigate, some of the most explosive political stories of the epoch.' He concludes: 'During the 1980s the mainstream media systematically sacrificed their journalistic integrity and became lapdogs of conservative hegemony – that is, the ideological tools of the corporate power elite.'

Press manipulation became a central strategy of the Reagan administration. Leslie Janka, a deputy White House press secretary who resigned over the exclusion of the press during the Grenada invasion, even commented: 'The whole thing was PR. This was a PR outfit that became President and took over the country. And to the degree then to which the constitution forced them to do things like make a budget, run foreign policy and all that they sort of did it. But their first, last and overarching activity was public relations.' (Hertsgaard 1988: 6) But in the face of this PR onslaught the press offered little resistance. Hertsgaard (ibid: 9) argues: 'As much through voluntary self-censorship as through government manipulation, the press during the Reagan years abdicated its responsibility to report fully and accurately to the American people what their government was really doing.'

Reagan had placed the revitalisation of the nation's intelligence system at the heart of his 1980 manifesto. The morale of covert action warriors, badly dented by Vietnam, was quickly restored. The CIA budget was increased by 15 per cent in 1982, 25 per cent in 1983. By 1985 the agency was the fastest growing major agency in the federal government. Knightley records: 'At one stage there were 20 different secret operations underway in Africa alone as the agency got back into business on a scale and with an enthusiasm unmatched since its heyday of the 1960s.' (op cit: 366) Central to the LIC strategy of the secret state is a media policy of silencing, mystification and lies.

Still the Vietnam syndrome persisted. Following the Vietnam trauma, the American public remained deeply divided over the wisdom and morality of interfering in the affairs of other countries. According to Richard Barnet, no more than 40 per cent of the electorate has ever subscribed to the official worldview that underpinned the intervention strategy. Thus for the most part Reagan, for all his noisy, militaristic rhetoric, resorted to secrecy and deception to carry out policies the administration felt unable to defend in open debate. (Barnet op cit: 217-218)

Yet in order finally to 'kick' the Vietnam syndrome and restore the military to their Second World War glory some notable victory in overt warfare, with substantial, glorifying media coverage, was desperately needed. This lay behind a series of military adventures during the Reagan years – all of them proved inadequate to the task. Only after the Gulf 'victory' could President

Bush finally pronounce the Vietnam syndrome 'kicked' and the fruits of that 'victory' rapidly crumbled to dust.

Grenada: the new militarist mission to escape the Middle East humiliation

On 23 October 1983, a Mercedes containing 12,000 lb of explosives was driven into the US Marine compound in Beirut by a member of a Shi'a militia and blew up killing 241 Americans, there to bolster the CIA-backed regime of President Gemayel. On the same day a bomb exploded at the French military headquarters in Beirut killing 58 soldiers. Another humiliating American retreat was put into motion.

But on a relatively unknown island of Grenada a crisis was unfolding which provided the US secret state with a perfect opportunity to assert itself and help erase the memory of the Beirut disaster. The four-and-a-half-year-old government of Maurice Bishop's People's Revolutionary Government (PRG) had been the source of constant concern to the US elite. With the Sandinistas' revolution toppling the US dictator ally Somoza in Nicaragua in 1979 and Castro's Cuba still surviving after decades of intense LIC diplomatic, economic, cultural warfare (see Freemantle 1983: 130-167), Bishop was seen as a further link in the chain of Soviet advancement in the region.

With internecine strife breaking out in the ruling PRG, Bishop was executed on 19 October, with Bernard Coard and General Hudson Austin forming a new revolutionary Military Council. On 21 October, the Prime Minister of Dominica, Eugenia Charles, as head of the Organisation of Eastern Caribbean States, is supposed to have requested US assistance in restoring 'order and democracy' to the island. But as McMahon argues it was not, as Reagan claimed (and the press dutifully reported), that the request dictated the US decision, rather it was the US that dictated the request – a scenario to be repeated between the US and Saudi Arabia in August 1990. (McMahon 1984: 153-165; Woodward 1987: 290-292; Mungham 1987)

Quigley also argues that OECS member countries violated their own treaty in voting for military action. The treaty allowed for military intervention only after 'external aggression' against a member country. In the case of Grenada there was no such aggression; nor did the OECS have the unanimous vote of all members as demanded by the treaty. (Quigley 1992: 201)

The secret mission the media missed

On 22 October, the Pentagon revealed that a naval task force, comprising two aircraft carriers and carrying around 1,900 marines, had been diverted from its course to Lebanon and was heading for Grenada. Operation Urgent Fury (as the Pentagon was to call it, in the glitzy, Hollywoody style that was to accompany all the US invasions of the 80s) was launched. For the US elite it was a significant moment. It amounted to the first large-scale military intervention in the hemisphere since the invasion of the Dominican Republic in 1965. Moreover, it was the first time special forces were deployed on a major scale since the launch of the revitalisation programme two years earlier. (Adams 1987: 221) The permanent war state was raring to go. All four US military services wanted a piece of the action – and they duly got it.

In all, 7,300 US military personnel and 300 police from Jamaica, Barbados and St Lucia were involved. As Smith (1994: 64) comments: 'Virtually every element in the US military played a role: airforce, navy, army (82nd Airborne), Marines, Army Rangers, Navy Seals, and Delta Force. If the Los Angeles Police Department had requested a role they would probably have gotten a piece of the action.' Above all, it was an attempt to wipe out the memory of a military humiliation (Beirut) with a massive, rapid, heavily censored raid.

James Combs argues that the Grenada invasion was significant in the emergence of a new kind of media spectacle warfare. He argues (1993: 278-279): 'Grenada was likely a preposterous military action producing no real results in terms of the array of power in the world, but it did help relegitimate the idea of intervention as beneficial and successful without producing a quagmire, nuclear exchange, large casualties and financial sacrifice by the citizenry...War was now to be conducted with not only concern with military tactics but also with how the war looked as dramatic narrative seen almost instanteously back home.'

All journalists were excluded from covering the invasion. The Joint Chiefs of Staff imposed total operational secrecy (OPSEC). The secrecy so integral to LIC strategies was now being applied to strategic invasions. Even White House spokesman Larry Speakes was not informed until after the first landings and had described the idea of an invasion as 'preposterous' in response to a CBS News inquiry on the eve of the operation. In the end, the press corps was kept off the island for three days. Some 400, mainly US journalists, were left stranded on Barbados.

A few journalists did try to reach the island by speedboat but were fired at by a US fighter plane and turned back. Gen. Norman Schwarzkopf, who led the military action (and later the US-led coalition forces in the Gulf), records approvingly in his autobiography how one of the military commanders, Vice Admiral Joseph Metcalf, responded to a question by one of the reporters involved: 'Admiral, what would have happened if we hadn't turned around?' with the words: 'We would have blown you right out of the water.' (Schwarzkopf 1992: 258) Two journalists did, however, manage to slip on to the island the night before the attack and were able to record the bombing of a civilian psychiatric hospital which killed 17 patients (four others were captured by the military and held for two days). (Rosenblum 1993: 125) Without their presence that 'mistake' might never have been recorded.

On 27 October, the first pool of 15 journalists and photographers were flown in to the island for a few hours accompanied by a military escort. Some 24 were taken on 28 October rising to 50 the next day. During the crucial first two days of the invasion, the US press significantly ignored the media ban and the dangers it imposed. Thus journalists failed to highlight the chances it gave the administration to manipulate public opinion for its own ends. As Hertsgaard (op cit: 221) comments: 'By the time the press worked up the courage to do more than clear its throat publicly about the censorship, three or four days after the invasion began, it was too late. The press had relayed enough government propaganda, sufficiently uncritically, so that the administration had successfully and irrevocably sold its version of the story to the public; the game of shaping public opinion was over and won for Reagan. In the process, the press had become, without knowing it, a passive accomplice in its own censorship.'

Grenada: the media spectacle testcase

On 27 October, the President appeared on television explaining directly to the public the rationale for the invasion. Such a development showed a sophisticated information policy – with the President able to present his message unfiltered by journalistic commentary or analysis. The carefully managed news conference with the American military appealing over the heads of journalists this time to the global community was to be an important feature of Gulf media strategy. Indeed, it was to prove to be a consistent feature of Thatcherite and Reaganite populism – with the heads of the secretive, centralised state using the mass media to articulate their views even over the heads of the traditional representative institutions (Parliament, Congress) to the public at large.

Administration lies

Nan Levinson (1991) describes Grenada as the 'uncovered invasion'. All the major features of the operation were distorted by administration lies, misinformation, secrecy – and, in the end, by journalistic bickering. All the justifications provided by the administration for the attack (dutifully reported in the press) were later deemed to have been spurious. (McMahon op cit: 144-167) Pentagon camera crews supplied propaganda pictures from Grenada (a device later to be used in the Gulf) of warehouses stocked with automatic weapons to 'supply thousands of terrorists' (according to Reagan). But once allowed on to the island, reporters found the warehouses were half empty, many containing cases of sardines while most of the weapons were antiquated. White House communications director David Gergen afterwards resigned in protest at the lying by his superiors. (Macarthur 1993: 142)

Casualties cover-up

The primary aim of the invasion, according to the administration, was 'to protect innocent lives'. Yet the invasion itself cost many people their lives. For some time the administration refused to reveal any casualty figures. In the end they said 18 Americans were killed and 113 wounded. The Cubans reported 24 Cubans and 16 Grenadians killed with 57 Cubans and 280

Grenadians injured. The Grenadian High Commission later suggested 1,500 Grenadians were killed. Half the 18 US dead were said to have been from 'friendly fire'.

Exaggeration of the threat

On the second day of the invasion, the US press reported official sources as saying that soldiers were meeting substantial resistance from 1,100 Cuban troops on the island with '4,340 more on the way', while a 'reign of terror' was endangering US medical students on the island. All of this 'information' was later found to be lies. As Garry Wills comments (1988: 356): 'The war was won because it could not be lost – the American invaders had a ten-to-one superiority over the defenders and all of the air and artillery weapons used.' On 31 October, the US State Department revised its earlier figures: there were, in fact, just 678 Cubans on the island of whom just 200 were soldiers. (Quigley op cit: 213-221) So much for administration claims that the island had become a massive base from which the Cubans and Soviets were planning to export 'terrorism'. But this exaggeration of the threat and invention of an enemy was to be repeated significantly during the later Gulf crisis.

Jan Servaes (1991) argues that Grenada was a test case for the 'disinformation war' later to be waged during the Gulf crisis. Savaes's study of six European 'quality newspapers' shows their coverage was influenced considerably by the disinformation campaign organised by the Pentagon. And as Parenti (1986: 51) comments: 'Objectivity means reporting US overseas involvements from the perspectives of the multinational corporations, the Pentagon, the White House and the State department and rarely questioning the legitimacy of military intervention (although allowing critical remarks about its effectiveness).'

Some of the most famous images to emerge from the invasion were of American students who had been evacuated from Grenada kissing the ground upon their return to the United States. These were distributed to news media around the world. But Hertsgaard (op cit: 227-228) shows how the press's uncritical coverage of this event served to reinforce administration justifications for the invasion. He writes: 'Only a handful of the students had actually kissed the ground upon returning home and subsequent reporting revealed that as a group the students were, in fact, divided on whether they had truly been in danger before the invasion. The disproportionate emphasis news accounts placed on students who did feel endangered, however, suggested that a virtual unanimity opinion existed among the students and moreover that it supported Reagan's justifications for invading.'

The Sidle Commission

In response to the protests lodged by some news organisations over the Grenada censorship regime, the Department of Defense set up a 12-member panel of journalists, journalist professors and military public affairs officers to study media-military relations. It was headed by General Winant Sidle, former chief of information for US forces in Vietnam and head of Martin-Marietta corporate public affairs. The Sidle report, released on 23 August, 1984, contained eight recommendations. Amongst the most important was one endorsing 'the largest possible pooling procedure to be in place for the minimum time possible'; another called for voluntary compliance by the media with security guidelines. Sidle proved to be yet another feature of the democratic facade of US politics – once the Gulf crisis exploded its most important suggestion, on the pooling arrangements, was completely ignored by the secret US state.

Libya and the secret war in Chad the media missed

On 21 May 1992, the *Guardian* carried four short paragraphs on Chad, the little reported country to the south of Libya. Some 40,000 people were estimated to have died in detention or been executed during the eight-year rule of Hissène Habré (1982-1990). A report of the justice ministry committee concluded that Habré had committed genocide against the Chadian people. Yet what the *Guardian* omitted was perhaps far more significant than the news it reported.

Away from the glare of the major media, the US secret state had conducted one of its most important secret wars against Libya during the late 1970s and 1980s, using Chad as its base. (Halliday 1981) Bob Woodward reveals that the Chad covert operation was the first undertaken by the new CIA chief Casey in 1981 and that throughout the decade Libya ranked almost as high as the Soviet Union as the *bête noire* of the administration. (Woodward op cit: 348, 363, 410-411) Mark Perry (1992: 167) even suggests that the CIA programme against Libya 'was one of the most extensive in its history'. Cockburn and Cockburn (1992: 123) suggest that US and Israeli intelligence worked together on the Habré coup.

But in late 1990, as the Middle East crisis developed, Libyan intelligence services in collaboration with their French counterparts (the French government having tired of Habré's genocidal policies) installed Idriss Déby in a secret operation as the new Chadian President. Jane Hunter (1991: 49) comments: 'Knowledgeable sources on Capitol Hill agreed that it was likely the Bush administration offered not to frustrate France's objectives in exchange for French co-operation in the war against Iraq.'

Back in 1981 Col Mu'ammar Gadaffi, President of Libya, had already survived a number of coup attempts organised in secrecy by the British and the French.[4] In the mid-1970s a British plan to invade the country, release polit-

---

4 Gadaffi had, perhaps paradoxically, undertaken a military training course in England in 1966. Yallop, David (1994): *To the ends of the earth: The hunt for the jackal*; Corgi; London records how the CIA had tolerated his 1969 coup that toppled King Idris. 'President Nixon, one of the world's original cold warriors, ably assisted by like-minded Kissinger, concluded that Mu'ammur Gadaffi held two aces – Libyan oil and his intense dislike of Godless Communism...The President decided that Libya's new leader was a man "he could do business with".' Yallop even reports that the CIA and Egyptian intelligence warned Gadaffi of a coup plot against him in 1970 while later in the year another plot was unmasked after the president acted on a tip-off from French intelligence. p. 210.

ical prisoners and restore the monarchy ended in a complete flop. In 1980, the head of the French secret service, Col Alain de Gaigneronde de Marolles, resigned after a similar French-led plan ended in disaster when a rebellion by Libyan troops in Tobrik was quickly put down. (Deacon 1990: 262-264)

Then in 1982, after Libyan troops had made an incursion into Chad, Hissène Habré was installed as president in a CIA-directed coup and from this base a covert war was waged on Libya. US official records indicate that funding for this secret war came from Saudi Arabia, Egypt, Morocco, Israel and indeed Iraq. Prades records the Saudis donating $7m to an opposition group, the National Front for the Salvation of Libya (which was backed by French intelligence and the CIA). But a plan to assassinate Gadaffi and take over the government on 8 May 1984 was crushed. (Prades op cit: 383; Perry op cit: 165) In the following year, the US asked Egypt to invade Libya and over-throw Gadaffi, but President Mubarak refused. (Martin and Walcott 1988: 265-266) By the end of 1985 the *Washington Post* had exposed the plan after congressional leaders opposing it wrote in protest to President Reagan.

Thrilled to blitz with Libyan bombings

Throughout the early 1980s Gadaffi was demonised in the mainstream US media as the 'terrorist warlord'. (Chomsky 1986) Libyan hit squads were said to have entered the United States, though this has since been revealed to have been a piece of Israeli secret service disinformation.[5] Reagan's list of terrorist states, issued in July 1985, comprised Iran, Libya, North Korea, Cuba and Nicaragua. (Segaller 1986: 120) And as Segaller (ibid: 130-135) argues, Gadaffi's anti-West rhetoric played into the hands of President Reagan. 'Terrorist' outrages at Rome and Vienna airports early in 1986 were both blamed on Gadaffi and Reagan declared Libya to be 'a threat to the national security and foreign policy of the United States'.

Frustrated in their covert attempts to topple Gadaffi (beyond the gaze of the media), the US government suddenly shifted its strategy. In March 1986, US planes patrolling the Gulf of Sidra were reported to have been attacked by Libyan missiles. But Chomsky (1991a: 124) suggests that this incident was a provocation 'enabling US forces to sink several Libya boats, killing more than 50 Libyans and, it was hoped, to incite Gadaffi to acts of terror against

---

5 Rusbridger, James (1989): *The intelligence game*; Bodley Head; London. Reports that CIA had been told by Israeli agent, the Iranian businessman Manucher Ghorbanifar, that Gadaffi had sent assassination squads to America to kill the president. 'This story had been used extensively by the Americans to drum up support against Gadaffi in the tame sections of the Western media even though they knew it was untrue. Ghorbanifar had also offered to pro-vide the CIA with intelligence about Iran in return for being allowed to smuggle drugs.' Ghorbanifar was later to act as an intermediary in the secret shipment of TOW missiles to Iran (to be known as the Iran/Contra affair). p. 80.

See also Yallop, David (op cit: 706). Also Joe Flynn, the infamous con man, was able to exploit Fleet Street's fascination with the Gadaffi myth. In September 1981, posing as an Athens-based arms dealer he tricked nearly £3,000 out of the *News of the World* with his story that the Libyan leader was 'masterminding a secret plot to arm black revolutionary murder squads in Britain'. See Lycett, Andrew (1995): 'I study my targets. I find out what makes them tick'; the *Independent*; 22 June.

Americans, as was subsequently claimed'. In the following month the US responded with a military strike on key Libyan targets. The attack was widely condemned. Adams (1987: 372) quotes a British intelligence source: 'Although we allowed the raid there was a general feeling that America had become uncontrollable and that unless we did something Reagan would be even more violent the next time.' In November, the UN General Assembly passed a motion condemning the raid.[6] Hussain (1988: 45) describes it as an act of 'imperialist aggression'. Yet the administration could not have hoped for a better media response.

For 11 minutes in the early morning of 14 April, 30 US Air Force and Navy bombers struck Tripoli and Benghazi in a raid codenamed El Dorado Canyon. Reagan dubbed Gadaffi a 'mad dog'. Two incidents on successive days earlier in the month had provided the excuse. In the first, four Americans died when an explosion blew a hole in a TWA plane flying from Rome to Athens. In the second a bomb explosion at La Belle Disco in West Berlin, frequented by US servicemen, killed three people.

Bleifuss (1990) records a report on 14 September 1990 on Radio *Deutsche Welle* suggesting that the CIA knew that a terrorist bombing of the disco was being planned but failed to maintain proper security – perhaps to give the Reagan administration a pretext to bomb Libya. Conor Gearty (1991: 83-87) comments: 'In so far as any blame could be allocated the Syrians appear to have been implicated in the first of these attacks and they were, and still are, suspected by many of having orchestrated the second.' Significantly newsrooms were informed of the planned air strikes beforehand – but all held back from reporting until after the raids, thus showing the growing complicity between media and the state over the handling of new militarist adventures. (Trainor 1991: 76)

According to Kellner, the bombing was a manufactured crisis, staged as a media event and co-ordinated to coincide with the beginning of the 7 pm news in the US. (Kellner 1990: 138) Two hours later President Reagan went on network television to justify the raid. Chomsky also argues that the attack was the 'first bombing in history staged for prime-time television'. (Chomsky op cit: 127) Administration press conferences so soon after the raid ensured 'total domination of the propaganda system during the crucial early hours'. He continues: 'One might argue that the administration took a gamble in this transparent public relations operation, since journalists could have asked some difficult questions. But the White House was justly confident that nothing untoward would occur and its faith in the servility of the media proved to be entirely warranted.'

---

6   Interestingly, Israel was one of the few countries to back the US over the raid. Yet when the Israeli representative at the UN came to justify his country's stance, he used evidence of Gadaffi's alleged commitment to terrorism taken from the German mass-selling newspaper *Bild am Sonntag* and the London-based *Telegraph*. Yallop (op cit) shows this evidence to have been 'pathetic'. p 695.

Backing Reagan came the ecstatic response of the media. Even before the attack, the media were urging military action against Libya. William Safire commented in the *New York Times* of 14 April, that if the US failed to attack 'the world will note who flinched, the recent war of nerves will have the wrong winner. Another US President will have been exposed as muscle-bound in the face of the challenge by a state terrorist and terrorism, victorious again, will continue to increase'. Then, following the raid, the *New York Times*'s editorial of 15 April commented: 'The smoke in Tripoli has barely cleared yet on the basis of early information even the most scrupulous citizen can only approve and applaud the American attacks on Libya...It's emotionally satisfying to say that Col. Gadaffi deserves whatever he gets.' Next day it editorialised: 'There have been times in the shadow war of terror when the tiger could do no more than snarl and twitch his tail – and there will be others. On Monday, America sent a justifiably different message. The tiger bites.'

The *Los Angeles Times* editorialised on 15 April: 'The West would shed no tears over the fall of Gadaffi, nor would Arab governments that live even closer to the psychotic tyrant.' And the *Washington Post*, of 15 April, enthused: 'President Reagan made a powerful case for his strike against Libya... US had reason and right to do what it did. It will be noted by Arabs that Ronald Reagan waited six years to hit back and then did so in a discriminating way – a too discriminating a way some of them may privately complain.' As was to be repeated during the 1991 Middle East massacres, the media tended to marshal emotions and mobilise patriotic sentiments around the drama of the action rather than critically explore the morality of the attack.

Libya and the precision myth

US press coverage stressed President Reagan's claims that the use of precision weapons had helped reduce civilian casualties. Similar claims were to dominate administration and media rhetoric during the 1991 Gulf massacres. The *New York Times* editorial of 15 April 1986, for instance, said the US 'evidently tried to avoid innocent casualties'. Yet Bob Woodward (op cit: 446) highlights the 'high-tech failure that was kept secret'. Eight, perhaps nine, F111 bombers each carrying four 2,000lb laser-guided bombs were to attack Gadaffi's own barracks at Splendid Gate. Some 32 bombs were supposed to strike the compound.

In the event, perhaps two hit their target. A number of F111s even had to turn back from the 14-hour, 2,800-mile flight from England. Even so, the media myth of hi-tech precision was to persist until the 1991 massacres and beyond. Col (Retired) David Hackworth, one of the most decorated soldiers in the US, commented after the raid: 'This big operation was a Pentagon attempt to impress Congress just when they're starting to cut back on the military.' (Chomsky 1991: 166-167) And Malcolm Spaven (1986) sees the bombing as being more about inter-service rivalry than international terrorism. (see also Dalyell 1987: 64)

The casualties cover-up

Gadaffi's barracks were located in a densely populated part of Tripoli while another target was in downtown Benghazi. As Quigley (op cit: 229) comments: 'Bombing at night, at high speed, in congested areas, by pilots with inadequate training, meant that mistakes and civilian casualties were highly likely in the Libyan raid. But they were a cost the administration was willing to pay.' The *New York Times* sought to play down this aspect of the raid. It commented on 15 April: 'Even if some neutral targets were struck and some civilians killed in the early morning raids, the US evidently tried to avoid innocent casualties. There is no way to say as much for Colonel Gadaffi and his terrorists whose purpose is to kill civilians.'

Yallop suggests that the main purpose of the raid was to kill the Libyan president. He quotes 'a member of the United States Air Force intelligence unit who took part in the pre-raid briefing': 'Nine of 18 F111s that left from the UK were specifically briefed to bomb Gadaffi's residence inside the barracks where he was living with his family.' (Yallop 1994: 713) In the event, the first bomb to drop on Tripoli fell on Gadaffi's home. Hana, his adopted daughter aged 15 months, was killed, his eight other children and wife Safiya were all hospitalised, some with serious injuries. The president escaped. But consider the outrage in the US media if a relative of Reagan had been killed by a Libyan bomb. There was no such outrage over the Libyan deaths. Following the April 1986 attack, reports of US military action against Libya disappeared from the media. But, away from the media glare, the CIA launched what Mark Perry (op cit: 166) describes as 'by far the most extensive effort yet to spark an anti-Gadaffi coup'. A secret army was recruited from among the many Libyans captured in border battles with Chad during the early 1980s.

The pool and the Gulf 1987: the first news blackout

The US attack on Libya was over far too quickly for any media pool system – as recommended by the Sidle commission – to be activated. On 7 April, it was revealed that pool reporters were kept two hours aboard the aircraft carrier Saratoga off Libya after Libyan missiles were fired at American planes on 24 March. The reporters were then taken from the ship without being told of the action. This sparked a strong protest to the government by the American Society of Newspaper Editors.[7]

The pool's first real test in a war zone came in July 1987 after one powerful section of the US secret state – then backing Iraq in its war with Iran – provided naval escorts for Kuwaiti oil tankers recently registered under American flags in the Gulf. But by mid-August the military had still failed to activate the pool. Eventually, several pools were placed on navy destroyers. But, according to Mark Thompson, of Knight Ridder, several reports from journalists on USS Fox were held up for nearly two days, at least one was

---

7   The *New York Times*, 7 April 1986.

changed by the Fox's commander before being filed and a photographer was refused permission to fly in a helicopter after the super-tanker Bridgeton was hit by a mine. (Woodward, Gary C op cit: 9)

The pool and the Panama invasion 1989

The Sidle recommendations were again to be totally ignored during the Panama invasion launched on 20 December 1989 (codenamed Operation Just Cause) – supposedly to arrest the country's leader, General Noriega, on drug charges. Some 24,000 troops participated in the invasion making it the largest US military operation since the Vietnam War. (Goldman 1991) For the first two days, media reports came from journalists detained in a warehouse. Some 100 additional reporters who accompanied the troops meekly returned home when they were told by the military they had no facilities to service them. (Rosenblum op cit: 126)

Gary Woodward (op cit: 11) argues that the media had no choice but to work alongside the military. 'But as the Persian Gulf War loomed, members of the press would have good reason to rethink the wisdom of ceding editorial prerogative of prior restraint to Pentagon planners. A general silence on this point throughout the tanker escort operation in 1987 and the later Panama invasion meant that coveted slots in press pools would come at a very high price.'

The casualties cover-up: again

In many respects the Panama invasion can be seen as another testing of a media/fighting strategy that was to be repeated during the Middle East massacres of 1991. At the heart of the Pentagon strategy was the representation of the attack as swift and clean. As Patrick Sloyan, of *Newsday*, commented, the muzzling of the press in Panama created 'the illusion of bloodless battlefields'. (Fund for Free Expression 1991) And, according to John R. Macarthur (1993: 16): 'What the administration prevented during the first thirty six hours of the Panama invasion were any eye-witness accounts or photographs of the shelling of El Chorrillo, the desperately poor neighbourhood in Panama City, where General Noriega's headquarters were located.'

The Pentagon was at first reluctant to provide any casualty figures. Only three weeks after the invasion did Southern Command say that 202 Panamanian civilians and 314 soldiers had died. Later it reduced the figure for military casualties down to 50. (Andersen 1991: 24) Yet the Spanish language press both within and outside the US (InterPress Service, *Echo* of Mexico) cited more than 2,000 deaths and approximately 70,000 casualties. The National Council of Churches and the Red Cross also estimated the total civilian deaths may have numbered 2,000 at a minimum. (Chomsky 1991: 164; see also Gellhorn 1990) A number of mass graves were discovered after the invasion.

Only 23 US soldiers were reported to have died in the operation. After *Newsweek* reported that as many as 60 per cent of these casualties may have resulted from US action (known in euphemistic militaryspeak, uncritically adopted by the press, as 'friendly fire'), the Pentagon announced for the first time that US action accounted for two of the 23 deaths and 19 of the 324 injuries. (Woodward, Bob 1991: 195)

Demonisation of Noriega

As was later to be echoed in media coverage of the Iraq-Kuwait crisis, much of the media coverage of the Panama invasion focused on the personality of General Manuel Antonio Noriega as newly defined by the Bush administration. He was accused of heading a huge drug-running operation and of brutally suppressing the results of an election a few months earlier. The shooting of a US military officer by a member of Noriega's Panamanian Defence Forces was said to be the final straw for the administration.

But such a 'human interest' focus downplays the history of US involvement with Noriega. He was recruited by the CIA's chief of station in Lima, Peru, in 1959 to provide information on his fellow students at the Peruvian Military Academy and his links with central American drug barons and US administrations were close, in particular while George Bush was briefly head of the CIA during the Ford administration (1975-1976). (Perry op cit: 110-115) In 1984, Noriega refused to accept the election victory of Arnulfo Arias and installed, to US applause, Nicolas Ardito Barletta in his place. But by 1989 Noriega had drawn the wrath of the Bush administration for refusing to co-operate in Col. Oliver North's plan to use a shipload of arms to accuse the Nicaraguan Sandinistas of smuggling weapons to the Salvadorean rebels. Then, more significantly, the administration wanted to revoke the Panama Treaties of 1977 according to which control of the Panama canal was to pass into Panamanian hands.

In addition, US military bases were to be phased out by the year 2000 (yet the Bush administration saw them as crucial staging posts for military intervention in Latin America). On 2 January, 1990, a Panamanian was due to be appointed head of the Canal Commission. These were among the major reasons for the invasion which, as Weeks and Gunson show conclusively, was in total violation of international law. It was condemned by the UN Security Council (though the vote was vetoed by US, UK and France) while the UN General Assembly deplored the intervention and demanded the immediate withdrawal of US forces from Panama. (Weeks and Gunson 1991) The 'human interest' bias of the coverage served to marginalise this critical historical background to the action.

In her analysis of the *New York Times* coverage of the invasion, Sandra H. Dickson (1994: 813) found that the single most prominent theme was that of Manuel Noriega as drug trafficker. Of the 344 themes present, 61 per cent were categorised as governmental or those the Bush administration used to describe the invasion while 39 per cent were coded as non-governmental or those that were contrary to or critical of the US invasion. She concluded: 'Although the *New York Times* provided a forum for critics to attack the US invasion of Panama, it still allowed US government officials to define and dominate the political debate.' (ibid: 815) Similarly, Gutierrez-Villalobos, Hertog and Rush (1994) found the mainstream news magazines, *Time* and *Newsweek*, offering little strategic opposition to administration policies over the Panama invasion.

Myth of the sudden response

The military invasion followed the failure of a CIA-backed coup attempt on Noriega months earlier. (James 1990) From July 1989 US forces conducted a series of provocative manoeuvres, condemned by the Organisation of American States, clearly intended to accustom Panamanians to US troop presence. On 2 July, US troops occupied two water processing plants and set up roadblocks throughout civilian neighbourhoods. As Hellinger and Judd comment: 'These manoeuvres dramatically raised tensions between US and PDF forces, a climate that probably contributed to the death of the US officer just before the invasion. None of this was reported by standard news organisations.' (Hellinger and Judd 1991: 53-54)

The Hoffman report

Following the Panama invasion, the Department of Defense indulged in its predictable ritual of commissioning a report – this time by Fred S. Hoffman, one of its former officials. He assigned specific responsibility for the failure of the pool system to Defense Secretary Dick Cheney and Assistant Secretary of Defense for Public Affairs Pete Williams. The report concluded that 'excessive concern for secrecy' prevented the Defense Department media's pool from reporting the critical opening battles and that the pool produced 'stories and pictures essentially of secondary value'. Williams and his staff promised to handle any future military operations properly.

Irangate no Watergate

While the US new militarist state machine felt more confident during the 1980s and ready to indulge in military attacks on the Third World, now that a media system had been developed which meant strategic actions could be shrouded in as much secrecy as straight covert actions, LIC strategy still prioritised covert warfare throughout the decade. The most infamous instance was the Reagan/Bush secret state's illegal deals with the Iranian government to send arms shipments via Israel, the money acquired being redirected to the Contra terrorists in Nicaragua. (Marshall, Dale and Hunter 1987; Simons 1992)

The foreign editor of the Hearst newspapers, John Wallach, first reported on contact between US and Iran in June 1985 and wrote about the arms sales six months later, but the story was denied by the White House and no one followed it up vigorously. (Pilger 1986: 570) Hertsgaard comments (op cit: 302) on the early marginalisation of the Irangate stories in the press: 'And so they floated past largely unnoticed, fortifying Reagan administration officials in the conviction that they could conduct whatever illegal or unpopular operations they wished without fear of detection.' The sales only hit the global headlines after an obscure Lebanese newspaper revealed them.[8] Closely linked to this scandal was the so-called October Surprise, according to which the Reagan election team made a deal with Iran to hold the American hostages until after the 1980 election and so deny Carter any of the benefits which would inevitably then fall on the President from the release. (Cohen 1991)

Kellner (1990: 88) argues that the October Surprise was 'perhaps the most explosive scandal of the Reagan years and the one most studiously avoided by the mainstream media'. Moreover, the congressional Iran/Contra hearings did more to cover-up the scandal than investigate it. Media coverage transformed Col. Oliver North, one of the principal organisers of the illegal shipments, into a national folk/cult hero. As Andersen (1992: 173) argues: 'Particularly in the absence of context, the focus on a character and personality is a convenient substitution for explaining a complicated and deliberately obscure political process. News coverage of the testimony of North emphasised the military man as a personality while the most damaging and serious of his actions remain secrets kept from the American public.'

Lance Bennett (1990: 123-124) endorses this view, commenting: 'The media seemed content to allow the government to investigate itself, assess the importance of the problem, define the solution and pronounce the denouement of the story. As a result, a scandal with deep institutional roots passed with only minor punishments handed out to minor actors deemed personally responsible for the breakdown in normal foreign policy making.' The administration had by November 1986 decided to make North the 'scapegoat' for the scandal – and the press were more than willing to adopt that agenda.

---

8   Ben-Menashe, Ari (1992): 'Nobody wanted the scoop', *Lies Of Our Times*; New York; June. Reveals the origins of the Irangate leak. Ben-Menashe was working for the External Relations Department of the Israel Defence Forces and a joint military intelligence-Mossad committee for Iran-Israel relations. The committee was involved in massive Israeli weapons sales to Iran – with tacit support of the Americans. Profits were used for Israeli intelligence activities. But then Oliver North set up his own operation in an attempt to sabotage the Israelis. 'We knew that his operation, with the assistance of the CIA, was skimming huge profits from the Iranian arms deals and channeling funds to the Contras; we also knew that this was in violation of US law at the time. I was asked to leak the story.' He discussed it with a number of leading US journalists. None could get it published. He ends rather cryptically: 'Why, I still wonder, was an insider like myself unable to get either *Time* or *Newsday* to touch the same story that the whole world ran with when it appeared, unattributed, in an obscure Lebanese journal?'

Rusbridger, James (op cit) suggests that the operation was leaked to the Beirut-based *Al-Shiraa* by Ali Akbar Rafsanjani, Speaker of the Iranian Parliament, on 3 November 1986, the day following the release of American hostage David Jacobsen. 'In Iran Rafsanjani had come under strong attack from Khomeini supporters who accused him of siding with America by accepting arms from the Great Satan and helping to get some of their hostages released. In order to extricate himself Rafsanjani gave details of the entire American arms-supply operation to the Lebanese magazine.' p. 83.

Hertsgaard (op cit) reports that when first questioned about the story in *Al Shiraa*, Reagan claimed there was 'no foundation' to the report. Documents subsequently released by Congressional committees investigating the affair showed the President, in fact, led a 10 November 1986 White House discussion aimed at concealing the details of the arms-for-hostages plans from the press and public p 321.

The Reaganite propaganda machine

Since the US elite outlined their programme for global dominance just after the Second World War, the media have been at the heart of this strategy. Thus that part of the Reagan Doctrine which prioritised the propaganda war was following a long-established tradition – but during the 1980s investment in the propaganda machine reached new heights. The budget of the US Information Agency rose to nearly $800 in 1986 – a 74 per cent leap since 1981. Reagan launched Worldnet, a $15m million a year project to link foreign journalists with policy makers by satellite. In October 1985 Voice of America began a 24-hour service to Europe. Radio Marti was launched to broadcast anti-Castro propaganda to Cuba; backing for *La Prensa*, the main opposition paper in Nicaragua, grew. (Hellinger and Judd op cit: 55)

Overt censorship by the Reagan administration

In addition during the 1980s, as Demac (1984) demonstrates, the administration took unprecedented steps to restrict and weaken permanently the power of the press through executive orders, legislation, intelligence service penetration of the media and tight controls on contacts between reporters and government personnel. To protect the new emphasis on covert activities, the Agents Identities Protection Act of 1982 criminalised any information identifying an individual as a covert agent, even if the information were to be derived from public sources. The 1984 Freedom of Information Act amendments further protected the CIA from public scrutiny. An Executive Order of 1981 established conditions for infiltration of academic and private institutions in the US. Attempts to impose even limited Congressional oversight of covert activities in the early 1980s failed dismally. As Dumbrell (1990: 157) comments: 'The constant invocation of national security and the genuine desire of members not to compromise sensitive areas of activity have seriously blunted the cutting edge of responsible oversight.'

National Security Directive 84 'amounts to a lifetime Draconian gag order on hundreds of thousands of government employees by applying to all federal employees secrecy obligations which were previously only applicable to employees of intelligence services', as Bennett says. (Bennett, J 1988: 32) CIA penetration of the media intensified and links between the defence industry and the media grew tighter. (Kellner op cit: 82-84) The press became a central force within a transnational corporate media structure that became increasingly centralised in the 1980s and directly committed to capitalist interests. With the ever-narrowing consensus between the two major parties and the media's obsession with the pseudo politics of image making, scandal, gossip, celebrity worship and sensation, the ideological and institutional machinery was in place which was to produce the media consensus on the Middle East massacres.

4 Ending history: the press and Saddam Hussein

New militarism, as a system aiming to resolve the problems of militarism within an advanced capitalist society, is dependent on a public largely depoliticised and, more specifically, ignorant of the political dynamics and history of the Third World. Kegley and Wittkopf (1987: 306) suggest that foreign policy makers in the US see public opinion as something to be shaped, not followed. They write (ibid: 307): 'Although public information may serve as a constraint on foreign policy it would be a mistake to ascribe too much importance to the limits it imposes. The ability of the public to constrain foreign policy (by defining a range of permissible policies) is undermined by the acquiescent attitude of most Americans toward most foreign policy iniatives.'

Significantly a survey carried out in the US during the conflict by Lewis, Morgan and Jhally (1991) found widespread ignorance of Middle Eastern politics and Western foreign policies. Media coverage of the Third World is premised largely on this ignorance and passivity and serves to reinforce them.[1] The popular press ignores the Third World – apart from certain sensational, exceptional stories (for instance, the Middle East massacres). The heavies perpetuate it through omission, ideological distortion, stereotyping and over-personalising.

Following the invasion of Kuwait by Iraqi soldiers on 2 August 1990, the press in the UK and US focused primarily on the personality of Saddam Hussein, President of Iraq. A number of controversies (the supergun affair, the execution of the journalist Farzad Bazoft, the interception of nuclear triggers bound for Iraq) had brought Saddam Hussein a certain amount of

---

1 Traber, Michael and Davis, Ann (1991): 'Ethics of war reporting', *Media Development*; London; October. pp 7-10. They comment: 'Ignorance of the affairs of a nation's ordinary people is useful in the construction of the image of the enemy. The less we know of the enemy the easier it is to create the image that we wish. The mass media have built up or, at least, reinforced a social cosmology which divides the world into angels and devils, the good and the bad.' p 9.

negative coverage in the Western media in the previous six months. Such coverage reflected the ambivalent attitude by the US/UK secret states to Saddam Hussein at this time.

But in general, people in Britain and America had before 1990 little knowledge of the politics of Iraq, the Gulf, or the personality of Saddam Hussein. Gary Woodward comments (1993: 21): 'An emphasis on spot news, the enormous cultural differences between Western and Islamic states, press dependence on frames of reference defined by the American government and a long history of insularity have all contributed to ignorance of the region.' Premised on this ignorance and reinforcing it, a massive propaganda campaign was launched by the press and media in general to demonise this formerly unknown character and legitimise the response of the Western powers to the Kuwait invasion.

The mystery of Halabja

The representation of Saddam Hussein effectively as Iraq only emerged in the months leading up to August 1990 and then completely dominated the coverage throughout all the British media. Before the Kuwait invasion, the principal bogeyman in the Middle East for the mainstream press was Iran. Searle demonstrates how the *Sun*'s racist venom was directed at this country throughout the 1980s. (Searle 1989) On 18 October 1987, after the US destroyed two Iranian ex-oil rigs in the Gulf, it commented: 'The Americans have enough firepower in the Gulf to render the country a wasteland. Maybe that would not be a bad thing for the rest of humanity.' (ibid: 36)

During the Iran-Iraq war (1980-1988) Iraq was in general referred to simply as Iraq or Baghdad. As significant sections of the West tilted towards Iraq so the personalising of that country through Saddam Hussein declined. When he was mentioned it was often in favourable terms. In their study of US press coverage of Iraq from 1979 to 1990, Gladys Engel Lang and Kurt Lang (1994: 47) also conclude: 'Most striking is Saddam Hussein's low news profile throughout these years; in only 4 per cent of all items examined was the man himself, his pursuit of military superiority or his sponsorship of terrorism a main or even subsidiary topic.'

Public opinion seemed to reflect press coverage, which in its emphases and tone, it could be argued, was reproducing state policy towards Iraq. The Langs (ibid: 44-45) mention a 1980 poll by Louis Haris and Associates which asked a national sample to identify which of 15 countries 'could be a threat to the security of the United States'. Iraq was mentioned by only 17 per cent, far behind USSR (84 per cent), Iran (56) and China (41). Again, in April 1986, a CBS/*New York Times* poll asked whether any other country in the Middle East besides Libya was responsible for international terrorism and a mere 1 per cent named Iraq. (ibid: 46)

Robert Freedman (1991) highlights stories in the Western press which spoke approvingly of Saddam's moves to privatise the economy in the mid-1980s and he was even compared to Thatcher in this context. In May 1989, the *Washington Post* referred to Saddam Hussein as 'pragmatic' As Ray and Schaap point out (1991: 9): 'This is a term the Establishment reserves for bad guys who usually do what we want them to.' A British television documentary on Iraq as late as February 1990 said of Saddam Hussein: 'He inspires great fear and equally great admiration.'[2]

Even the press coverage coverage of the chemical bombing of Kurds in Halabja on 16 March 1988 was notable for its comparative restraint. (Rose and Baravi 1988) Yet more than 5,000 civilians were killed and another 7,000 maimed for life. Timmerman (1991: 293) suggests the gas was a hydrogen cyanide compound the Iraqis had developed with the help of a German company. Made in the Samarra gas works, it was similar to the poison gas the Nazis had used to exterminate the Jews more than 40 years earlier. Survivors interviewed by Human Rights Watch/Middle East confirmed that the bombs were dropped from Iraqi and not Iranian planes since they flew low enough for their markings to be legible. (Human Rights Watch 1995: 70). Human Rights Watch also list 60 villages Kurdish villages attacked with mustard gas, nerve gas and a combination of the two over the previous two years. (ibid: 262-265)

Little blame was levelled personally at Saddam Hussein in the press for the Halabja atrocity. No Hitler/Nazi jibes emerged. The *Guardian* of 17 March 1988 was typical: 'It is hard to conceive of any explanation for the chemical bombardment of Halabja other than one which Iranians and Kurds offer – revenge.' The madness of Saddam Hussein, his lust for power were nowhere identified as the causes of the outrage. While a 24 March editorial defined the atrocity as 'Iraq's latest and greatest war crime' it mirrored the government's position on the war taking no side and calling for a ceasefire. At the same time the press gave considerable prominence to US government claims that Iranians were also responsible for the chemical attacks. *The Times* carried prominently the report headlined 'US evidence suggests Iran also use chemicals' while the *Guardian* quoted a Reuters report of US State Department spokesman Charles Redman claiming: 'There are indications that Iran may have also used chemical artillery shells in the fighting.'

Six weeks after the attack, a UN report, made by a Spanish military doctor, Col. Manuel Dominguez Carmona, concluded it was impossible to say whether Iraq or Iran or both were to blame. (Bulloch and Morris 1992: 144) In February 1990, a US Army War College report concluded that Iraq was not responsible for the Halabja massacre and that 'it was the Iranian bombardment that had actually killed the Kurds'. (Pelletiere et al 1990; Yant

---

2   See Simpson, John (1991): *From the house of war*; Arrow Books; London. He writes: 'Before the war it was customary for journalists and academics writing about Iraq to take some at least of the carefully marshalled demonstrations of love and support for Saddam Hussein at their face value...Among western academics specializing in Iraq, Peter Sluglett of Durham University and Marion Farouk-Sluglett of the University College of Wales were in a minority when they questioned whether ordinary Iraqis provided Saddam with anything more than lip-service.' p 9.

1991: 109) Was this mere US government-inspired disinformation since Iraq was then a close ally? Certainly the media at the time of Halabja raised serious questions about the supposed guilt of Iraq. These doubts were completely absent in the coverage of the 1990 crisis and later massacres. The Halabja bombing, rather, featured prominently in all the demonisation propaganda directed at the Iraqi leader.

Bazoft ambivalences

The ambivalence of the elite's approach to Saddam Hussein at this time was most apparent in the coverage of the hanging of *Observer* journalist Farzad Bazoft on 15 March 1990. An explosion had destroyed the al-Hillah plant north of Baghdad on 17 August 1989 and Bazoft had travelled there with an English nurse, Daphne Parish, taking photographs and even soil samples.[3] After being arrested by Iraqi security police he had 'confessed' to being an Israeli spy. (Timmerman op cit: 357-358) Immediately following the hanging British intelligence leaked information that Bazoft had stolen £500 from a building society ten years earlier. According to John Pilger, MI5 was acting on behalf of the Thatcher government 'desperate for any excuse not to suspend its lucrative business and arms deals with Saddam Hussein'. (Pilger 1992a)

The *Sun*'s 'exclusive' headline went: 'Hanged man was a robber'; the *Mail*'s: 'Bazoft a perfect spy for Israel'; *Today*'s: 'Bazoft was an Israeli agent'; a *Sunday Telegraph* editorial condemned Bazoft as a spy, likening investigative journalism to an offence against the state. The investigative journalist Simon Henderson also argued that Bazoft was a spy. He concluded: 'At no time did the British admit that Bazoft had been spying, nor did Iraq flesh out its allegations. The reason was clear: if Britain admitted to the spying the two countries would have had to break off diplomatic relations.' Neither country wanted this. 'So the Bazoft incident was left to die down.' (Henderson 1992: 214-216)

Yet it is false to stress the pro-Iraqi stance of the US/UK elite during the 1980s. Competing sections of the US secret state were dealing differently with Iraq. There was massive covert support most of which only became known in 'Iraqgate' scandals in both the UK and US after February 1991.[4] The CIA engineered a secret 'tilt' towards Saddam Hussein in 1982 just as Iranian Revolutionary Guards were threatening to break through Iraqi defences. Intelligence and military links were expanded after Reagan was re-elected for a second term. (Perry 1992: 381-383) As Friedman comments

---

3   Daphne Parrish gives her version of events in (1992): *Prisoner in Baghdad*; Chapmans Publishers; London.

4   The best account of the Matrix Churchill trial of October 1992 appears in Leigh, David (1993): Betrayed; Bloomsbury; London. On the follow-up Scott Inquiry, see: (1994): *Not the Scott report: Thatcher, Major, Saddam and the merchants of death*; *Private Eye*; London; November. The Scott report, which finally appeared in February 1996, was largely a whitewash. Also revealed in 1996 that SAS had trained Saddam Hussein's bodyguards. See August, Oliver: 'Britons trained Saddam guards', *The Times*; 17 January.

(1993: 31): 'By 1986 the White House was steeped in the covert ethic. The off-the-books operations involving the diversion of profits from arms transfers to Iran in contravention of the law prohibiting aid to Nicaragua, were eventually exposed and became known to the public as the Iran/Contra affair. The equally egregious and simultaneous covert aid to Iraq however remained secret.'

By the beginning of 1990 a number of British newspapers (in particular the *Observer*, for obvious reasons) were calling for the elimination of Saddam Hussein. A series of revelations focused on Iraq's growing military might. In March, UK customs in Operation Big Bertha confiscated eight Iraqi-bound steel tubes, manufactured by a Sheffield company and believed to be for a 40-ton 'supergun'. On 28 March, a joint US/UK customs operation seized at London's Heathrow airport 40 electrical capacitors said to be used as nuclear triggers. Thus the *Mirror*, for instance, was able to editorialise on 23 July: 'Hussein is a tyrant without any scruples who obeys no rules,' and described him as a bloodthirsty tyrant and 'butcher'. Black and Morris suggest that much of the anti-Iraqi information appearing in the press at this time originated from Israeli intelligence. (Black and Morris 1991: 518)

The end of history? Reinforcing the myths underlying new militarism

The ideological framework legitimising the response of the Western elites to the Kuwaiti crisis (of which hyper-personalisation was an important ingredient) had, to a considerable degree, been provided some months earlier by an obscure writer in an equally obscure American magazine. Francis Fukuyama, deputy director of the US State Department's policy planning staff, in the summer 1989 edition of the *National Interest*, had contributed a 16-page essay entitled 'The end of history?' (1989)

Heralded by all the major media outlets in the West, Fukuyama was rapidly to become the intellectual guru *par excellence* of the day. Like all popular theories his was at root breathtakingly simple. The end of the Cold War, the collapse of the Soviet Union, had proved the victory of consumerist Western democracy over totalitarian marxism. 'What we may be witnessing is not just the end of the Cold War or the passing of a particular period of postwar history but the end of history as such; that is the end point of mankind's ideological evolution and the universalization of Western liberal democracy as the final form of human government,' he wrote. (ibid: 3)

Western elites could not believe their luck. Here was a man who seemed to offer intellectual respectability to their triumphalist feelings over the collapse of the Soviet Union. The intellectual flavour of the previous year in the US had been provided by historian Paul Kennedy, whose *Decline and Fall of the Great Powers: Economic change and military conflict from 1500 to 2000* (Unwin and Hyman; London 1988), had given much scope for the American imperial elite to indulge their fears of vulnerability. Now Fukuyama's theories could help replace Kennedy's introverted anxieties and pessimism with an unabashed optimism about the global possibilities of American-led capitalism. The ideological implications of Fukuyama's fundamentally simple theories were extremely varied. For instance, it was to articulate and in the process help justify the silencing of the history of the Middle East and of other non-capitalist/Arab/Islamic histories which the Western elite and mainstream media sought to achieve during the Gulf crisis.

Equally, the Fukuyama theories served to legitimise the silencing of the history of Western imperialism both past and present in the region. In many ways, too, the theories articulated some of the most potent contradictions in the US elite's worldview. On the one hand they sought to escape the traumas of the past (as in Vietnam) into the triumphant, ever-present and mediacentric 'now'; yet on the other hand they were unable to escape the grip of the past. Moreover, central to Fukuyama's argument is a belief that liberal democracies of the US type are inherently peaceful. Most intriguingly of all, Fukuyama promotes an illusion of demilitarisation just at the moment when the US military was running 'out of control'. Thus the end of history theory articulated to a mass audience the myth of demilitarisation so crucial a component of new militarism.

Ideological function of the human interest story

The hyper-personalisation of the Kuwaiti crisis can be seen as an extension of the Fukuyama project. For in the process an enormously complex history was grossly over-simplified and distorted while attention was detracted from other important social, political, geostrategic, religious and environmental factors.

The human interest angle, of which the Saddam Hussein coverage was a manifestation, is deeply embedded in the journalists' culture. Nor is it confined to the popular press. An ideological consensus informs all the mainstream media and an integral feature of it is this human interest bias. (Keeble: 1994: 158-170; 267-270) The human interest bias is built in to the professional routines of journalists – the interview, the source, the profile, the human descriptive 'colour' form the essential basis of most mainstream journalism. Such a bias also makes economic sense: people are intrigued by other people; revelations of people's secrets form the basis for countless news stories and features. As John Taylor sums up: 'The concept of news as human interest has remained stable because it has consistently sold newspapers. These stories are the most widely read in both tabloids and broadsheets. Their appeal carries across the differences between men and women, young and old, middle class and working class.' (Taylor 1991: 2) Indeed, the human interest focus reinforces the media's function as entertainment above that of political informant, analyst or critic.

The human interest bias is all the more predictable when the press deals with dictators such as Saddam Hussein. The Iraqi leader, since becoming president in 1979, had taken over full control of the state apparatus. He commanded all aspects of foreign and domestic policy and ruthlessly eliminated his opponents. When dictators are 'friends' of the West the personalising of their coverage can be muted. When they become 'enemies' and the focus of assassination attempts the size of their personal power and their monstrosities provide the press with all the propaganda 'ammunition' they need.

While usually pursued unproblematically by journalists, the human interest focus still serves many complex ideological purposes. As Curran, Douglas and Whannel argue, human interest is not simply a neutral window on the world but embodies a particular way of seeing. (1980: 306) Accordingly, the possibility of basic structural inequalities is rejected while non-historical forces of 'luck, fate and chance' are represented as dominant within a given, naturalised world. Paul Kennedy (1986) sees the human interest bias as an indication of the potency of the conservative historical ideology which prioritises human interest factors above deeper underlying, contextualising factors.

This view is reinforced by Sparks (1992: 39) who argues: 'The popular conception of the personal becomes the explanatory framework within which the social order is presented as transparent.' The media fail to convey the 'social totality' comprising 'complex mediations of institutional structures, economic relations and so on'. Similarly Chibnall (1977: 26) suggests that the personalisation of politics and the media is 'perhaps the most pervasive product of the cultural fetishism of modern society'. Issues are increasingly defined and presented in terms of personalities 'catering for the public desire for identification fostered by the entertainment media'. Events are, consequently, to be understood, 'not by reference to certain structural arrangements and social process but either a) as the work of individuals or b) through their effects on individuals'.

Hitler Hussein

One of the most dominant features of the coverage of the Iraqi invasion of Kuwait was the focus on Saddam Hussein as the new Hitler. The *Telegraph*, of 3 August, wrote: 'President Hussein's decision to invade Kuwait is proof of his Hitlerian determination to get his own way.' Robert Harvey, in a leader page feature, contributed: 'For once the overworked comparison with Hitler is apposite.' The *Mail* editorial of the same day commented: 'Like a rerun of Hitler's invasion of Czechoslovakia in the 1930s, the Iraqi dictatorship has flouted international opinion and grabbed a small but wealthy neighbour. Nothing justifies this outrage.' In the *Sun* of 4 August, Dr John Laffing, described as an expert on Arab affairs and author of 109 books including *The Arab mind* and *The man the Nazis couldn't catch*, wrote that 'power-crazed tyrant Saddam Hussein was exposed yesterday as a Fuhrer freak who models himself on Adolf Hitler' and had set up a shrine to Hitler.

On 5 August, the *Sunday Times* said of the Iraqi invasion: 'It was a strategy on Hitlerian lines: the annexation by blitzkrieg of a weak neighbour.' The *Observer* editorial of the same day commented: 'Why this Hitler of the Gulf

has to go'. 'It is going to be desperately difficult to get out of this one with-
out the exchange of rocket fire. If the comparison with Hitler holds good, it
may prove impossible.' And the editorial continued: 'Comparing people to
Hitler can be counter-productive as Sir Anthony Eden (over Nasser) and
Nicholas Ridley (over Chancellor Kohl) both found to their cost. But in
Saddam Hussein the world is facing another Hitler ... He has the same kind
of expansionist ambitions and brutal lack of humanity. Like the German
Fuhrer he has an underlying vision of an all-powerful Iraq funded by oil and
backed by force.'

The *Independent* of 3 August editorialised: 'The appetites of dictators grow
with what they feed upon as Europe learnt to its cost when dealing with
Hitler.' And its profile of 11 August began: 'In the overworn comparison
with Hitler and Stalin there is a kernel of truth. For he shares the secret of
great dictators – he understands the psychotic relationship between fear and
love.' The *Mirror* intoned: 'Saddam Hussein is the Adolf Hitler of the Arab
world. If he isn't stopped now the West will pay a heavy price.' A similar
focus was made in American press coverage. The Gannett Foundation study
found 1,035 mentions of Saddam Hussein as Hitler from 1 August to 28
February 1991 in the print media. (Gannett 1991: 42) On both sides of the
Atlantic the analogy was reinforced in cartoon representations. Macarthur
comments (1993: 72) : 'Hardly any reporters were heard challenging the
President in his Hitler comparisons at press conferences.'

Yet the Hitler angle did not appear to politicians and the press 'naturally' –
it served a number of important ideological, propaganda purposes. With the
collapse of the Soviet Union, the spectre of the 'communist threat' could no
longer be raised as a justification for US military action. As a propaganda
tool the Hitler threat was remarkably efficient: it was simple and seemingly
unproblematic. In popular rhetoric, Hitler has been transformed into an
enormous symbol of evil and danger. Focusing on the enemy as a Hitler
could only serve to direct massive emotional negativity to that single person
– and at the same time elevate the moral purity of the forces lined up against
him. As the *Independent* leader of 3 August commented with commendable
clarity: 'Since the changes in Russia some people have been lamenting the
lack of a convincing enemy: Here he is.'

Saddam Hussein was and remains a brutal dictator. The *Independent* profile
of 11 August commented: 'President Saddam has achieved the apotheosis of
the totalitarian ideal.' On that kind of basis the myth can flower. Yet for 10
years the superpowers were happy to cultivate Iraq as a 'friend'. During
those years there were many opportunities for the press to put the Hitler
label on Saddam Hussein. The Ba'ath party, indeed, had fascist origins, being
formed in Damascus in 1941 out of an aid committee set up by Aflaq and
Bitar to assist Rashid Ali's Nazi-backed revolt in Iraq. (Bulloch and Morris
1991: 53-54) One of the first mentions of Saddam Hussein as Hitler
appeared on 16 September 1988. Hazhir Temourian wrote: 'Saddam
Hussein, the little psychopath who clearly believes he will get away with

emulating his hero, Hitler, must be punished with the powers of the civilised world.' But this was in the 'leftist' *New Statesman and Society*. (pp 20-22)

All the post-August 1990 Hitler hype sought to say implicitly: 'There have been many horrible dictators since 1945 but Saddam Hussein is the worst of all.' By no sensible historical criteria could the validity of that assertion be assessed: it is merely serving rhetorical, ideological and ultimately political/military purposes. Thus the *Sun* reported on 3 August: 'The Beast of Baghdad inherited the title of the world's most evil dictator when Rumania's President Ceaucescu was executed last Christmas day.' John Kay compiled a feature on the '10 dangerous despots that deal in death'. Predictably, top of the (somewhat eccentric) list – missing out such dictators as the US-backed Marcos, Papa Doc, Pinochet, Zia, and Deng Xiaphing – came Saddam Hussein. Then came Gadaffi, the 'mad dog dictator who believes Shakespeare was an Arab called Sheik Spear'; 'potty' Pol Pot, Kim Il Sung; Hafez Assad of Syria; Noriega, Castro, Stroessner of Paraguay, Ramiz Alia and Idi Amin. Norman McCrae commented in the *Sunday Times* of 30 December: 'Saddam Hussein is an archetype of the Third World's nastiest dictators with a recently reiterated record of torture actually worse than that of the Gestapo.'

The endlessly repeated Hitler analogy represented a highly selective, ideologically motivated use of history by the US and its prominent allies. For its essential purpose was to draw on pre-Cold War rhetoric to silence many histories – in particular the imperial roles of the US and UK in the Middle East and more globally. As Bennett comments (1994: 32): 'The vivid, personalized framing of Saddam Hussein as Hitler made a clean historic break with past administration policies toward Iraq and established a new historical and emotional reference from which opinion formation could begin anew.' For Britain and America the confrontation against Iraq could be represented as a new struggle, a crusade even (Christian metaphors being used prominently throughout) to reverse the aggression of a brutal dictator. In this context, according to Barney Dickson (1991: 43), the post-imperial rhetoric of global responsibility could be invoked.

The Hitler analogy also served a critical role in the complex, multi-faceted propaganda project to highlight the military option above the diplomatic one – after all Hitler was removed only by force. (Glasgow University Media Group 1991: 3) As Christopher Layne comments (1991) : 'The 1930s analogy rests on the assumption that "aggression" must be resisted, not appeased whenever it occurs because it will snowball unless firmly stopped.' It was a sort of variation of the Cold War/old order domino theory which drove the US into the debacle of Vietnam. Those who questioned the Bush agenda were thus labelled 'appeasers' (returning again to pre-1939 rhetoric) and thus saddled with all the negative connotations of that word. It served to highlight Saddam Hussein and the country he was supposed to run as a powerful, global threat which needed to be tamed or destroyed if President Bush's 'New World Order' was to be established.

Thus it was a crucial element of the ideological mystification that sought to represent the conflict as a legitimate war between two credible armies when in reality it was very different – an unnecessary slaughter of thousands of innocent civilians and conscripts. David E. Morrison (1992: 18), in his detailed analysis of public responses to media coverage of the 'war', records how most interviewees reproduced what they both heard and saw in the media. 'He was like Hitler, He didn't care. I mean the way he treated people' is one representative view quoted.

Behind the Hitler hype – contradictions

Yet there were many more ambivalences and contradictions in the Hilter angle which the press significantly evaded in their sensationalist, unproblematic coverage. Hitler, after all, had drawn considerable support from sections of the ruling elites in Europe and north America (in the City and Wall Street) in the six years leading up to war. (Sutton 1976; Ponting 1991: 47) He was seen as a useful bulwark to the more serious threat of Soviet communism. And his authoritarianism and racism appealed to many in the elite.

Equally, Saddam Hussein was most effectively appeased from 1980 to 2 August 1990 by significant sections of the ruling elites in America, the West and East in general. This ambivalence was rarely highlighted in the media. Iraqgate/Saddamgate had to wait two years before emerging (rather tamely since this was election year after all) in the States and even longer in Britain. The emphasis on Second World War rhetoric (with references to 'the allies', the 'liberation of Kuwait', even the planned amphibious landing by the Marines all reinforcing its emotive power) also distanced countries such as Germany and Japan from the UK/US military adventure. (Sadria, Mojtaba 1992)

After the massacres, with Saddam still in power (and with the US maintaining its pre-invasion policy of ambivalence towards the Iraqi regime) the Hitler analogies suddenly disappeared from the media. The analogy was exposed as an ideological device to legitimise the US/allied stance. Once the complexities of the Middle East and the ambivalences, contradictions and hypocrisies of the US strategy emerged after the massacres, the Hitler analogy with its crude over-simplification, faded away.

Madman Saddam

Along with Saddam as Hitler, the other dominant aspect of the coverage of Iraq after the Kuwait invasion was to represent Saddam as mad. On 7 August, John Kay wrote in the *Sun*: 'Britain's elite SAS regiment could assassinate crazed Iraqi President – and defuse the growing Gulf crisis in one blow.' The *Guardian* editorial commented: 'In the two years since the Gulf war ended it has been at times hard to decide which of the two damaged regimes that staggered out of that bloody conflict was the more deranged or the more dangerous.' The *Mail* of 3 August, in a centre spread headlined 'A new Hitler plots his empire', described Saddam Hussein as a megalomaniac.

The *Express* headlined: 'Mad despot who wants to rule the Arab world'. The story beneath gave prominence to a piece of Mossad disinformation which was to feature regularly in the press in the lead up to the massacres. It reported : 'This week an Israeli graphologist who examined his handwriting at the request of the secret service Mossad – without knowing the identity of the author – ruled that he is in urgent need of psychiatric treatment.'

Linked to this representation was the emphasis on Saddam (and by association those who supported him) as being a barbarous, brutal beast. In effect, the press was portraying him as a monster, non-human, uncivilised and thus worthy of any treatment dealt him. The *Mirror* profiled him on 3 August: 'Already he is a mass murderer, a man guilty of genocide, a monster who has used gas and chemical weapons on civilians and enemy troops and whose war with Iran cost half a million lives.' On 7 August, the *Sun* evoked the animal metaphor in this obscene way: 'A stone lifted at the Iraqi embassy in London yesterday and a reptile crawled out.' They were referring to ambassador Shafiq Al-Salih who supposedly shrugged when asked the fate of British 'hostages' in Iraq. The paper continued: 'We hope an American B-52 wipes the crooked smile from his lips.'

In much of the coverage Saddam is presented as the embodiment of evil. The *Mail* of 3 August: 'Hussein is known to approve 30 types of torture. They include mutilation, gorging out of eyes, cutting off the nose, sex organs and limbs, hammering nails into the body, burning with hot irons and roasting victims over flames.' What is striking about this dominant genre of Saddam profiling is the way in which he is represented as existing in a natural state of bloodthirsty anarchy in which none of the normal human factors operate. The history of British/American imperialism, political, religious, environmental dynamics play no part in this biography. It is completely untouched by history. There is little concept of Saddam Hussein as a diplomat. Thus the dominant representation remains extraordinarily one-dimensional and consistent throughout the crisis and massacres.

As Prince argues on these anti-historical projections and images (1993: 244): 'Iraq was thereby exiled from the modern world and the 20th century, banished to a nameless, pre-civilised period, effectively distanced in spatial, temporal and moral terms from the West.' And in placing Saddam Hussein within the context of the violent history of Iraq, Efraim Karsh (1993: 64) argues: '...he has been largely a captive of the political system in which he has operated, and in which naked force has constituted the sole agent of political change.'

The profile in the *Mirror* of 3 August is typical of press coverage. The Iraqi tyrant is said to have swept to power on 'a wave of blood – by killing and torturing his way to the top'. Then follows a list of atrocities committed by Saddam. No historical explanations or contextualisations are given. He appears to have lived in a timeless zone of barbarism. 'He ordered little children to be tortured in front of their parents. Other youngsters were buried alive…Now he heads an evil empire of death squads and employs 100,000 secret policemen to spy on his people.' It continues: 'Five schoolboys were publicly shot after being whipped, beaten and burned with cigarettes because their parents opposed him.' And so on. The *Sun* the same day quotes a British Foreign Office diplomat: 'What he can't eat or make love to he kills'. And Margaret Thatcher's much quoted comment on 5 August: 'We can't let the law of the jungle triumph' reinforced this demonisation process.

Similar kinds of stresses were made in the US press. Mary McGrory, in the *Washington Post* of 7 August, described Saddam Hussein as a 'beast'; A.M. Rosenthal in the *New York Times* of 9 August attacked him as 'barbarous' and 'an evil dreamer of death'. On 19 January in the *New York Times*, David Levine's cartoon, called 'Descent of Man' showed a Clark Gable figure transformed into gorilla, ape, snake and finally Saddam, surrounded by flies. Focusing on Saddam as an unpredictable animal could only serve the ideological purpose of marginalising the diplomatic track – for how could such a 'person' be expected to be trusted or engage in rational negotiation? Yet such a focus incorporated certain contradictions which the press negotiated only awkwardly.

For instance, if Saddam was a madman then he was no credible threat. How could a madman wage a credible war? So alongside the stress on the madness was a querying of that dominant line in some of the less one-dimensional coverage. Thus Paul Johnson in the *Mail* of 3 August: 'Like Col Nasser before him he is a boastful, self-glorifying liar and so easy to ridicule. But he is a more formidable strategist than Nasser and much more dangerous.'

The *Mirror* quoted a 'western diplomat' as saying 'He is utterly ruthless. But he is definitely not mad.' On 26 August, the *Sunday Times* profile of Saddam Hussein concluded: 'To psychologists the Iraqi president is clearly suffering from psychosis – a condition manifested by a detachment from reality.' But it adds carefully: 'Psychosis or not, Saddam still remains a formidable and unpredictable opponent.'

Saddam trapped within the frame of popular culture

The crisis, with all its immense complexities, was from the outset represented within the dominant frames of popular culture which represent reality as a simple fight between good and evil. As Gilbert Adair said: 'Saddam Hussein himself has become a concentration of pure malevolence, of a type instantly, irresistibly, reminiscent of the villains in James Bond movies.' (Adair 1991) And Roy Greenslade, editor of the *Mirror*, later commented: 'We covered the war in a fairly mainstream, tabloid way. Here was a recognisable enemy. Saddam was an evil man. That was the great assumption.'

John Schostak develops this theme. He writes (1993: 85): 'By evoking the experiences now overlaid with the mythology of the Second World War, Hussein's actions and the West's counter actions could be explained simply and simplistically to the public. The complex history of involvement by the

West in Middle Eastern affairs, which had allowed tyrants to arise and be supported was largely glossed over. The invasions and subversions carried out by Western powers all over the world could be ignored in this simplistic drama echoing the fight of good over evil.'

According to William F. Fore (1991: 52), the mass media are the devices used by the controllers of our culture to keep it simple. In this they reproduce the rhetoric of the political elite. For instance, President Bush told Congress: 'I have resolved all moral questions in my mind: this is a black versus white, good versus evil.' This moralistic, anti-historical rhetoric, reproduced in the press, helped portray the Kuwait invasion as an inexplicable and irrational undertaking. The press reinforced their anti-Iraq propaganda project by covering the developing crisis within the stereotypical frames deeply embedded in popular culture and in the journalists' dominant news value systems. As Jim Lederman, in his study of the US coverage of the Palestinian intifada, comments: 'Journalists, as professional storytellers, need sharply defined and vivid characters, preferably ones that can be identified easily by the audience as good guys and bad guys.' (Lederman 1992: 18)

Edward Said and Rana Kabbani have outlined the way in which orientalist myths and anti-Islamic clichés are so embedded in Western perceptions. (Said 1981, Kabbani 1991; 1994 orig 1986) And Stuart Hall (1995: 21) has argued that representations of the 'savage barbarian' lie at the centre of racist ideology. Moreover, in a series of Hollywood blockbusters in the years leading up to the Gulf crisis, Middle Eastern characters served as symbols for greed, primitive behaviour and violence. In films such as 'The wind and the lion' (1975), 'Black Sunday' (1977), 'Rollover' (1981) and 'The little drummer girl' (1984) the Orient was viewed as underdeveloped, inferior and the source of chaos, violence and corruption. (Prince op cit: 238-248)

The demonisation of Saddam Hussein fell within these racist frames according to which 'Arabs' and 'Islamic fundamentalism' (14) were from the late 1980s coming to replace collapsed 'communism' as the new 'enemy' for the Western elite. (Power 1991) Moreover, while Hollywood demonised the Arab world it also responded to the aggressive international posture of the Reagan administration by producing a series of invasion and rescue films (such as 'Iron Eagle' of 1986; 'The Delta Force', of 1986; 'Death before dishonor' of 1987 and 'Navy Seals' of 1990) that implicitly argued the need for strong US presence overseas. Prince argues: 'Films like 'Top Gun' and 'Rambo' dramatised the heroic ideals of empire and the aggressive heroes of these narratives functioned as personifications of a national will and warrior spirit encoded by the foreign policy rhetoric of the Reagan period.' (op cit: 240) Roy Greenslade later admitted pointedly: 'I can see now that our coverage in the *Mirror* was built on a lot of anti-Iraqi bias, an anti-Moslem bias and an anti-Arab bias.'

Along with the racism in the coverage went a remarkable degree of heavily loaded sexist imagery. Anthony Easthope (1986: 63-65) has highlighted the four essential ingredients of the representation of war in the popular media: defeat, combat, victory and comradeship. For the Western, predominantly male elite (indeed, the only women to feature in the story with any prominence are Margaret Thatcher – and she is kicked out mid-way – and April Glaspie, the US ambassador to Iraq in July 1990 – and she ends up the principal scapegoat) defeat was to occur in the invasion of Kuwait. Significantly this invasion was most commonly described by politicians and media as a 'rape'. (Combat and comradeship were to come with the trial of war; victory was to come in the end – but it was to prove only illusory.)

The sexual voraciousness of Saddam Hussein (and Iraqis/Moslems in general) was a dominant theme in the popular press coverage of the crisis and massacres. The innocence of tiny Kuwait was constantly reaffirmed in contrast to the brutality of Saddam who (according to the dominant frame) had personally 'systematically raped' his 'peaceful neighbour'. Under Secretary of Defense Paul Wolfowitz had asked whether Americans would 'let a man like that get his hands on what are essentially the world's vital organs?' Rape, in fact, has been constantly used throughout American history to legitimise military/political offensives. A popular genre of colonial literature featured white women being captured and raped by native Americans while during the Spanish-American war, Hearst newspapers highlighted the kidnapping of a light-skinned Cuban woman to justify US intervention. More recently, President Bush used the sex attack on a US officer's wife in Panama as a pretext for invading that country while the rape of a white woman by a black convict was used by his election campaign team to smear Dukakis in 1988.

Saddam Hussein as the archetypal bad dad

Anne Norton has traced a significant element of the press coverage of Saddam Hussein in the representation of the archetypal bad father. (Norton 1991) 'Arab hyper masculinity,' she argues, 'is in every sense a domestic matter. Academic and popular accounts of Hafez al-Assad, Saddam Hussein and Gadaffi emphasise their dictatorial domestic rule, their unrestrained use of domestic violence.' Within popular culture, one of the fullest expressions of this domestic dictator appears in the film 'Star Wars' (so famous President Reagan called his space militarisation programme after it) with Darth Vader, the dark father armed with an almost (but not quite) invincible war machine that must be stopped. This stereotype was most effectively deployed by the press in their coverage of the Western 'hostages' and, in particular, the meeting between some of them and Saddam Hussein late in August 1990.

According to Jean Baudrillard the prominence given to the hostages' story in the Western media embodied his hyper-real 'non-war'.[5] 'The hostage has

---

5   Baudrillard, Jean (1991): 'The reality gulf', the *Guardian*, 11 January. A lively critique of Baudrillard's 'no Gulf War' thesis appears in Norris, Christopher (1992): *Uncritical theory: Postmodernism, intellectuals and the Gulf War*; Lawrence and Wishart; London. See also Kellner, Douglas (1989): *Jean Baudrillard: From Marxism to Post-modernism and Beyond*; Polity Press, Cambridge and (1990): *Television and the crisis of democracy*; Westview Press, Oxford.

replaced the warrior. Even by pure inactivity he (sic) takes the limelight as the main protagonist in this simulated non-war. Today's hostage is a phantom player, a walk-on who fills the impotent vacuum of modern war. So we have the hostage as the strategic site, the hostage as a Christmas present, the hostage as a bargain counter and as a liquid asset.'

In reality, the public had become the real hostages – to media intoxication. 'We are all manipulated in the general indifference...we are all in place as strategic hostages.' Indeed, a survey conducted by Shaw and Carr-Hill (1991: 12) found a large percentage of newspaper readers 'not affected' at all by the massacres – 44 per cent, for instance, of *Sun* and *Star* readers. Certainly the hostages story competed with the demonisation of Saddam Hussein as the most prominent of the pre-massacres period – in both the national and local press. It is easy to understand why. Here were all the ingredients of an archetypally 'good story':

- It provided strong local/national/patriotic angles.

- And strong 'human interest' angles.

- It had a strong emotional/melodramatic content with all the stereotypical good versus evil elements: innocent 'ordinary folk' surviving only at the whim of brutal 'enemy' heavily personalised in the form of mad Saddam.

- It provided 'ordinary' people with the rare opportunity to attain 'heroic' stature.

- 'Ordinary' people could be represented as victims of a fate over which they had no control, caught up quite by chance in the brutalities and complexities of modern realpolitik of which they are normally just passive spectators.

- The hostage story reinforced the representation of Saddam Hussein as a 'bully' and the West, more generally, as innocent victims.

- It provided the opportunity to stress traditional 'family values' and, by association, helped in the representation of Britain and the United States as families under threat. A similar stress on the family occurred during the Falklands/Malvinas 'war', as Taylor identifies (1991: 97). In the absence of any pictures, the press had the problem of keeping up interest. Thus, 'they anchored their coverage to the home front, telling the story of the Task Force as if it were the story of a family'.

- Moreover, there were strong emotive connotations of the word 'hostages' (given Western media coverage of the Beirut hostages and particularly in America associations with the hostages held in the American embassy in Tehran after the fall of the Shah in 1979). Significantly the Iraqis attempted to counter the ideological force of the word 'hostages' by calling them 'guests'.

- Allegations of sexual assault on some women hostages provided the press with titillating 'sex/sensational' angles.

Thus, hardly a day went by from early August 1990 until late December without a hostage story being given enormous prominence in the press. After a while they acquired a certain repetitive, ritualistic, theatrical dimension.

Jostein Gripsrud (1992) locates the sensationalism and personalisation of the popular press in the melodrama of the 19th century stage. 'Melodrama was didactic drama, designed to teach the audience a lesson. Today's popular press also teaches the audience a lesson, every day. It says that what the world is really about is emotions, fundamental and strong: love, hate, grief, joy, lust and disgust. Such emotions are shared by all human beings, regardless of social positions and so is "general morality": crime does not pay...' (ibid: 87)

Gripsrud argues that the melodramatic imperative of the popular press indicates a popular resistance to abstract, theoretical ways of understanding society and history. Yet 'it is deeply problematic, not least because it is deeply ahistorical'. (ibid: 88) Sensationalist media coverage, then, is the archetypal representation of an 'end of history' culture. Gripsrud goes on to develop the ideas of Jurgen Habermas over 'the classic public sphere' by suggesting the media emphasis on so-called personalities and private lives of public figures may be said to contribute to an erosion of the public sphere. 'It is part of a tendency to distract the public from matters of principle by offering voyeuristic pseudo insights into individual matters.' (ibid: 90)

In relation to the hostages story, the melodramatic imperative of the press meant they focused wherever possible on the most vulnerable, the most horrific – thus children, babes and mums take centre stage. The *Mirror* front page headlined on 20 August: 'I'll keep your kids until I win: Butcher's new threat'. Underneath, the report ran: 'The babes of British families held in Kuwait were made prisoners of war last night. Evil Saddam Hussein vowed to keep the several hundred British children trapped in the Gulf until he gets his way...There was no hint of compassion from the Iraqi dictator who has threatened to let babies starve and use hostages as human shields.' On page seven of the same issue, the *Mirror* reported: 'Our babes in the grip of the crazed butcher.' Underneath the copy ran: 'Even unborn babies are at the mercy of Saddam.' Next day it was reporting: 'Iraq last night threatened to eat any British or American pilots shot down over their territory. The astonishing warning came from a Baghdad government official as Saddam Hussein seized more Western hostages for use as human shields.'

All this is crude anti-Iraqi propaganda, preparing the public to support a war in a far-away country they knew little about. As if to articulate the *Mirror's* own response, a man is quoted as saying 'It's frightening but I think it's time to send the multi-national force into Iraq.'

When bad dad meets hostages in Baghdad

The demonisation of Saddam, the heroism of the hostages, the melodramatic imperative of the press and the mediacentrism of new militarism all come together in the coverage of Saddam Hussein's meeting with a group of British hostages. On 23 August the Iraqis released film of their president meeting a group of British hostages. Saddam was dressed in civilian clothes. He appeared relaxed and friendly. Here, then, were images which totally contradicted the demonising propaganda of the Western media.

The meaning of images is never naturally given. Someone appears to be crying: are they overjoyed, afraid, sad, or maybe they just have a fly in their eye? Maybe they are not even crying. Interpretations will differ and contradict each other. Post-modernist theorists such as Baudrillard argue that it is no longer possible to identify a concrete objectivity according to which the reality as represented in the media can be assessed. Opposing this view John Fiske (1992: 49) argues that the 'powerless' in society seek to subvert the dominant values by revelling in stories that expose the hypocrisies, secrets and lies of the powerful, the great and the good.

He writes of the popular press: 'One of its most characteristic tones of voice is that of sceptical laughter which offers the pleasures of disbelief, the pleasures of not being taken in. This popular pleasure of 'seeing through them' (whoever constitutes the powerful 'them' of the moment) is the historical result of centuries of subordination which the people have not allowed to develop into subjection.' But Curran and Sparks (1991) oppose this view of polysemy (in which a multiplicity of meanings is possible) by prioritising the notion of 'preferred reading'. In relation to the coverage of the hostages' meeting with Saddam Hussein, the press's 'preferred reading' was totally unambiguous. 'The Great Pretender: Butcher uses British kids in sick TV stunt' headlined the *Mirror* on 24 August. The kind daddy of the image was transformed into the supremely evil, monstrous bad dad.

Central to the demonisation of Saddam Hussein was the representation of the Iraqi leader as a cunning propagandist to which the Western vulnerable state could easily fall victim. As the *Sunday Times* of 26 August commented: 'The White House realises it is engaged in an all-out propaganda war with Saddam and Bush's political advisers are considering ways to counter his media offensive as the battle for support in the Arab world intensifies.' In a way, this contradicted the other dominant theme of the coverage which was to stress his madness and unpredictability. Such an unstable man could not command a propaganda machine of global reach. But still the evil propagandist theme was to persist through the massacres. Even when his army was being massacred the press could still represent the Iraqi leader as a credible threat – by virtue of his 'grotesque' propaganda powers.

Such representation also pictured the anti-Iraq coalition as vulnerable and on the defensive (the myths of vulnerability and defence being essential to the new militarist, strong state). Notice how in the *Sunday Times* comment (above) the US elite with its highly sophisticated, massively financed, global-reaching propaganda machine is represented as caught unawares by Saddam and left 'considering ways of countering' Saddam's offensive. According to

Norton, the press coverage of the meeting showed Saddam Hussein as 'a figure of phallic danger'. The press transformed the meeting into an archetypal confrontation between good (little English boys, described as 'terrified', 'squirming') and evil (the 'cynical', 'sickening', 'utterly repulsive' Saddam Hussein). The ultimate achievement of a secretive society is to expose the secret wiles of an 'enemy'. Hence the media focus on Saddam's stunt when he 'tried to mask his brutality behind the guise of a kindly uncle' (according to the *Mirror*).

The event provided the media with an opportunity to represent the children (Elliott Pilkington and Stuart Lockwood) as acting out some of the David and Goliath fantasies of warfare/confrontation with the 'evil tyrant': 'A plucky boy of four aimed a punch at Saddam Hussein as the tyrant tried to shake hands with him in a sickening TV charade. Elliott Pilkington put his tiny fist up in rebellion expressing the only way he knew the rage of Britain's helpless hostages.' In typical press fashion, an 'expert' is drawn in to support the bias of the coverage. 'Last night a psychologist examining the video said: "You could see little Stuart was terrified by the attention he got from Saddam simply through the way he was holding himself."'

One of the boys featured in a widely-distributed photograph of the event, Stuart Lockwood, was given star billing when he arrived in Britain on 2 September. 'I was brave in Baghdad', headlined the *Mirror*, seemingly putting words into the young man's mouth. But without any hint of self parody the paper proceeded to destroy its previously carefully contrived story by quoting his mum: 'Glenda said she was not frightened when an army officer turned Stuart's head around and forced him to look at Saddam during the TV interview. She said: "There were times when we were frightened but that wasn't one of them. Stuart is only five years old. I really don't think he was really aware of the situation".'

In some ways, the coverage of the hostages meeting can be seen as a metaphor for much of the press handling of the crisis and massacres – the reality shrouded in patriotic-inspired, sensationalist stereotyping, blatant mystifications, distortion and exaggeration.

5 Silencing the history of the Middle East: the linkage taboo

Missing the why? factor

E very student journalist learns the basic five 'w's (who, what, where, when, why) and the one 'h' (how) of hard news first paragraphs (known as intros). Yet journalists feel most at home with the who, what, when and how of events coverage. And they usually see these elements unproblematically. The why factors (the causal linkages) are usually very complex – and are often missed out or handled very superficially or stereotypically.[1] This was very much the case over the Kuwait invasion. Very little space was given to the reasons for the invasion. Most of the coverage dealt with the here and now of the invasion itself (the who, what, when and how): the advance of the Iraqi troops, the flight of the Kuwait leadership, the response of the international elites; the build-up of allied troops in Saudi Arabia.

Some background coverage focused on the oil dispute between Iraq and Kuwait. This might be considered an important immediate cause of the invasion but the many underlying linked causes (or the 'profound' causes as

---

1   Morrison, David (1992): *Television and the Gulf War*; John Libbey and Co; London. He concludes: '...what is interesting is that the news was more likely to feature the objectives of the war than reasons for the war. In other words, the news tended to adopt a political/militaristic perspective rather than a political/causation perspective.' The reasons supplied on television largely reproduced the government's agenda: To liberate Kuwait – 54 per cent; To uphold international law – 15 per cent; Fear of Hussein's expansion capacity – 6 per cent; To ensure world wide oil supply – 4 per cent; Failure of diplomatic means – 7 per cent; Other – 14 per cent. p 77.

Curtis, Liz (1984): *Ireland and the propaganda war*; Pluto; London also highlights the absence of relevant contextualising in much of British media coverage – in this case of Ireland. 'The British media's emphasis on "factual" reporting of incidents, concentrating on "who what where when" and leaving out the background and significance, appears to be objective and straightforward but is, in fact, very misleading. This type of reporting

defined by Paul Kennedy[2]), largely ignored by the press, were far more significant. Nelson and Olin (1979) highlight the political and ideological foundations for assumptions about causes of wars. Liberals, they suggest, tend to stress the role of individual personalities and the psychological stresses on major decision-makers. Radicals, in contrast, argue that the real causes of international conflict lie in long-term factors such as economic competition, imperialism, nationalism and racism. Thus underlying the press's stress on the Saddam factor were specific ideological assumptions.

The taboo on linkage in defence of US strategic and political interests was almost a metaphysical denial of the complexities of Middle Eastern politics. As Edward Said commented (1992: 2): 'Linkage means not that there is but that there is no connection. Things that belong together by common association, sense, geography, history are sundered, left apart for convenience sake and for the benefit of US imperial strategists...The Middle East is linked by all sorts of ties, that is irrelevant. That Arabs might see a connection between Saddam Hussein in Kuwait and Israel in Lebanon, that too is futile. That US policy itself is the linkage, that is the forbidden topic to broach.'

The myth of the overriding oil factor

On 3 August 1990, the *Express* presented its 17-day countdown to the crisis. All blame is directed at Saddam. On 17 July he accuses Kuwait and the United Arab Emirate of flooding the oil market and driving down oil prices. Next day he accuses Kuwaitis of stealing oil from wells on the disputed border. On 24 July tension escalates when US announces a (defensive) warship and aircraft staging exercise in the Gulf. On 25 July Saddam summons the US ambassador in Baghdad for 'a dressing down'. Next day Kuwait and UAE pledge to abide by new quota agreement. July 31: Diplomats say Iraq has massed 100,000 troops on Kuwait's borders.

Thus the vast and complex history of the world's dependency on Middle East oil is shrunk to just 17 days.[3] Since 1901 when the British first obtained con-

---

provides the audience with details of age, sex, occupation, type of incident, injuries, location and time of day. But such information says nothing about the causes of the incident making violence appear as random as a natural disaster or accident.' p 107.

Lederman, Jim (1992): *Battle lines: The American media and the Intifada*; Henry Holt and Company; New York stresses a more practical factor: 'A newspaper reporter tied to a six hundred word slot on the foreign news page and the radio reporter limited to thirty five seconds have little opportunity to explain complicated issues that may lie behing the event.' p 16.

Liebes, Tamar (1992): 'Our war/Their war: Comparing the Intifada and the Gulf war on US and Israeli television', *Critical Studies in Mass Communication*; Annandale, VA. Vol 9 No.1 pp 44-55. Stresses the lack of contextualisation in the media coverage. 'Even the occupation of Kuwait and Saddam Hussein's human rights violations receded as the dynamics of the conflict and the ultimatum, the mobilisation, the logistics, the diplomacy, the preparations for the land war took centre stage.' p 53-54 The same could be said of the press coverage.

2 Kennedy, Paul (1986): 'A.J.P. Taylor and profound forces in history', *Warfare, diplomacy and politics: Essays in honour of A.J.P. Taylor*; (ed) Wrigley, Chris: Hamish Hamilton; London pp 14-29.

3 Bromley, Simon (1991): 'Crisis in the Gulf', *Capital and Class*; London; Summer pp 7-14 Highlights oil factor from leftist position.

cessions to search for oil in Persia the development of Middle East oil fields has grown to the extent that by the late 1980s they supplied 71 per cent of Japan's consumption, 67 per cent of Italy's, 47 per cent of France's, 38 per cent of Germany's, 28 per cent of the UK's and just 17 per cent of the United States'. (Reich 1987) The Middle East and the Gulf possess at least 66.3 per cent of global oil reserves. In comparison, the US has only 4 per cent. Saudi Arabia has estimated reserves of 252,000m barrels compared to the US's 35,000m. (Abrahams 1994: 22)

In 1979, President Carter's own doctrine stressed America's commitment to protecting the flow of oil (and petro-dollars so crucial for funding US impe-rialist adventures) in the face of any 'enemy' (Soviet) advance. (Tanzer 1992) Moreover, President Bush and his son together with many members of his administration had personal financial interests in Gulf oil which were large-ly ignored by the mainstream press.[4] Bush's own Zapata Offshore Oil Company had drilled the first well off Kuwait some 30 years earlier. (Yant 1991: 87) Friedman reports how six days after the Kuwait invasion, Bush signed 'conflict of interest' waiver documents on behalf of Secretary of State James Baker and ten other cabinet officers and officials allowing them to participate in 'current United States policy-making discussions, decisions and actions in response to the Iraqi invasion of Kuwait'. (Friedman 1993: 170) Moreover, secret Saudi monies have helped bolster Western elites – funding, for instance, the Marshall plan and the Contras. (Laurens 1992).

Abrahams comments: 'Saudi Arabia willingly does imperialism's dirty work. It was responsibile for financing the Afghan counter-revolutionaries to the tune of billions of pounds: it was a conduit for money and arms to the Contras in Nicaragua and it is the main financier of reactionary Muslim fun-damentalist movements devoted to the eradication of communism and socialism in the Arab world.' (op cit: 23) Other oil-rich Gulf states are close-ly linked to the West through investments and high-tech military orders. Private investors from Saudi Arabia, Kuwait and the United Arab Emirates have holdings in the US worth $150 billion. In addition, government-fund-ed agencies of Saudi Arabia, Kuwait, Qatar, Oman and Bahrain hold an esti-mated $200 billion in overseas investments. (Schiller 1992: 39)

---

4   landers, Laurie (1992): 'Restricting reality: Media mindgames and the war', *Beyond the Storm: A Gulf crisis reader*; (eds) Bennis, Phyllis and Moushabeck, Michel; Canongate; Edinburgh. pp 160-172. Highlights involvement of President Bush's policy advisor Brent Scowcroft with Kuwait Petroleum Corporation. p 168.

See also Colhoun, Jack (1992): 'The family that preys together', *Covert Action Information Bulletin*; Washington; Summer. pp 50-59.

And Dexter, Fred (1991): '*Ménage à trois*: Oil, money, BCCI and the CIA', *Covert Action Information Bulletin*; Washington; Winter. Shows that as the Irangate hearings revealed, Saudi Arabia was to become one of Washington's favourite sources of vast unvouchered money for secret operations during the Reagan years. pp 46-48.

See also Tisdall, Simon (1992): 'Bush gave Baker waiver over Iraq'; the *Guardian*; 19 May.

Yet, contrary to press reports that warned of a new oil crisis, there was, in fact, never any danger of Iraq's invasion of Kuwait disturbing the global oil economy. As Philip Agee argued (1991: 22), access to Middle East oil for the industrialised countries was never threatened. 'The producers, including Iraq, have to sell to sustain their own economic and development projects. They get no benefits from either withholding oil or forcing the price too high. On the contrary, in doing so they hurt themselves.' The global industrial community had learned the lessons from the two previous crises – of 1973, when Gulf OPEC ministers raised the price of oil by around 140 per cent, and 1978-1979, when the Iranian revolution cut supplies. (Glavanis 1991)

The principal importers of oil diversified their energy consumption reducing their reliance on oil, enormous stocks were built to deal with any emergencies while prices were kept relatively low with the control of the market falling away from OPEC to the industrialised consumer countries. (Stork 1986; Roberts 1995: 198-199) Despite the oil embargo on Iraq and the firing of the Kuwaiti oil fields; despite the media whipping up fears of a major crisis in the Gulf, it can be argued there was never any danger of an oil shock in 1991.[5] As Van Evera comments (1991: 13): 'The price of oil was not at stake in the Gulf. Thus Iraq's seizure of the Gulf would have posed little direct threat to American sovereignty or prosperity. An expanded Iraq would have been a dominant regional power but would have remained a minor world power with little influence beyond the Middle East. It could not have threatened the security of the US or its Western industrial allies. Nor would its expansion have injured democracy since the Gulf states are not democratic...The containment of Iraq serves American interests if the US intends to sustain its security guarantee to Israel.'

Had Iraq retained Kuwait it would still have controlled fewer net resources than Saudi Arabia. In 1986 Iraq plus Kuwait GNP was $62.3 billion; Saudi $77.1 billion. The enlarged Iraq would still have been a minor world power, producing only 1 per cent of Gross World Product. In contrast, the US produces 27 per cent of GWP while Nato states together produce 50 per cent of GWP. 'With this small economic base even an enlarged Iraq could not have built a military machine that could match the

---

5   Chomsky, Noam (1992): 'After the Cold War: US Middle East policy', *Beyond the Storm* (op cit). pp 75-87 Argues that the US and UK are not necessarily opposed to high oil prices. The sharp price escalation in 1973 was in many ways beneficial to their economies – trade balance with oil production rose and the US and UK began to profit from their own high-priced oil in Alaska and the North Sea. pp 85-87. He suggests: 'The US would follow essentially the same policy if it were 100 per cent in solar energy, just as it followed the same policies pre-1970 when it had little need for Middle East oil.' pp 79-80.

See also Shelley, Toby (1991): 'Burying the oil demon', *The Gulf War and the new world order*; (eds) Bresheeth, Haim and Yuval-Davis, Nira; Zed Press; London. pp 166-176. He writes: 'The crisis in the Middle East has not been accompanied by an oil shock because all the fundamental influences on the market have been directly or indirectly under the control of the industrialised consumer countries.' p 174.

militaries of the industrial West.' (ibid: 12) It could also be argued that Iraqi complaints about Kuwait's over-production and capture of the Rumaila oil field were legitimate. But this view was never heard in the US or UK press. Stork and Lesch comment (1990: 13): 'Iraq's complaints in 1990 about Kuwait's over-production sound all too plausible in a region where people have an acute memory of the manipulative role of Western companies and governments usually with the eager compliance of the local beneficiary regime.'

The myth of Saddam's threat to Saudi Arabia

The notion promoted relentlessly in the mainstream US and UK press of President Saddam Hussein as the threat to the global economy is entirely dependent on the myth of the unique awfulness of the Iraqi invasion of Kuwait and the marginalisation of many other invasions during the Cold War period. The Indonesian invasion of East Timor (1975), the Soviet invasions of Hungary (1956) and Czechoslovakia (1968), Morocco's seizure of Western Sahara in 1975, the US invasion of Panama (1989), even the Syrian invasion of Lebanon (which was to follow in October 1990) are just a few obvious cases. But there were many others. For instance, in November 1971 the Shah of Iran with US backing sent his troops to occupy three islands belonging to the United Arab Emirates.

The Saddam threat is also based on the supposed danger the Iraqi army posed to taking control of Saudi Arabia's massive oil fields, containing a quarter of the globe's reserves. The *Sunday Times* of 5 August was typical. In debating the possible Iraqi invasion of Saudi Arabia, it reported that the weather was exceptionally hot 'but this should prove no obstacle to the Iraqis many of whom are battle-hardened by eight years' conflict with neighbouring Iran'. Its editorial envisaged the Saudi takeover, leaving Iraq 'the unchallenged regional superpower capable of dictating oil policy for the entire Gulf repository of 65 per cent of the world's oil reserves.' It continued: 'That is the Western nightmare writ large; an evil, anti-Western despot with a stranglehold on the main source of the West's lifeblood.'

A strong 'balancing' case can be made out to suggest no danger ever existed. But this was never heard in the US or UK press. CIA officials, in any case, have since conceded that at 'no time was there any evidence Saddam contemplated such a move'. (Cockburn and Cockburn 1992: 354) And according to Stephen Dorril, an MI6 survey of friendly intelligence services in the Gulf found a consensus believing that Iraq did not intend to invade Saudi Arabia. (Dorril 1993: 408) Darwish and Alexander (1991: 286) argue that 'once Kuwait had been secured Iraqi deployments were entirely defensive and the much cited move towards the Saudi border was merely the extending of front lines and the fortifying of defensive positions ... Not only did the Iraqis have no intention of attacking Saudi Arabia, they also avoided the sort of provocative actions that may have precipitated a war.'

Moreover, the ironies of the US defending the profoundly repressive regimes of the Gulf were rarely highlighted significantly in the press.[6] For instance, the *Sunday Times* of 13 January 1991 gave this totally uncritical picture: 'Pre-invasion Kuwait was an immaculately clean desert kingdom. Traditional Islamic values survived while billion pound oil riches sustained one of the best health systems in the world, the first modern university in the Gulf and a centre of international finance.'

The representation of the Kuwait invasion as a sudden 'naked act of aggression' was profoundly anti-historical. Iraq's border dispute with Kuwait, its claims on the islands of Warbah and Bubiyan and for an access to the Gulf were, in fact, all long-standing. An unsuccessful attempt to annex Kuwait had been made in 1932, just after independence and in 1961, just after Kuwait gained independence. In 1938, the Kuwait emir's advisory council recommended union with Iraq – but was prevented from doing so by the British. By the late 1980s Iraq was keen to develop close relations with Saudi Arabia. A friendship agreement had been signed and after the invasion of Kuwait Iraq was at pains to stress its friendship with Saudi Arabia. King Hussein of Jordan always insisted that Iraq had no intention to invade the kingdom. King Fahd was quoted on 7 August as feeling confident there was no threat. Salinger and Laurent argue that the Arab world desperately tried to resolve the crisis on the basis of Iraq's non-intervention in Saudi Arabia only to find their efforts undermined by pressure from the United States government. (Salinger and Laurent 1991: viii)

---

6   Armstrong, Scott (1991): quoted in Valerian, Richard: 'Talking back to the tube', *Columbia Journalism Review*; New York; March/April. pp 24-26. Focuses on the failure of the press to highlight the significance of the setting up of the $50 bn Command, Control, Communication and Intelligence infrastructure in Saudi Arabia during the 1980s. 'Without this understanding it is impossible to explain how 600,000 people were so rapidly deployed. And it is impossible to appreciate how entangled we are with the Saudis. Without this Saudi infrastructure the American war machine is an unco-ordinated mass of independent appendages.' p 26.

Aruri, Naseer (1992): 'Human rights and the Gulf crisis: The verbal strategy of George Bush', *Beyond the Storm* (op cit). pp 305-324. Argues on Arab states in general: 'It may be said this is a disaster area in terms of human rights. Irrespective of the type of government, republic, emirates or kingdoms and irrespective of ideological alignment or foreign policy orientation whether aligned with the West or the anti-Iraqi coalition or not, most Arab regimes fall short of the minimum international requirements for human rights.' p 310.

See also Franklin, Stephen (1991): 'The Kingdom and its messengers'; *Columbia Journalism Review*; New York July/August. pp 24-27. And Lennon, Paul (1991): 'Relative values in a time of war'; the *Guardian* 21 February. Highlights the failure of the media to report an Amnesty International report on torture, detention and arbitrary arrests in Saudi Arabia. 'It is common knowledge that fear of not being granted visas was the only consideration in withholding coverage of that embarrassing story. War kills, corrupts and obliges you to be tactful about strange bedfellows.' Ryan, Sheila (1992): 'Countdown for a decade: The US build-up for war in the Gulf', *Beyond the Storm* (op cit) Shows (pp 91-102) Saudi expenditure per soldier $223,592 annually compared with $66,000 for the United States or $6,960 for Iraq. The CIA has also assisted the ruling family in establishing a substantial internal security force. p 97.

See also *South* editorial (1990): 'Fuelling the new arms race'; London; November. The most damning critique of Saudi Arabia appears in Aburish, Said K (1994): *The rise, corruption and coming fall of the House of Saud*; Bloomsbury; London.

Cockburn and Cohen (1991: 21) report that sources close to King Hussein of Jordan and Yasser Arafat, PLO chairman, were claiming that Saddam Hussein had agreed to withdraw as long as the Arab summit of 3-4 August held back from criticising Iraq. 'According to this version of accounts, Mubarak agreed to the deal but changed his mind and denounced Iraq when the USA offered to write off billions of dollars of Eqypt's debt.' On 5 August, Saddam Hussein summoned Joe Wilson, the US *chargé d'affaires* in Baghdad, to say Iraq had no intention of invading Saudi Arabia. This message was relayed to the State Department but then on 6 August a prominent story in the *Washington Post* had the Iraqi leader claiming he would invade if the Iraqi pipeline was cut.

Cockburn and Cohen comment: 'In other words, within moments of the invasion, a faction within US policy-making circles, determined to press forward to war and to the destruction of Iraq as a regional power, was already manipulating the record with diligence and success. There are also accounts that, in his first trip to persuade King Fahd to accept US troops, US Defense Secretary Dick Cheney used satellite photographs selected to demonstrate an Iraq poised for invasion, whereas subsequent photographs refuted such claims.' (ibid: 21-22; see also Salinger and Laurent op cit: 137-138; and Aburish, Said K. 1995: 175-178)

The scenario of diplomatic openings from Baghdad being dismissed by the US/UK and marginalised or ignored by their mainstream media was to be repeated on a number of occasions. Heikal (1992: 249) reveals that on 8 August, a prominent Palestinian businessman sent a message by fax to Washington indicating Baghdad's willingness to withdraw from Kuwait, to allow the restoration of the Sabah family. In addition it sought an Iraqi presence on Bubiyan island, a settlement of Iraqi debts and compensation. It was completely ignored. Heikal adds: 'In President Carter's day this would probably have been seen as an opening bid leading to secret talks but Bush had decided there was nothing to discuss.'

Other offers came from Iraq on 9 August, 19 August, 21 August, 23 August and 2 January; on 24 September (from French President Mitterrand at the UN), on 21 October (by the Saudi defence minister). King Hussein of Jordan, Russian President Gorbachev, the Algerian government and the PLO all made concerted efforts to promote a diplomatic solution – all of them rejected by the Bush administration and marginalised by the press. (Cockburn 1991; Niva 1992) In any case, the US military later generally admitted that Iraq was without the logistical support facilities to invade and occupy Saudi Arabia.

Jean Edward Smith (1992) even argues that President Bush committed himself to using force against Iraq the day before Cheney's meeting with King Fahd of Saudi Arabia though insisting publicly he was merely trying to protect Saudi Arabia. The Saudi Arabian Joint Forces Commander, General Khaled Bin Sultan (1995: 313), provided some authoritative support for this view when, in his memoir of the 'war', he revealed that from the moment Iraq invaded Kuwait, America was planning an offensive strategy.

The myth of the Kuwait surprise

Considerable evidence suggests that the US fully expected an Iraqi invasion of Kuwait in early August. Some even argue that the US encouraged the invasion. (Yousif 1991) Yet the dominant view represented 'the world' as vulnerable and being taken by surprise. Peter Pringle, for instance, in the *Independent on Sunday* of 2 December 1990 wrote: 'Considering that the Pentagon had no contingency plan for opposing Saddam, President Bush responded to the invasion of Kuwait with a strikingly grand commitment.'

The border row with Kuwait had been intensifying over a decade, coming to a head in the years following the 1988 ceasefire in the Gulf War. US satellites over the Gulf would have provided evidence of troop build-ups. On 25 July, Col Said Matar, who was based at the Kuwaiti consulate in Basra for 14 months before the invasion, told his government that an Iraqi invasion was planned for 2 August. Following the ending of the 1980-1988 Iran/Iraq war, Iraq replaced Iran as the major Middle East threat in the eyes of American military strategists. (Sultan, Khaled Bin op cit: 313) Just before the invasion, Gen. Schwarzkopf, who was to lead the coalition forces, was playing computer war games (codenamed 'Internal Look') in which the scenario was an Iraqi invasion of Saudi Arabia through Kuwait. (Pilger 1991; Atkinson 1994: 107) Nigel Gillies, Command Public Information Officer at Headquarters United Kingdom Land Forces, also revealed that US Centcom (the re-named Rapid Deployment Force) at Tampa in Florida had carried out an exercise using the scenario of a Kuwait invasion. He continued: 'This exercise validated the requirement for two major press centres – one in the Saudi capital at Riyadh, and the other much nearer the scene of any action at Dhahran.' (Gillies 1991: 12)

The secret anti-Hussein strategy

Heikal (op cit: 173-174) suggests that a CIA unit had been working closely with the Kuwait government since 1984 and that they had encouraged Kuwait's provocation of Iraq over the oil dispute. At a meeting between top Kuwaitis and William Webster, CIA chief, in November 1989, it was decided 'to exploit the deteriorating economic situation in Iraq so that we can press its government to accept designation of our frontiers with them'. Continuing its covert support for Iran, the meeting agreed that Kuwait should re-programme its relations with Iran and reinforce its alliance with Syria.

The Glaspie scapegoat

The *Express*, in its backgrounder on the invasion, had described the American ambassador, April Glaspie, as having been given a 'dressing down' by Saddam Hussein on 25 July. The opposite had occurred. It was a very friendly meeting, in fact. In early September, the Iraqis released an English translation of the session, the accuracy of which was never denied by the Americans (and carried in full in Salinger and Laurent op cit 47-62). Saddam Hussein is quoted as claiming that economic war was being waged against his country and that $25 was not a high price for a barrel of oil. Glaspie replied: 'We have many Americans who would like to see the price go above $25 because they come from oil-producing states.' She then said the US had 'no opinion on the Arab-Arab conflicts, like your border disagreement with Kuwait'.

On 28 July, President Bush sent a note of friendship to Saddam Hussein. On 31 July, John Kelly, assistant secretary of state, told the Middle East sub committee of the House of Representatives that if Iraq invaded Kuwait 'we have no treaty, no commitment which would oblige us to use American forces'. On 1 August, a day before the invasion, the Bush administration approved the sale of $695m of advanced data transmission devices to Iraq. Glaspie was later allowed to be scapegoated by the administration, being blamed for not indicating clearly to Saddam US warnings over any invasion plans. She was quoted as saying: 'Obviously I didn't think – and nobody else did – that the Iraqis were going to take all of Kuwait.' This suggests that people might have expected the Iraqis to take some of Kuwait.

This does not imply that the Iraqi invasion of the whole of Kuwait was expected by a significant section of the US secret state. They probably expected a seizure of the northern oil fields and islands. Once the whole of Kuwait was taken the Americans quickly saw the military opportunities – and took them. The mythology of the surprise is partly based on allegations (quite commonly voiced in the press) that the CIA and British secret service had committed appalling blunders in not halting the Iraqi advance. But if the advance was seen as potentially beneficial to the US then these allegations are spurious.

Silencing the Iraqi dimension

Immediately following the invasion the focus for the causes of the ensuing crisis was directed by the press entirely on Iraq. America/Britain/France were nowhere part of the problematic. In fact, this was the consensual perspective maintained throughout the British media. Yet the press coverage of Iraq was totally overshadowed by the demonisation of Saddam Hussein. Saddam became Iraq. As the *Sunday Times'* profile commented on 29 July 1990 (just before the Kuwait invasion): 'Today Saddam Hussein is Iraq.' Such a focus remained consistent throughout the press during the crisis and massacres.

It thus rendered invisible the complexity of the rich social, political, cultural history of Iraq and its people, the Iraqi regime's diplomatic manoevrings during the 1970s and 1980s and its attempts to assert an Arab nationalism, particularly in the post Camp David period. Iraqi coverage was all too one-dimensional. As Matthew Rendell indicated, the military strategy adopted by the US-led coalition presupposed the existence of a 'monolithic entity called the Iraqi nation which can be represented by single voices'. He continued: 'The relationship between journalists and the military might hinge on the need of the military to think in terms of monoliths. After all, if an army is not fighting on behalf of a stable, unquestionable entity, then what is it doing?'[7]

Thus, only after the massacres ended on 28 February did an image of Iraq emerge which was not a monolithic unity but one which had been falling apart for years. Members of the groups who had been opposing the regime, drawn from the rich variety of ethnic and religious communities in the country – Kurds, Shi'as as well as Arabs, Turkomans, Persians, Sunnis and Chaldean Christians – had been slaughtered.

Silencing the role of British imperialism

Missing from most of the coverage was a sense of the extraordinary impact Western imperialism had (and continued to have) on the country and the resentments that flowed from it.[8] The dominant new militarist ideological consensus has, in fact, eliminated the very notion of imperialism from the mainstream discourse. Clearly the carve-up of the Middle East and Gulf by the imperial powers after the First World War contained the roots of the current crisis. The region's nations had been born through secret diplomacy – and their fates continue to be profoundly affected by the imperial powers' covert activities.

During the war the Arabs had been promised independence in exchange for support against the Turks. But secretly the Sykes-Picot agreement between Britain, France and Czarist Russia divided the Arab world between Britain and France. (Anderson and Rashidian 1991: 3-8) Iraq was created by joining the Ottoman provinces of Mosul, Baghdad and Basra. Its borders with Kuwait and Nejd, the territorial core of what was to become Saudi Arabia, were fixed in arbitrary fashion by Sir Percy Cox, British High Commissioner for Iraq, in November 1922. Kuwait was given a 310-mile coastline with several deep water ports. Iraq was given a mere 36 miles of coastline and just one deep water port which it had to share with Iran.

A monarchic structure was imposed on Iraq by the British in 1922 with the installation of Sharis Hussein's son, Faisal, as King (and with son Abdellah becoming King of Transjordan). And though the country technically gained its independence in 1932, it was still effectively under the rigid control of the British. And the British ruled the territory, considered of strategic significance in relation to India, with an iron hand. It also proved a useful training ground for the infant RAF which was able to provide a relatively cheap and

---

7   Rendell, Matthew P. participated in the discussion with Stewart Purvis, ITN editor, at the Royal Society of Arts, London, on 12 June 1991, on the theme 'The media and the Gulf War'. He is quoted on page 742 of the *RSA Journal*; London; November 1991, No 5423.

8   See Pilger, John (1991): 'The brainwashing of Britain', the *Guardian*; 8 February while Chomsky, Noam (1986): 'Thought control in the USA: The case of the Middle East', *Index on Censorship*; London; July/August provides some useful historical background to the coverage of the 1991 massacres. pp 2, 11, 23.

effective method of maintaining security in the southern marshes and north-land mountains – using chemical weapons against Kurds (an imperial policy little mentioned in background articles in the press during the build-up to the massacres).

The leading academic historians of Iraq, Marion Farouk-Sluglett and Peter Sluglett (1990: 42-45). describe the rule of Salih Jabr on behalf of the British as 'one of the most repressive regimes to come to power in the Middle East in the first half of the century'. Under the premiership of Nuri Said all polit-ical parties were banned, leading communists were executed in public, the press was heavily censored, terrible poverty gripped the mass of the popula-tion. More liberal forms of government were never considered. The overall concern was internal stability and stronger government.

Indeed, an awareness of the legacy of British imperialism in Iraq was almost totally missing from the press coverage. One clear exception was the report-ing by Robert Fisk in the *Independent*. For instance, under the headline 'History haunts the new Crusaders', he commented on 9 August 1990: 'The European powers who have taken the place of the Turks brought only pain to the Arabs, ignoring earlier promises of independence and dividing up the Arab lands into competing tribes ... Since the end of the Second World War, Arabs have struggled to shake off the humiliation of their history.' And one of the very rare acknowledgements of the role of Western imperialism in the crisis was made by columnist Robert Harris in the *Sunday Times* of 12 August 1990. But he did so in a feature supporting the build-up of coalition troops: 'Most of us, if we gave the matter thought, will probably agree, how-ever reluctantly, that we have no other course. We should be clear, however, how costly this policy may prove and we should give it its proper name – imperialism.'

Silencing the role of American imperialism and its covert wars

The complex, offensive role played by America historically in the region was hardly ever identified in the press. The dominant ideological frame eliminat-ed this perspective – America was seem primarily as the vulnerable defender of the New World Order, resisting the 'naked aggression' of a brutal dicta-tor. As the historian Richard W. Van Alstyne comments (1974: 6): 'In the United States it is almost heresy to describe the nation as an empire.' It might be useful to highlight just a few of America's covert and less covert imperial activities marginalised or eliminated by the dominant consensus of the new militarist state.

The 1952 coup in Egypt

Founded in 1947 the CIA, according to Phillip Knightley, rapidly became a state within a state. Between 1947 and 1953 its activities expanded six-fold largely in the covert operations section. Knightley suggests it had been licensed, effectively, to conduct 'a secret Third World War'. (Knightley 1986: 248) J.K. Galbraith described this as 'the licence for immorality'. (Galbraith

1977: 242) CIA activities had global reach – but the Middle East was always a crucial theatre of operations. In 1952, the CIA paid $3m ($50m today) into Swiss bank accounts to persuade General Mohammed Neguib to organise a coup on 22 July 1952 to oust King Farouk of Egypt. (Rusbridger 1989: 115-116; Copeland 1989: 142-171) Neguib proved to be merely a front man for Col. Gamel Nasser who took over in February 1954 and who for a while was courted and heavily financed by the CIA. (Freemantle 1983: 34-35; 103). But he rapidly turned firmly anti-Western and became the target of two CIA and one SIS (British secret service) assassination attempts. (ibid: 168; Bower 1995: 190)

CIA coup of 1953: Iran

In 1951, Dr Mohammed Mosaddeq of Iran nationalised the Anglo-Iranian Oil Company, introduced parliamentary elections and sought to reduce British influence in the country. In their seminal analysis of US press coverage of Iran, Dorman and Farhang (1987) showed how the dominant representation of Mosaddeq shifted from that of a quaint nationalist to that of a lunatic and Communist dupe. They say: 'Nowhere in the prestige press coverage of 1951 nationalisation was there a serious look at the specific grievances of Iran towards British oil interests, nor was Britain's historical role in Iran explored in depth. The press was content to portray the British as relatively innocent bystanders caught in a whirlwind of fanaticism and mindless nationalism.' (ibid: 42)

In 1953, the CIA (through Operation Ajax) and British intelligence (through Operation Boot) helped plan a coup which ousted Mosaddeq and restored the Shah, who had been the chief partisan of Nazi interests in Persia during the Second World War. (Rusbridger op cit: 114; Copeland 1989: 187-191; Curtis 1995; Fisk 1997) The top CIA operative in Iran was Kermit Roosevelt, a grandson of President Theodore Roosevelt, who revealed the agency's role in his book *Countercoup: The struggle for the control of Iran* (McGraw Hall; New York; 1979). He was assisted by General H. Norman Schwarzkopf, father of the 1991 Gulf 'war' general. Key Iranians were bribed, a massive propaganda campaign frightened people about a Soviet takeover, anti-Mossadeq factions in the army were supplied with American equipment. The US press, according to Dorman and Farhang, 'ignored, overlooked or dismissed the possibility of US involvement in the affair'.

Thereafter, the Shah proceeded to develop one of the most savage and oppressive regimes of this century. (Chomsky 1988: 176) With Britain withdrawing from the Gulf and American elite still smarting from the Vietnam disaster, President Richard Nixon and his security adviser Henry Kissinger made Iran the focal point of their Middle East strategy, agreeing to sell virtually any conventional arms the Shah wanted. By the time of the 1979 revolution, the $20 bn American sales to the Shah had made him the biggest arms customer in history. Yet Dorman and Farhang show how, despite the Shah's appalling record on human rights, the US press acted primarily as apologists for him and uncritical supporters of the consensus policy towards him.

CIA and the Ba'athist coups of 1963 and 1968

The CIA played significant roles in the coup of 1963 which brought the Ba'athists (and ultimately Saddam Hussein) to power in Iraq. (Bulloch and Morris 1991: 55-56) Bulloch and Morris also report that the 1968 coup which returned the Ba'athists to power was also done 'in the interests of the CIA'. (ibid: 56) America's responsibility for helping create the repressive conditions which ultimately led to the Iranian revolution of 1978-79 and then the Iran-Iraq war of 1980-88 was never acknowledged in the press. Equally, Iraq began its 'tilt' towards the West in 1975 with its first purchases of arms from France. In 1979, it condemned the Soviet invasion of Afghanistan while its invasion of Iran 'had at least tacit American support as well as the active backing of some of the Shah's former generals', according to Bulloch and Morris. (ibid: 75)

Brian Crozier (1994: 162-163) records President Sadat of Egypt saying in an interview with him on 10 November 1980: 'I knew in advance of Saddam Hussein's intention to attack Iran. He went to Saudi Arabia to seek the advice of King Khaled, who gave him the green light. Khaled told the Americans who also gave Saddam Hussein the green light.' America's (and Britain's) massive covert support to Iraq between 1980 and 1990 was seriously underplayed in the press after August 1990. It clearly could not be totally ignored. But it was generally passed over as a mistake – one which the global community had to learn from. Thus the *Express* editorial of 3 August commented: 'In large part Saddam is the West's own Frankenstein monster. We have armed and encouraged him. Now he is rampaging free, a danger to all. If there is to be any chance of maintaining some semblance of international order the West will have to be prepared to rattle its own sabre. And be further prepared to use it.'

The CIA began passing sensitive data to the Iraqi regime through King Hussein (on the CIA books for the previous 20 years) two years before Iraqi-US diplomatic relations were formally restored in 1984. (Yousif 1991: 62) Friedman reports how America, Britain and France all provided tactical military advice to the Iraqis in the battlefield. (op cit: 38) From 1987, the CIA engaged in secret bombing missions against Iranian sites (ibid: 42; see also Woodward, Bob 1987: 439) Between 1985 and 1990, the Reagan and Bush administrations approved $1.5 bn sales of advanced products to Iraq. By the end of the 1980s, Washington had approved a total of $5 bn in loan guarantees for Iraq, making it one of the biggest recipients of US largesse. (Friedman op cit: 104)

Even more significantly, US arms trading to Iraq continued after August 1990. President Bush and Secretary of State James Baker ignored Jordan's violations of the UN embargo after the Kuwait invasion. 'Between 2 August and 4 October 1990, the State Department approved twelve new military equipment orders worth five million dollars, including items such as spare parts and components for TOW missiles, helicopter components for the AH-1S Cobra, 105-mm cartridges for artillery shells and conversion kits for the M-16 rifle.' (ibid: 172) But the scandal of covert support to Iraq (Saddamgate/Iraqgate) had to wait two years before emerging (somewhat tamely – since it was election year, after all) in the US.

RDF: the gun waiting to be fired?

Nothing more exposes the myth of the 'defensive' United States than the creation of the Rapid Deployment Force. Indeed, it could be argued that by 1990 so much doctrinal theory and financial investment had been directed at this force and to the Middle East strategic region in general that, with the decline of the Soviet Union, the US military was desperate to find an 'enemy' to give it 'a piece of the action' and provide it with some legitimacy.[9] Originally conceived as a small, flexible, quick strike force to protect US interests in the Gulf and elsewhere following the Iranian revolution of 1979 it rapidly expanded into an enormous fighting force ready for action. It was renamed CENTCOM in January 1983 with responsibility for preserving/promoting US interests from the Horn of Africa and the Arabian peninsular to Pakistan with more than 200,000 US military personnel at its disposal.

The command did not establish new fighting units; rather forces earmarked for other theatres could be called upon. Special bases were built up: the UK island of Diego Garcia, for instance, was depopulated to make way for the military installations. Up to $1.1 bn dollars was spent on improving ports and airfields in Oman, Somalia, Kenya, Egypt, Morocco and Portugal for RDF purposes. British forces were also closely integrated into RDF exercises. But all this developed without any public/media debate in either the US or UK. As Stephen Goose commented (1989: 98): 'The United States is spending billions of dollars to restructure and equip its armed forces so they can intervene more effectively in the Third World, and yet there has been little debate about the implications of those actions.' By August 1990, it could be argued, the RDF was like a 'loaded gun' waiting to be fired.

Silencing the Israeli link

The Israeli link in the Middle Eastern crisis was subtly silenced by the dominant ideological consensus. Since the 1950s the bedrock of US policy in the region has been its devoted support to Israel. Democratic Senator Robert Byrd of West Virginia, on 1 April, 1992, indicated for the first time the level of financial backing: some $53 bn between 1949 and 1991 – equivalent to 13 per cent of all US military and economic aid over the period. (Neff 1992; 1992a) It became the crucial link country in the US's secret war strategies with

---

9   Ryan, Sheila (1992): 'Countdown for a decade: The US build-up for war in the Gulf', *Beyond the Storm* (op cit) pp 91-102.

the CIA providing it with large subsidies to penetrate Africa in the 1960s in the US interest and later in Asia and Latin America. (Hersh 1991: 5) Israel was the crucial power whose roles were to contain the Soviet's supposed aggressive designs on its southern flank during the Cold War years; to contain Arab nationalism, and to oversee the West's control over the oil supplies. Cultural and political ties cemented the alliance.

Israel, it has been argued, rates as one of the most terroristic of states. (Rose 1986) Yet it is rarely defined as such in the Western media. It refuses to withdraw from the occupied territories as demanded by the United Nations; it conducted a brutal war against the Palestinian intifada; it has regularly committed attacks against 'enemy' states. In 1981, for instance, it bombed the Iraqi nuclear plant at Osiraq. In 1982 its invasion of Lebanon ended in disaster and with thousands killed.

In 1985, it bombed the Tunisian headquarters of the PLO, killing 75 people. The UN Security Council condemned the raid as an act of armed aggression, the US alone abstaining. Mossad, the Israeli secret service, and the Abu Nidal organisation, which, some commentators argue, it has largely infiltrated, have over the years eliminated through assassination three of the four founding fathers of the Fatah wing of the Palestinian Liberation Organisation.[10] There is enough evidence to demonise the state of Israel if the media ever wanted – but it never does. In contrast, 'Arab terrorism' is a constant reference point in the Western media.

Just as Saddam Hussein was concerned to link the Iraqi invasion of Kuwait with the Israeli invasion of the West Bank, Golan Heights and Gaza in his negotiating position of 12 August 1990, so the US was equally determined to deny any linkage. (Abu-Lughood 1992) Such a policy was seen as compromising with the aggressor. But Halliday argues that for Iraq the promotion of the Palestinian cause was far from a cynical move since it continued a policy established well before the formation of the Ba'ath state in 1968. (Halliday 1991: 223-224) The PLO had set up its HQ in Baghdad after being bombed out of Tunis and saw advantages in an alliance with the growing major Arab power. (Jahanpour 1991) For Iraq, support for the PLO could be associated with Saddam Hussein's mounting anti-imperialist rhetoric and advocacy of the cause of the Arab masses against their Western-backed, corrupt, and over-wealthy rulers. Yet the media followed the Bush agenda, demonising Saddam Hussein, and representing Israel as the innocent, 'vulnerable' nation. (Ahmed 1991: 18)

---

10 Seale, Patrick (1992): *Abu Nidal: The world's most notorious terrorist*; Arrow Books; London. He writes: 'Of the four founding fathers of Fatah only Arafat remains. Muhummad Yusif al-Najjar was killed by an Israeli assassination squad in Beirut in 1973; Khalil al-Wazir (Abu Jihad) was killed by Israeli commandos in Tunis in 1988.' He suggests that Abu Iyad, Arafat's No. 2, was killed by Abu Nidal, possibly on the orders of the Israelis, in January 1991, on the eve of the Gulf massacres. Seale argues strongly throughout the book that Abu Nidal is an Israeli agent – though the evidence, he admits, can never be conclusive. p 324.

Iraq's ambition to gain strategic parity with Israel lay behind much of the political dynamics of the 1988-1990 period. Since 1960 Israel has developed a nuclear weapons programme, first with French assistance, then with covert South African aid. Following revelations to the *Sunday Times* (on 5 and 12 October 1986) by Mordechai Vanunu, a former employee of the Dimona nuclear research centre, it was by the late 1980s estimated to have at least 200 nuclear weapons, making it one of the largest nuclear powers in the world.

The Vanunu revelations came after a report in the *Observer* (of 2 February 1986) that Israel, with financial backing from Iran, had developed a missile capable of carrying nuclear weapons. Yet Israeli politicians have only very rarely admitted to the existence of their nuclear arsenal. They cannot be open about it: America is prevented by law from aiding nations developing nuclear weapons. To admit their existence would render all those billions of dollars of aid illegal. So the Great Lie is maintained. Throughout the demonisation of Saddam Hussein as a nuclear threat in the run-up to the Gulf massacres, the press never chose to 'balance' their coverage with reference to the Israeli arsenal. (Kaku: 1992) In effect, one of the most dominant factors in Middle East politics was silenced out of existence. Moreover, Turkey is a nuclear state by default being home to a vast Nato arsenal including 450 nuclear-capable artillery, 90 surface to air missiles and 36 short range ballistic missiles. Turkey is never represented as a nuclear 'threat' in the press. It's a friend to the West, after all. (Ehteshami 1987: 149)

6 New militarism and the making of the military option

Immediately following the Iraqi invasion of Kuwait of 2 August 1990 virtually all the London-based national press opted for a military response. The new militarist consensus emerged blazing verbal guns. Even the governments of US and UK at the time played a dual role, calling for diplomacy but warning of military retaliation. Most of the press had no time for talk – they wanted war and right now. From 3 August Fleet Street was on a virtual war footing.

The ideological framing was perfectly simple and consistently maintained. Immediately diplomacy and sanctions were downplayed (or identified with 'appeasement'); the Saddam 'monster' threat was emphasised and the military option prioritised. The language was always fighting and fiercely patriotic. On 3 August in the *Mail*, columnist Paul Johnson wrote (under the headline: 'Force – the only answer to this despot'): 'One thing is certain – half measures are not going to be enough. Threats of economic sanctions and fiddling about at the UN will simply confirm Hussein's judgment that he has got away with it.' He continued: 'All the requisite forces – air, land and sea – should be promptly despatched to the area, a task force created, a commander appointed and instructions clearly given to meet any further act of aggression by Iraq with force...Force or the convincing threat of force is the only language he has ever understood.'

By 4 August the *Mail* was highlighting the war option this way: 'Two military moves would force Hussein out of Kuwait, say defence experts. They are a frontal attack across the Saudi Arabian desert and a massive bombing assault on nuclear and chemical weapons factories around Baghdad. The Gulf nations would need help from the US and European troops in an operation backed by precision bombing techniques developed principally by the US and Britain.'

The *Mirror* argued: 'Presidents Bush and Gorbachev supported by Mrs Thatcher and President Mitterrand should meet immediately to agree a unified plan of action against him. The lesson of history is that appeasement never brings peace or security but means only a harder and bloodier fight later on.' Under the headline 'What can the world do now?' the paper wrote: 'If Saddam refused to withdraw Bush could order selective strikes against Iraqi targets like military and oil installations.'

On 4 August, the *Mirror*'s page one headline ran: 'Stay put or it's war' with the focus on the military logistical build-up. On 6 August, it reported: 'The military option seemed more likely as it was reported that Defense Secretary Dick Cheney was heading for Saudi Arabia.' By 8 August war was almost breaking out: 'Battle stations' was the headline. 'The allied fleet dwarfs Iraq's navy of five missile frigates and 38 patrol craft. But President Saddam Hussein can call up 450 combat planes for air strikes.' On 9 August (almost intoxicated by war fever) it declared: 'US on brink of war with Iraq.' And its editorial commented sternly: 'Saddam Hussein was given his last chance to "pull back from the brink". If he refuses it will mean war...If war comes we shall pray it will be won quickly and decisively.'

The *Sunday Times* of 5 August began its page one lead: 'The threat of large-scale war in the Middle East increased dramatically last night as America prepared to dispatch B52 bombers to the region in an effort to deter Iraq from invading Saudi Arabia.' Saudi and Turkish preferences for an Arab solution were described as 'a problem'. Its editorial ruled out a military operation 'at least for now'. 'The logistics of mounting it against a ruthless ruler prepared to use chemical weapons, with almost 1m battle-hardened troops and more tanks than Rommel, Eisenhower and Montgomery combined had in North Africa, are just too formidable.' The implication being that when the logistical problems were sorted out, then was the time to attack.

Just one week later the *Sunday Times* was backing all-out war. Its editorial commented: 'There will be no real purpose to the American expedition until Mr Bush faces up to the harsh fact that President Saddam will have to be removed, sadly but inevitably, by force...The reason why we will shortly have to go to war with Iraq is not to free Kuwait though that is to be desired or to defend Saudi Arabia, though that is important. It is because President Saddam is a menace to the vital Western interests in the Gulf – above all the free flow of oil at market prices which is essential to the West's prosperity.' For the *Sunday Times*, Britain's biggest selling Sunday 'quality', the backing for military action to topple 'madman Saddam' became the obsessive, simple theme of all its Gulf editorials from early August onwards.

The *Independent*: not independent?

The *Guardian* and the *Independent*, however, stood out against this war-mongering campaign. The first (while following the dominant consensus in prioritising the military build-up in its news coverage) was to maintain editorially a sceptical eye towards the Bush/Thatcher/Major agenda, backing the negotiations/sanctions option until the outbreak of hostilities. As principal feature writer Martin Woollocott explained: 'We were somewhat divided at editorial meetings. Some saw war as inevitable; some saw ways out and for them diplomacy was of major interest. The *Guardian* is traditionally anti-imperialist and we tend to take a hard look at the motives of the major powers.'

The *Independent*'s approach was different. Until 17 August it backed the negotiations option with a series of editorials stressing the diplomatic route. For instance, on 13 August it responded positively to Iraq's 'encouraging' negotiating offer in which it linked Israel's occupation of the West Bank and Gaza with the Iraqi intervention in Kuwait. 'For the West to overthrow Saddam Hussein by force would be to emulate his behaviour in Kuwait.' On 15 August, it was critical of US acting aggressively in imposing a blockade of Iraq. On the following day it saw Iraq's treaty with Iran as increasing the danger of war. 'It is therefore more necessary than ever to move carefully and to give mediation a chance.' On 17 August, it concluded: 'It is in the UN's long-term interests to seek a negotiated settlement.'

Everything suddenly changed on 20 August. Then the *Independent* joined what Edward Pearce of the *Guardian* dubbed the Editors for War group. Saddam had to be stopped now, it pronounced. Next day it commented: 'Stability will not return to the region while Saddam Hussein remains in power and the only argument he understands is force.' On 22 August, its earlier commitment to negotiations was dumped: 'Iraqi offers to negotiate should be treated with the utmost scepticism. Deeds not words are required from them.' On 24 August, it declared: 'The logic of the American and British line in the Gulf leads to war sooner rather than later.' Harvey Morris, in charge of the *Independent* Gulf desk during the crisis and massacres, suggested that the sudden change came about after the editor fully examined the implications of the Iraqi invasion. He denied there was any pressure on the paper to shift its editorial stance.

The pro-war consensus in the US

A similar prioritising of the military option occurred in the American media with the press and television reinforcing each other. The dominant debate was over the pros and cons of military strikes – not over the nature of any diplomatic solution. There was virtually no questioning (as in Britain) of the decision to send so many troops to the Gulf. News coverage highlighted the logistical build-up of forces, the most prominent columnists urged war. On 5 August, Jim Hoagland, *Washington Post* chief foreign correspondent, wrote: '...the political characteristics make this a rare case where the United States would be unwise not to use force'. On 19 August, Henry Kissinger, President Nixon's security adviser, in a syndicated article, called for a 'surgical strike' against Iraq, a view backed by William Safire in the *New York Times*, and by editorialists in the *Wall Street Journal* and *National Review*.

On 11 September, the *Washington Post* reported a *Post*-ABC poll that gave 74 per cent approving the decision to send forces to the Gulf. Given the bias of the reporting, such a finding was not surprising. Propaganda can be quite effective in a climate of 'moral panic' whipped up by the media. Even so, 26 per cent were opposed to the sending of troops, a large group which were given hardly a voice in the press. Editorials tended to express little criticism of the Bush agenda. Thus the *Washington Post* commented on 8 August: 'In response to Iraq's aggression, the world's security system is now going into operation as it should. Forces are gathering under many flags and President Bush is leading the gigantic enterprise with skill.' The *Chicago Tribune*, on the same day, under the headline 'US must be ready for tough fight' editorialised: 'The risks of firmness are ultimately smaller than the dangers of appeasement.'

Dorman (1991) highlights the pro-Bush agenda that the US uncritically adopted following the Iraqi invasion of Kuwait. 'By accepting the frames offered by Bush the press helped to limit debate at the time when it would have done the most good – before we got in so deeply that the war became inevitable.' He suggests that, with Congress on vacation, the press simply did not know whom to turn to for critical reaction to the President's initial policy. 'In other words, when it comes to foreign policy if a member of Congress does not say it, it isn't likely to be covered.' The *New York Times* commented: 'President Bush has drawn a line in the sand, committing US forces to face down Saddam Hussein. The costs and risks are momentous, going well beyond US military operations in Lebanon, Grenada and Panama. On balance he has made the right choice in the right way.'

Certain quibbles emerged when, shortly after the November elections Bush virtually doubled the number of troops to 430,000. The *Washington Post* argued that the President should seek congressional approval for the move; the *Los Angeles Times* complained that Bush had not done enough to convince the American public of the rightness of the goals in the Gulf; the *Atlanta Constitution* and *Chicago Tribune* were largely supportive. In their analysis of US coverage of the crisis and 'war', Abbas Malek and Lisa Leidig (1991: 15) argue that the 'press behaved more like a propaganda arm of the government promoting the idea of the inevitability of the war in the Persian Gulf'.

Iraq: the necessary global threat

Running through all the coverage on both sides of the Atlantic was the representation of Saddam Hussein personally as a global threat: the world was threatened and the world (united) was reacting in defence. In order to legitimise the massive build-up of troops the threat of the 'enemy' clearly had to be exaggerated. As Associated Press veteran Mort Rosenblum (1993: 117) later admitted: 'From the beginning all of us bought the myth that a nearly naked emperor was clad in triple-ply armor.' There was constant reference to 'Saddam' possessing a 1 million-strong army of battle-hardened soldiers, the fourth largest in the world. This was blatant disinformation which ran through the whole of the US/UK press.

But in this way new militarist societies (dependent on relatively small armies and increasingly on small special/covert forces and very expensive, low-man-power, high-technology weapons) are subtly able to represent much weaker and less sophisticated militarist societies – such as Iraq – as more powerful than they really are. In fact, the bigger the size of the Third World army, the less effective it is in combat with a professional First World force. Morale amongst conscripts is often low to non-existent as both the Argentinians (in the Falklands in 1982) and later the Iraqis were to prove. Moreover, Iraqi troops were known to have performed badly in the 1980-1988 war with Iran when thousands had deserted. (Faleh Abd al-Jabbar 1992: 5-6) Rather than 'battle-hardened', a more apt description for the Iraqi army in 1990 would have been 'battle-weary'. But it was never applied.[1]

Saddam's potential as a global threat was linked to his 'terroristic' ambitions and stressed in the propaganda campaign to actualise the growing possibility of war to the public who might otherwise feel completely uninterested in a military adventure in a far-away unknown part of the world. Thus the *Sunday Times* of 5 August on Saddam: 'From his massive command bunker outside Baghdad he put into operation what could be the first stage of a plan to reshape the Middle East and create potential mayhem for the world's economic and political order...Iraqis in their dark green uniforms are known by their fellow Arabs as the Prussians of the Middle East. Blooded in the Gulf war they are regarded as invincible. The army is the biggest in the region and is reckoned to be a match for Nato's powers such as Britain, let alone the Kuwaiti police guard.'

Its editorial warned: 'Iraq could be the unchallenged regional superpower capable of dictating oil plans for the entire Gulf repository of 65 per cent of the world's oil reserves. That is the Western nightmare writ large: an evil

---

1   See Abbas, A (1986): *The Iraqi armed forces, past and present in Saddam's Iraq: Revolution or reaction?*, CADRI/Zed Books; London pp 220-222.

    Also Cook, Nick (1990): 'Iraqi air power', *Jane's Soviet Intelligence Report*; London; October. On the poor performance of Iraqi pilots in the war with Iran, he comments: 'Air combat in the eight-year conflict was almost non-existent.' And Friedman, Norman (1991): *Desert victory: The war for Kuwait*; Naval Institute Press; Annapolis, Maryland. He comments: 'It may be that the Western powers, having backed Saddam during the Iran-Iraq War, could not admit that his forces had been less than competent, even in their triumph in 1988. The evidence was certainly there, in more than a decade of military disaster: against the Israelis, against the Kurds, against the Iranians during much of the war. All of these cases had been well-documented.' pp 112-113.

    While the press represented the allies, in contrast, as relatively inexperienced in battle compared to the Iraqis, Friedman argues the opposite. The US army had made enormous investment in the National Training Center in the Mojave Desert where its troops could fight mock battles. New technology, in the form of lasers whose hits could be immediately scored and tabulated, made these battles realistic. 'Thus, in enormous contrast to previous wars, the US Army which came to Saudi Arabia in 1990-1991 was already somewhat battle-hardened and battle-wise.' p 121.

anti-Western despot with a stranglehold over the main source of the Western lifeblood.' On 3 August, the *Mirror* asked: 'What can the world do now?' Iraqi was described as militarily 'very strong'. 'He has a well-trained army of a million men who fought an eight-year-long war against Iran. He has thousands of tanks, and artillery pieces, some MIG fighter bombers and ground to ground missiles. And chemical weapons that he has used before.'

The myth of the global threat was accompanied by the myth of the global response to the invasion. As President Bush said at a news conference on 22 August 1990: 'This is not a matter between Iraq and the USA. It is between Iraq and the entire world community, Arabs and non-Arabs, all the nations lined up to oppose aggression.' An editorial in the *New York Times* of 12 August described Bush as 'leader of all countries'. Central to the US strategy of globalising the conflict was its cynical manipulation (largely ignored by the mainstream press) of the United Nations to which it owed, at the time, several hundred million dollars. This was crucial in providing it with the facade of unanimity and the foundation for its 'new world order' rhetoric. The US was to fight a 'good' war against an 'evil' enemy. With UN backing it was also to fight a legally 'just' war.

In fact, the world was deeply divided and confused over the invasion. America, through a mixture of ruthless diplomacy and bribery, won over sufficient support in the UN to create an appearance of 'world support'. But in the end only 26 countries (out of 160) joined the coalition (many of them with tiny, token forces) with only 11 taking part in the offensive action in Kuwait. News of the massive opposition globally to the build up to war was marginalised throughout the US and UK press. Massive nationwide anti-war demonstrations and sit-ins were largely ignored by the US and UK press. This was a profoundly American war. But even in the United States there were deep divisions, the final votes for military action only clearing the Senate on 22 January by 53 to 47 and in the House of Representatives by 250 to 183 – hardly evidence of a national consensus for war which the media were intent on representing.

Hyping the inevitability of war

Most of Fleet Street and the US press represented war in the Gulf as inevitable – from the beginning of the crisis up to the launch of Desert Storm. Many prominent journalists genuinely believed in the war's inevitability from the early days of the crisis. Martin Woollacott, of the *Guardian*, for instance, commented: 'War *was* inevitable from September. Neither side could make the necessary concessions because the purposes of the two sides were too radically opposed. A Middle Eastern leader had taken unilateral action to challenge the West's authority. And the prestige gained had to be wiped out.'

But the constant representation of the inevitability of conflict, it could be argued, served the ideological and political purpose of rendering opposition marginal and doomed to defeat. It amounted to a sophisticated means of disempowering anti-war voices. From 3 August 1990, the press concentrated on the military build-up in the Gulf – the implication behind virtually all the coverage being that it would shortly be put to use in a war. Thus, the *Sun*, on 7 August, under a headline 'Yanks on warpath', began its report: 'America's mighty war machine was gearing up last night for a military strike as patience in the West finally ran out.' This focus was reinforced with a 'You the Jury' feature which gave a *Sun* poll result of 22,991 to 177 in favour of military action. By 9 August, it summoned up Second World War imagery in this way: 'President Bush spoke with Churchill-like gravity to the American people in a TV address that virtually prepares the world for war.' Next day it reported the allies and Iraq standing 'ready to do battle today'.

The *Sunday Times* identified in an editorial of 12 August the reasons why 'we will shortly have to go to war with Iraq'. On 6 November, the *Daily Star* carried what it claimed was a 'world exclusive': 'War this week: Iraq raid go ahead'. The front page of the London *Evening Standard* of 30 November maintained: 'Iraq may strike at any moment.' (Keeble 1991) The *Mirror* constantly prioritised the military option, made only token gestures towards the diplomatic option and kept up war fever by forever representing the 'world' as on the brink of battle. The Iraqi offer of 12 August, linking withdrawal from Kuwait with other occupations in the Middle East, was ignored by the paper. But on 15 August it was writing: 'It is not yet known if Saddam is prepared to negotiate with the West over his invasion of Kuwait.' On the same day it suggested Turkey's army had been put on a war alert after Saddam Hussein's jets had blitzed Turkish villages just inside Iraq.

The *Mirror's* Ramsey Smith on board HMS York on 16 August was already quoting soldiers as being ready to fight. With those same phrases that were to be repeated time after time over the following months, Petty Officer Mike Lough was quoted: 'I would much rather just get the hell out of here and go home. But we are under no illusion. If the job has to be done then we will have to do it. It is as simple as that.' Professional duty was eliminating all moral, political dilemmas for the soldier – just as was happening for so many journalists. On 22 August the paper headlined: 'War is inevitable warns Mitterrand: French expect air strike in 28 hours.' Three days later it was headlining: 'Countdown to war'. Saddam Hussein was said to be set 'to plunge the Gulf into all-out war within hours'. It quoted an interview with Gen. Ariel Sharon, a leading member of the Israeli Cabinet, in another of proprietor Robert Maxwell's papers, the *European*, (so using news as a publicity stunt) to the effect that the West would have to go to war 'without delay' to curb Saddam.

Consistent with the Bush agenda to promote occasionally peace and yet prepare for war, the *Mirror*, suddenly on 28 August, carried an editorial 'Give peace a chance'. War, it said, was not inevitable. Mrs Thatcher should give peace a chance. Such views accompanied a story on President Bush supposedly backing a UN peace bid. They didn't last long. The next day it was keeping up the war fever with the report: 'Tyrant Saddam Hussein was warned yesterday that half a million Iraqis could die if he sparked off a war with further military action.'

On 17 September, under the headline 'Let's blitz Saddam', it reported: 'If war starts, the American air force wants to decapitate Iraq by bombing President Saddam Hussein, his family, his senior commanders, his palace guard and even his mistress.' Such reports fed the demonisation of Saddam, but in military terms were highly questionable: these were just the people who were to escape once the massacres began, protected in their secret bunkers. Those to die, rather, were the thousands of innocent conscripts. (Glasgow University Media Group 1991: 2) By 12 October, it was saying 'Hurd paves way for war in the Gulf'. On 31 October the paper was suggesting Saddam Hussein had put his army on alert for an invasion within the next few days. On 1 November, war was said to be 'imminent'. On 22 November, it highlighted 'Rambo' Star Sylvester Stallone calling for a pull-out of US troops and a nuclear attack on 'Saddam Hussein': 'In that way no American would get hurt.'

Roy Greenslade, editor of the *Mirror* at the time, has revealed that not only was a *Mirror* journalist assigned by the newspaper's proprietor Robert Maxwell to sell encyclopeadias published by one of his companies in Saudi Arabia (and threatened with the sack when he refused) but that all the paper's leaders were being written by the Maxwell himself. (Greenslade 1992: 208) From early August they kept up a constant cry for war. Accompanying a near hysterical support for Israel 'the West's only real friend and trustworthy ally in the Middle East', and criticism of President Bush for 'playing footsie with Syria's President Assad' (November 26) was a profound contempt for Saddam Hussein.

On 25 October, for instance, under the headline 'The way to win', the editorial commented: 'Saddam Hussein is clever as well as ruthless. Mrs Thatcher should be strongly supported in her determination to bring him to book by military means...An overwhelming pre-emptive strike at night against planes on the ground, arsenals and headquarters would save hundreds of thousands of lives.' The same line was repeated on 27 November. It was blaming the Ministry of Defence for appeasement on December 13 for supposedly banning 'Christmas carols for our boys in the Gulf'.

On 8 January, it criticised the Labour Party for preferring sanctions to war. 'Too late to chicken out' it claimed. 'Giving Saddam another breathing space would mean more deaths and terrible injuries among our forces.' The Mirror Group was at the time the only one on Fleet Street providing any consistent support to the Labour Party – not from any kind of principled stand but, it could be argued, out of a simple, capitalist desire to exploit a gap in the market. Now, on an issue as crucial as the Middle Eastern crisis, the *Mirror* turned against Labour.

Roy Greenslade has since argued that, in pushing the 'war is inevitable' line, he hoped that the British press might have impressed on the Iraqis the allied commitment to action and thus encouraged them to retreat from their invasion of Kuwait. He said it was certainly easier for the *Mirror* to back the war option once Mrs Thatcher was replaced as Conservative leader by the less jingoistic John Major.

Silencing the anti-war voices: *Daily Mirror* case study

Along with the prioritising of the military option went the virtual exclusion of anti-war voices. Hallin (1986) has identified the historic 19th century compromise established between press and government according to which the press abstained from radical criticism of the state in exchange for access to government sources. Journalists are, effectively, agents of the state, reproducing the dominant ideological values, defining the limits of acceptable discourse and marginalising/delegitimising/eliminating radically critical voices. Kellner (1990: 98-99), along with the Italian political theorist Antonio Gramsci, modifies this view arguing that the media serve to negotiate and mediate significant democratic tensions and crises in the interests of the elite hegemony.

Nowhere was the press's propaganda role more apparent than in the press coverage of the crisis and massacres. Voices objecting to the sending of troops to the Gulf were virtually non-existent. And those who advocated using the troops as an offensive force (sooner or later) were privileged far above those who saw them merely as supporting the sanctions policy. (Flanders 1992: 160-172)

For instance, over the first six days of the crisis the *Mirror* used 67 quotes but only two of them were opposed to the military option. One was from the anxious husband of an air hostess stranded in Kuwait at the time of the Iraqi invasion (7 August); the other was from the stepfather of a stewardess caught in the invasion. In both cases, an assumption could be drawn that both men were speaking out of selfish concern for the fate of their relatives. Once that danger was removed an implication could be that they might support war. None of these anti-war voices came from a principled, articulate political voice of opposition to the military build-up.

The extraordinary complexity of the Arab responses to the crisis was almost completely ignored by the press. (Azzam 1991) Arab views were almost totally excluded. (Keeble op cit) More generally, they were represented stereotypically as hysterical, violent supporters of Saddam Hussein. Jim Hoagland, associate editor and chief foreign correspondent of the *Washington Post*, wrote on 7 August 1990: 'He [Saddam Hussein] is so hated at home that his defeat, even by foreign forces, will be greeted by deliverance by his own nation and by much of the Arab world.' Arabs, he claimed, were too weak to 'deliver the blow themselves' and Reagan's decision to bomb Libya in 1986 was the right model for Bush to follow.

On 17 August, the *Mirror* carried a profile of Maryam Rajavi, who was supposedly Iraq's youngest general. 'And like the highly trained, battle-hardened women under her command she is a total fanatic.' Running contrary to this general thrust, was a report on 22 August focusing on British wives of Jordanian men calling for a diplomatic solution to the crisis. Yet the paper still managed to headline this story 'Arab wives on warpath' transforming a call for peace into a war cry and at the same time perpetuating the stereotype of the violent, fanatical Arab (in fact, they were British wives). 'The women, who have made their homes in Jordan, accused the Prime Minister and President Bush of threatening world safety because of greed for oil.' Just four women were quoted.

Given the sexist bias of the paper, a picture accompanying the story featuring some attractive women must have helped in its selection. Significantly the picture was repeated when five days later the paper used the letters page to articulate what amounted to its own criticisms of the diplomatic option. Under the headline 'Wailing women' a reader wrote: 'How ridiculous of the British women who married wealthy Arabs to voice their strident uninformed attacks on this country at a carefully rehearsed press conference in Jordan. And their talk of starving Iraqi kids sounded like crocodile tears in view of their obvious prosperity.' People calling for peace are, thus, identified with stridency and ignorance; the implication is that they are ruthless propagandists and wealthy hypocrites. The *Mirror* is, at the same time, delegitimising a view it strongly opposes.

Those politicians, such as Tony Benn and Edward Heath, who were identified with the peace movement, were vilified. On 7 September, for instance, the paper attacked Benn in this way: 'Tony Benn belongs in a mausoleum, ex-Prime Minister Jim Callaghan said yesterday. He is leading a broadside against his old colleague who is leading the campaign for a Commons vote against action in the Gulf. "As far as my friend Mr Tony Benn is concerned I am sure that one day a statue will be erected to him in that mausoleum for people whose self righteousness exceeds their intellectual ability."' The implications are clear – Benn is ignorant and self-righteous; those who support war are presumably intelligent and genuine. There is no pretence at balance, a counter quote from Benn himself, say.

Given the failures of the Labour Party and Democratic Party in the US to promote the diplomatic option with any conviction (Rogers 1992: 275) the peace movement in Britain and the US lacked any strong institutional base and this, in part, accounted for the marginalisation of peace voices.

Naked propaganda

Just before the launch of Desert Storm a man and woman streaked naked at a Tottenham Hotspur football match in protest. Here was a perfect story for the *Mirror*. Of course they carried a picture of the two (discreetly) starkers but then, given their sexist bias, only focused on the woman involved. A whole page was given over to her 'naked truth about her nude New Year sprint' but – apart from the short quotation 'I decided to do it as a way of drawing attention to the crazy war that could soon break out' – she was given no space to articulate her views. Instead, the story concentrated entirely on the event, how a woman PC handled her, what her brother, father, grandfather felt. The human interest bias of the press is seen here demonstrating one of its prime ideological functions – to depoliticise the profoundly political.

The myth of popular support: Polls and the manufacture of public opinion

Opinion polls play a crucial role in new militarist societies serving largely to create rather than reflect public opinion on crucial issues. The Middle East crisis of 1990-1991 provides a perfect case study. The central myth of the massacres is that up to 80 per cent of the British public supported the use of the military option. In the forward to his collection of journalism articles on the massacres, Brian MacArthur (1991: 10), of the *Sunday Times*, articulates the dominant view, reproducing this figure to suggest that the British press, in their unanimous support for the war, were once again reflecting the wishes of the public.

Not only does this view discount the views of those 20 per cent who, even according to his reading of the polls, did not support the war and thus were unrepresented (20 per cent reflected in electoral support being quite substantial). It also ignores the fact that Labour, the party leading in the polls at the time, was pressing the case for sanctions when Desert Storm was launched. More significantly still, the MacArthur view obscures the complexities of polling results. Ultimately it is based on a partial reading of polls in both the US and UK which were heavily manipulated towards promoting the war option. (Cockburn 1991) As Fouad Moughrabi (1993: 40) argues: 'Opinion surveys presume that people have access to information which informs their attitudes. In reality, of course, the majority of the public has only the information that the media provide, especially about foreign policy issues. In the case of the Middle East, information is often selected and interpreted so that it reinforces existing sterotypes and creates new ones.' He suggests that polls provide major private and public institutions 'a powerful tool to shape, domesticate and manage public opinion'.

People's views are very often confused; they contain ambivalences, contradictions; they can change quickly, they are based, often, on ignorance and prejudice. Sometimes people may be afraid to give their true feelings/thoughts to a questioner; they may even want to make fun of the whole process and give any response. People lie. They have learnt to imitate the state's secrecy and so keep their true feelings secret.

Views are often influenced by the way and tone in which the question is put, by the personality of the questioner. During the early 1980s, for instance, 80 per cent of Britons polled said they supported Nato. But when asked to spell out Nato and explain what it was only 40 per cent could.[2] Ask people if they supported the 'independent nuclear deterrent' and a majority would say

---

2   Berrington, Hugh (1989): 'British public opinion and nuclear weapons', *Public opinion and nuclear weapons*; (eds) Marsh, Catherine and Fraser, Colin ; Macmillan; London. pp 18-36

'Yes'. Ask them if they supported a nuclear deterrent which, if ever used, would lead to the deaths of thousands and possible global holocaust only a minority would support it. Similarly, views can be manipulated by restricting the range of questions. This was particularly the case during the Middle East crisis.

Journalists often interpret polls unproblematically. And they are drawn to them because they appear to provide 'objective' statistics. (Dionne 1992: 154-156) Polls are often manipulated to deliver a particular result. Newspaper coverage of polls usually reinforces this intended result. Moreover, when polls can be interpreted in the interests of the elite (or a prominent section of it) then journalists highlight them; when they produce results embarrassing for the elite the results are twisted or they are quickly forgotten.[3]

How the polls silenced the peace option.

In August 1990, following the Iraqi invasion of Kuwait, Gallup asked a series of questions on the crisis. (Wybrow: 1991) The views expressed were extremely contradictory. Some 85 per cent were said to approve of President Bush's action 'to prevent an Iraqi invasion of Saudi Arabia'. Note: they did not support an offensive war against Iraq. Moreover, when asked: 'Do you think the present crisis in the Middle East will be over quite soon or do you think it will go on for a long time?' 72 per cent thought it would go on for a long time. Only 20 per cent thought it would be over quite soon.

At this time the vast majority of the British press were calling for all-out war against Iraq. But most people opposed this view. They supported the defence of Saudi Arabia if attacked (the attack, of course, never came). They thought the crisis would last a long time (thus ignoring the arguments of Fleet Street editors who were calling for war now) and were presumably preparing to hold on while a diplomatic solution was worked out. When asked about the outcome of the crisis, in fact, the majority 58 per cent, thought there would be no war.

Most significant of all, none of the Gallup questions invited people to ponder the various aspects of the diplomatic/sanctions option. All the questions were about military and military-related issues. In this way, it could be argued, the polls reinforced the military option so vigorously promoted in the media. No questions were asked on the possibilities of a compromise solution. How many people supported the Iraqi attempt to link withdrawal

---

3   Glasgow University Media Group (1985): *War and peace news*; Open University Press; Milton Keynes. Devoted important sections of their study into television coverage of the Falklands to opinion polls. They conclude that television completely distorted poll findings in the interests of the government's strategy. 'The polls showed attitudes were very complex. Until well into the crisis a majority thought that the issues did not merit losing British life.' A poll, just before the landings, also showed that 76 per cent of the population wished the United Nations to administer the islands pending a diplomatic solution. 'Little of this appeared on ITN.' p 19. See also pp 136-143; 305-308 on the theoretical issues raised by opinion polls.

from Kuwait with Israeli withdrawal from the Occupied Territories? What if Iraq was to be offered the northern Kuwaiti oilfields and UN forces were placed on the border? What about a Middle East peace conference being set up to negotiate all the region's controversies? And so on. These possibilities were hardly ever envisaged by the pollsters. The bias of the public debate on the crisis, it could be argued, was manipulated subtly to promoting the war option.

Worst still, the polls introduced into the public domain a debate about the totally unacceptable. People were not asked their views about a Middle East conference, they were asked if the use of nuclear weapons was legitimate (some 26 per cent were in favour). In this way the polls subtly introduce the possibility of nuclear holocaust into the public domain. Throughout the crisis Gallup asked if people preferred a military assault or a blockade 'that might have to last for a very long time'. The majority was always in favour of the blockade: 63 per cent in September to 55 per cent in December. In the last Gallup poll before the launch of Desert Storm only 31 per cent supported a military assault.

Adding to the complexities, throughout the crisis people voted roughly 60 per cent in favour of military action if the economic blockade alone was found to be failing. But this was never established. The last CIA assessment before the launch of Desert Storm indicated exactly the opposite – that the sanctions were having a crippling effect on the Iraqi economy. But the American elite just could not wait to 'kick Saddam's arse' (as they so often declared). In December, Mori asked five questions for the *Sunday Times*.[4] All of them involved debates around the military option. The majority were in favour of war. But the peace option was nowhere explored. In this way, the limits of legitimate debate are set by the polling organisations and the media they serve.

A similar bias was evident in US polls. A *Washington Post*/ABC News poll taken 30 November to 2 December asked: 'If Iraq does not withdraw from Kuwait should the United States go to war with Iraq to force it out of Kuwait at some point after 15 January or not?' Some 63 per cent responded yes to war, 32 responded no and 15 per cent expressed no opinion. A *Wall Street Journal*/NBC poll conducted 8 to 11 December asked:: 'Would you favour or oppose the US going to war against Iraq if Iraq does not withdraw its troops from Kuwait by the United Nations' deadline of 15 January?' Some 54 per cent backed war, 34 were opposed, the remainder expressed no opinion. But as Michael R. Kagay comments (1992: 107): 'In answering questions framed in such a "use force or not" format a respondent who wished to pressurise Iraq to get out of Kuwait was seemingly offered only one way to accomplish the goal – war ... Had a method of pressurising Iraq short of war been offered, perhaps more would have chosen that instead.'

---

4   *British Public Opinion*: newsletter of Market and Opinion Research International; London; December 1990 p 5.

Press manipulation of public opinion

On 24 August, the *Independent* published an NOP poll on the crisis. Out of 13 question categories, seven were based on the presumption of the inevitability of war. None of the questions explored the possibilities of the diplomatic option. Again the poll raised the possibility of the use of nuclear weapons. But this time, the *Independent* raised a new and, it could be argued, equally unacceptable question. It asked if people would support an undercover team to be sent to Iraq to assassinate Saddam Hussein.

This was clearly built on the massive demonisation campaign against the Iraqi leader that was being pursued in the British media and the accompanying glorification of the role of the SAS. Some 61 per cent of people supported this suggestion. But most crucially, the question failed to point out that such an act would break international law. In the United States a number of television shows asked similar questions of their audience with similar results. Such questioning points to an important element of new militarist society. During the 1950s and 60s the CIA indulged in many coups, assassinations, mass killings. But they were largely secret. Now, in the context of the democratic facade of the new militarist state, the secret state thrives in a political climate which can tolerate the open debate over what was once hidden action. Assassination of heads of government is now a legitimate, unproblematic political option – but only when a friendly state calls for it.

Soon after the Iraqi invasion of Kuwait, the British press reported uncritically President Bush authorising the CIA to assassinate Saddam Hussein. None of the reports pointed out that such action is unlawful. But when the Iranian Ayatollah calls for the death of one British writer (which is equally unacceptable) the outrage expressed reaches fever pitch. In his coverage of the NOP poll, *Independent* journalist Peter Kellner merely reinforces the military option. The parallels he draws are all with previous wars – the Falklands, Suez, Second World War. At this stage in late August the launch of Desert Storm is months away. But for Kellner and the *Independent* (and the British press in general) war was inevitable. Once again the Hussein Hitler line is promoted (though no specific Hitler question was asked): 'There is a widespread belief that Britain faces a modern version of Hitler but that any resort to military force should have the backing of the UN.'

He goes on to discuss the dilemmas posed if Thatcher and Bush attacked without UN blessing. No such pondering over the possibilities of a negotiated settlement. And he concluded: 'A reasonable guess is that a quick decisive war in the Gulf would attract public acclaim – almost whatever methods were used short of nuclear retaliation.' In other words, the scene was being set early in August for the conflict. In the poll, some 87 per cent supported the blockade to persuade Iraq to withdraw; some 66 per cent supported military action but only if the blockade failed to end the occupation. The failure of sanctions to move the Iraqi troops was never established. In fact, the poll could easily be interpreted to promote the need for diplomacy to avert the need for military action. The *Independent*, and the press in general, was committed to a completely different agenda.

The art of ignoring polls

On 16 January 1991, on the eve of Desert Storm, the *Guardian* published an ICM poll. Only 54 per cent of people backed the use of force. Some 32 per cent favoured all action short of the use of force; as many as 13 per said Britain should not get involved. In other words, here was a major polling body on the eve of the massacres revealing that only a slim majority backed the military option.

ICM, unusually, asked a question about the peace option. Some 31 per cent said there should be a link between a general conference on the Middle East (including the Palestinian question) and any settlement of the Gulf crisis. So on the most controversial aspect of the Iraqi strategy on the Gulf crisis, the poll found a sizeable minority in support. But perhaps even more significant, the poll found a high percentage (24) were unable to express an opinion. Not surprising since the possibility of a Middle East conference had been virtually ruled out by the press.

The art of distorting poll results

On 22 October, the *Mirror* carried a rare article on the US peace movement which it described as 'ominous': 'Yanks come home American protesters tell Bush.' But in opening the report the paper said that 86 per cent of people in Britain 'believe our boys should launch a military strike against the Iraqi tyrant'. No poll at that time was producing such a result. It was an invention. But it became an accepted truth. Such is the potency of the press in new militarist societies.

7 The apparatus of silence

The routinisation of self censorship

The 1991 Gulf war was accompanied by what many commentators have identified as unprecedented levels of government censorship and control. John Pilger, for instance, commented: 'During many years reporting wars and coping with propaganda I have never known such manipulation in a self-proclaimed free society.' (Pilger 1991) Journalists were the real prisoners of war, trapped behind the barbed wire of reporting curbs, according to William Boot. (Boot 1991: 24) Alex Thomson, ITN Channel Four News reporter during the conflict, used the same image: 'The pools were a prison.' (Thomson 1992: 82) Leaders of the International Federation of Journalists (IFJ), representing journalists from 50 countries, met in Brussels during the war and endorsed a tough statement criticising the level of secrecy in Gulf coverage. It warned that 'media controls being applied by the allies are in danger of descending to levels of censorship which have become routine in Iraq'.[1]

Very few journalists were allowed to travel with the troops; very little actual combat was observed; most journalists were confined to hotels in Saudi Arabia. Those journalists who tried to evade these constraints were harassed by the authorities – and sometimes even by other colleagues. Yet the importance of these overt, interventionist strategies by the state should be placed in context. Journalists have tended to exaggerate their importance.[2] It helps promote the myth of the adversary press. Governments tend to emphasise their censorship moves because they are felt to be in accordance

---

1 Appears in 'Journalism in the firing line', an article for publication issued by Aidan White, general secretary of the Brussels-based IFJ, on 26 February 1991.

2 In a *Times/Mirror* survey during the 'war', more than three-quarters of the respondents felt the military was not limiting information and almost 60 per cent thought the Pentagon should exert tighter controls on the press. Quoted in Woodward, Gary C. (1993): 'The rules of the game: The military and press in the Gulf War', *The media in the Persian Gulf War*; (ed) Denton, Robert; Praeger; Westport CT p 22.

with 'the public mood'. But, in reality, censorship operates on far more subtle levels.

Even where a journalist – such as Robert Fisk of the *Independent* (with considerable experience of covering Beirut and the Lebanon war) – was opposed to many aspects of the war and worked with other colleagues outside the official media structures as so-called 'unilaterals' their impact on the overall coverage in their newspaper was negligible. Godfrey Hodgson, foreign editor, said that over a six-week period, with an average of more than four pages given over to the crisis each day, the paper used pool copy on fewer than half a dozen occasions – from a correspondent attached to an American group. (Hodgson 1991a: 14) The *Independent* editorially was firmly behind the US-led coalition's strategies over the massacres so that Fisk, together with other colleagues who worked as unilaterals, could have little impact on the crucial ideological bias of their newspaper. Thus it shared with all the other papers the massacres agenda – which was largely set by the military.

As Don McKay, who reported from Bahrain for the *Mirror*, commented: 'One had one major fear: the commander of the air base could have us kicked off the island at any time. We were just there door-stepping. We could have been bounced anytime.' According to John Macarthur (1993: 95), 'many journalists simply thrill to the excitement of military conflict and are easily swept up by the martial spirit of the moment. Others see war as an opportunity for self-promotion. For most part, the anchors, editors, bureau chiefs and reporters who expressed themselves publicly during the Gulf crisis seemed to be apolitical, respectful of power and careerist to a fault'.

Constructing the 'theatre of war'

Paradoxically, while the essential elements of the fighting were shrouded in secrecy certain features of the strategy were exposed as perhaps never before. The press before the launch of Desert Storm were able to detail the action plan: first the air strikes, then the ground campaign sweeping round the west flank of the Iraqis to encircle them. All this was to be quite quick (contradictions with the 'monstrous, global, Saddam' theme were not explored). In other words there was an element of theatre/film about the US-led coalition's censorship regime. New militarism had conjured up not a war but the illusion/Hollywood show of a 'war'. So the coalition forces acted each day as if according to a pre-arranged script. This is exactly how Fuad Nahdi, one of three *Los Angeles Times* reporters in Riyadh, described it. 'The first press conference of the day would be at 7.30 am. From then on you knew exactly what the line for the day was going to be. The script had been written beforehand and I felt like the reviewer of a good play or film.'

Given the absence of any credible enemy, the controllers of the coalition's war effort sought to manipulate the conflict and the public response to it. Today the theme (or, in American jargon, the 'spin') will be 'victory in sight'. The next day the theme will be 'Let's not get too confident, there is still a long way to go.' After Iraq broadcast pictures of captured POWs, the message became: 'Saddam must be punished for his war crimes.' And so on. Each day, representatives of the White House, Pentagon, State Department and CIA met to plan the 'spin' for the day. White House spokesman Marlin Fitzwater would test the message at the late morning briefings where no cameras were allowed. The message could then be fine-tuned for the later State Department and Pentagon briefings which were both filmed and likely to make the evening news. (McDaniel and Fineman 1991: 154)

Symbolic purpose of the censorship regime

So the censorship regime served essentially ideological, symbolic purposes – it was an expression of the arbitrary, monopoly power of the military over the conduct of war. The military, according to the myth, went into the Vietnam war with their hands tied behind their back (by traitorous media and peacefreaks). Now, after the trial engagements in Grenada, Libya and Panama, the military wanted to show they were in control. Censorship was used not so much to preserve military security but to promote a positive image of the massacres.

In many respects the press went on to a war footing immediately after 2 August 1990. No particularly draconian censorship was needed once hostilities began – the press had already proved themselves meek and pliable to the secret state's media manipulation techniques as during normal times of 'peace'. As Michael Traber and Ann Davies (1991: 8) comment: 'It is clear that the military manipulated the media in a way similar to the way government authorities manipulate the media all the year round.' The pro-war consensus was quickly established in August 1990; hostilities were always represented as being inevitable somewhere in the near future. The US-led coalition forces were glorified, Saddam was demonised. The crucial ideological, patriotic frame was set and was never to shift even after the massacres were over.

Setting up the censorship regime

Despite the recommendations of the Hoffman and Sidle reports in the United States (and the *Fog of War* report in the UK)[3] stressing the importance of setting up temporary pooling arrangements immediately upon the start of any major crisis, US Defense Secretary Dick Cheney first refused to allow any journalists to accompany the troops on 8 August. On 13 August, a 17-member press pool was formed by the US government drawing representatives from each news medium – seven from television, five from news agencies, two from the press, two from magazines and one from radio.[4] And within 12

---

3   Mercer, Derrik (1987: 375-386): *Fog of War*; Heinemann; London. See also Steeden, Richard: *The reporting of war in the British press: Does the public have a right to know?* Unpublished MA thesis, University of Sheffield Department of Librarianship, September 1991. Highlights well the failure of MoD guidelines to follow the most significant recommendations of the *Fog of War* report.

4   The initial 17 pool journalists came from AP, UPI, Reuters, CNN, National Public Radio, *Time*, Scripps-Howard, *Los Angeles Times*, *Milwaukee Journal*.

days of the Iraqi invasion Navy Captain Ron Wildermuth, Gen Norman Schwarzkopf's chief of public relations, had produced a 10-page document, code-named *Annex Foxtrot*, in which he wrote: 'News media representatives will be escorted at all times. Repeat: at all times.'

Bowing to the inevitable, Margaret Thatcher's government allowed in a press pool of 16 to accompany the military later in the month. The three nationals were chosen by the director of the Newspaper Proprietors' Association, John Page, drawing their names from a hat. Four of these pools visited Saudi Arabia up to mid-September when, the MoD said, interest fell off. The pool was reactivated in October though more interest was shown by the regional media at this time. Hamish Lumsden, chief press officer at the Ministry of Defence, said that by December 1990 40 British journalists were 'in theatre' in the Gulf getting bored and wanting to get home by Christmas.[5]

According to Steve Anderson (1990), fear of being booted out of Saudi Arabia obsessed reporters in the lead up to Christmas 1990. 'Saudi Arabia isn't known for its hospitality towards foreign journalists and only allows 20 to enter a year. At the moment they are host to more than 800 predominantly American and British and most with entry visas that are valid for one month only. These have either expired or are about to and there are concerns that too much rocking the boat could lead to expulsion with no defence from the military minders.' Boredom was the other major problem. 'No drink, no women and no story.'

US reporters covering the build-up of forces in the Gulf complained they were rarely able to talk to the troops. Escorted visits were infrequent and usually lasted one night. Public affairs officials claimed the appearance of journalists would distract units from their war preparations. AP's veteran war correspondent Edie Lederer commented: 'The access to troops coming into Saudi Arabia and to servicemen and women deployed in the field for months was far too limited. I think this was deliberate. I believe the military's policy was "no access, no bad stories".'[6]

British plans for dealing with reporting during the hostilities were devised by a team at the MoD including Brig. Bryon Dutton, director of army public relations, Capt. Mike Sant, Hamish Lumsden, and Mike Barnes, the final guidelines being officially launched at the MoD by Hugh Colver, chief public relations officer, on 14 January. They had, in fact, been drawn up by the Media Advisory Service (which is attached to the Cabinet Office) for use in times of national crisis. While the MoD claimed the country was not 'in crisis' the guidelines were brought in all the same.

---

5   Lumsden, Hamish interviewed September 1992 at MoD, London. He said the MoD had consulted with the Saudi authorities and had managed to persuade them, with some difficulty, to increase the number of accredited journalists to 60 and 90 technicians. But to what extent were the MoD using the Saudi's media shyness/repressiveness as an excuse to limit the number of accredited journalists?

6   From letter to Pete Williams, assistant Secretary of Defense for Public Affairs at the Pentagon, (dated 27 August 1991), by Edie Lederer.

Amongst the Americans a series of meetings were held between 13 media representatives and Defense Department officials to plan restrictions in the war zone but they failed to come to any consensus and the guidelines went through four draft stages.[7] On 14 December, the Assistant Secretary of Defense for Public Affairs, Pete Williams, issued a memo to the media saying that 'pool material' would be subjected to 'security review at source'. There was also introduced a new concept of 'Phase Three'. This 'would begin when open coverage is possible and would provide for unilateral coverage of activities. The pools would be disbanded and all media would operate independently, although under US Central Command escort'.

The US guidelines were finally released on 7 January 1991 and following criticisms by American editors a reduced version was issued a week later.[8] As in Britain, the establishment of 'voluntary' guidelines in the United States was a subtle move by the authorities. Most importantly they avoided potential legal problems of prior restraint (as emerged during the 1971 case when the court upheld the *New York Times*'s first amendment right to publish the Pentagon Papers during the Vietnam War). (Kleinwachter 1991: 6) In theory they allowed the press freedom to publish ultimately at their own discretion – yet in reality the numerous pressures were there to make them conform.

The ground-rules identified 12 categories of information not to be reported.[9] Most related to force levels or operational security but they did include the category of 'embargoed information until expiry of the embargo' which, effectively allowed any information to be restricted, without explanation, simply by declaring it embargoed.[10] In the end, overt censorship of copy was

---

7 DeParle, Jason (1991): 'Long series of military decisions led to Gulf War news censorship', *New York Times*, 5 May. See also LeMoyne, James (1991): 'A correspondent's tale: Pentagon's strategy for the press – Good news or no news', *New York Times*, 17 February.

8 *Ground rules and Guidelines for Desert Shield* appear in (1991) *The media and the Gulf War*; (ed) Smith, Hedrick; Seven Locks Press; Washington DC. pp 4-12. Intriguingly the guidelines were accompanied by this note: 'The following information should not be reported because its publication or broadcast could jeopardise operations and endanger lives.'

9 *Index on Censorship*; London; April/May 1991 Vol 20 No 4 and 5. p 52. Ground rules indicated the following categories of material that were 'non-releasable': no specific locations should be used when filing stories; journalists must remain with their military escorts at all times and follow instructions, and information (except where already released) on the following subjects should not be published without consulting MoD or in-theatre public relations staff: number of troops; number of ships and aircraft; numbers regarding other equipment; names of military installations or specific locations of UK or allied military units; information regarding future operations; information regarding security precautions at military installations; photographs that would show levels of security at military installations or name specific locations of forces or installations; rules of engagement details; information on intelligence collection activities, including targets, methods and results; information on current operations against hostile targets; and information on special forces and their operational techniques.

10 Article 19: *Bulletin* No 13; London: 'Silent Kingdom: Suppressing freedom of expression in Saudi Arabia'. The US-led coalition forces were defending Saudi Arabia, a distinctly totalitarian regime. during the massacres. Article 19 comments: 'Free expression is controlled through a highly effective bureaucracy of censorship and people who do attempt to express critical opinions face punishments which routinely include ill-treatment, torture and even

to provide only a few niggling problems for journalists. Only five dispatches among 1,300 filed during the war were referred to the Pentagon and only one, which referred to allied intelligence activities, was ultimately suppressed, according to Rick Atkinson. (1994: 160)

Pooling the press pack

Some 800 journalists (reporters, editors, producers, photographers, technicians) were in the international press corps in Saudi Arabia by December 1990. On 17 January, a US Air Force C-141 cargo plane left Andrews Air Force base with 127 news media personnel on board. And by the start of Desert Storm, the total number of journalists in Saudi Arabia had reached around 1,400. Given that 2,000 habitually attend the conventions of the major political parties in the United States this is a relatively small number to cover an event of such global significance. A third of them were based in Riyadh, the capital, where the Allied Joint Information Bureau was situated in the Hyatt Hotel – most of the remainder in Dharhan. A few were based in Muharaq in Bahrain and Riyadh journalists were occasionally taken to the air base at Tabuk. Eighteen were with the Marines in amphibious ships; seven were with the US Air Force Combat Pool based at Al-Kharj; 19 were covering the navy at sea while eight were with the medical corps.

The French observed their typical independence, established in the Novotel Hotel three miles away in Riyadh. Only 11 journalists were allowed into their pool. Each day they were flown by SIRPA (*Service d'information de l'armée francaise*) to somewhere near the front line.[11] The journey there would take two hours, they would stay for half an hour under military escort at all times, and then fly back for two hours. Not surprisingly the journalists did not like this arrangement.

The highest contingents in the press corps were from Britain (150 in Saudi Arabia – just 60 journalists and 90 technicians, sound crew or producers) and the US (700 plus). Out of these British and American journalists were assigned places in the pools accompanying the military, the UK and US thus symbolising their power over the global communications networks. (Boyd-Barrett and Thussu 1992) Three places went in the pools to reporters from

---

execution. An array of laws and regulations ensures near total suppression of all political, religious and academic views and activities contrary to those of the government. The right to establish political organisations or trade unions is prohibited by law.' As John Naughton commented, the media tended not to dwell on this aspect of the coalition's cause: 'It did not dwell on the medieval repressiveness of the Saudi regime, the curious habits of the Al Sabah family business in Kuwait or the irony of suddenly finding Syria fighting on "our" side.' (the *Observer*, 3 March 1991)

11 Giroud, Emmanuel (1991): *'Journalistes et militaires: Une cohabitation difficile'*, *Mediapouvoirs*, Paris, July/August/September. pp 153-161. He quotes journalist Jean-Luc Mano on the pooling arrangements: 'It was like a mini Club Mediterranean – with a visit to the pottery on Monday, water ski-ing on Tuesday etc.' A series of articles critical of the media coverage of the massacres by the French press appeared in '*Medias Mensonges et Democratie*', *Le Monde Diplomatique*, February 1992. See also Conesa, Pierre (1992): *'Analyse strategique de l'information'*, *La persuasion de masse: guerre psychologique, guerre mediatique*; Robert Laffont; Paris pp 121-144.

countries other than the US or UK. Only 43 were with the ground units at the start of Desert Storm, rising to 132 with the army and Marines at the launch of the 'ground offensive'.

The British contingent was formed into six Media Response Teams (two attached to British armoured brigades, two with RAF bases, one with the Royal Navy, another at Muharaq). In addition, there was a 13-person Forward Transmission Unit (including Kate Adie of the BBC, Keith Dovkants of the London *Evening Standard*, Stephen Sackur of BBC Radio, Robert Moore of ITN, and Gordon Airs of the *Glasgow Record*) to oversee the sending of copy and film by fax and satellite to London.

But after a while, the FTU members, according to Keith Dovkants, 'got tired of seeing the war at second hand'. He added: 'We all started pressing to get in on the action and so we converted ourselves into an MRT. We were camped in a berm at Wadi al Batin but we did get to go on a couple of artillery raids. And that turned into something quite good and pretty exciting.' All the FTU members were given pills in case of Iraqi attacks. Keith Dovkants commented: 'I just didn't take them. I don't like taking pills anyway. I thought if worst comes to worst I'll just take a deep breath.'

Kate Adie was, in fact, the only woman in the British pools.[12] Fidelma Cook, senior reporter for the Glasgow *Sunday Mail*, had a visa request rejected because 'there are no facilities for ladies on board ship'. (Sebba 1994: 276). In contrast, according to Edie Lederer, there were 'tons' of women in the US pool. It was one of the most impressive aspects of the Gulf reporting for her, confirming the high status gained by women in the US media.[13] The *Washington Post, Los Angeles Times, Philadelphia Enquirer* and *Newsday* were among those newspapers with women representatives in Saudi Arabia.

Non-pool reporters were supposed to remain permanently in their hotels for the duration of the war, dealing with the pooled copy and producing other reports based on press conferences by the military. (Fialka 1992) Aidan White, IFJ general secretary, expressed concern over how so many reporters were left sitting in cocktail bars watching wall-to-wall coverage on the US television networks. 'If there is glamour in the work of war reporting, there is precious little of it today in the Gulf,' he said. As James Meek, of the *Scotsman*, records: 'They had little to do but eat in lavish restaurants – sometimes over-eating to compensate for lack of alcohol – pore over bland military briefings, watch CNN and pester the military for more access.'[14] Journalists ended up interviewing themselves.

On 12 February, the Pentagon, in response to complaints over exclusion, announced the formation of five more seven-member press pools. Of the

---

12 On media sexism, with specific reference to the representation of Kate Adie, see Macdonald, Myra (1995): *Representing women: Myths of femininity in the popular media*; Edward Arnold; London/New York p 49

13 Lederer, Edie interviewed by telephone, August 1995.

14 Quoted in *Reporting the war* (op cit) pp 24-25.

previous 15 US pools only two were assigned to ground forces, the rest covered ships or airbases. (Thomson op cit: 67) On 23 February, Dick Cheney announced the suspension of all press briefings and pool reports as the so-called ground offensive was launched – again more a symbolic, theatrical act demonstrating the power of the military and administration over the media rather than one determined by operational security considerations. It was virtually unprecedented: there had been no equivalent blackout during the Korean War and only two very brief blackouts during the Vietnam War. Predictably the blackout was quickly broken by Cheney himself after just 12 hours and the first reports of the new offensive came some ten hours after they were filed.

In creating pools the military knew they were tapping into an essential feature of the journalists' culture where privileged access to sources is an everyday element of professional practice. Yet seen from another perspective the special accreditation that pooling involved was fiercely opposed by the Americans and British in the UNESCO controversy of the 1970s and 1980s over the New World Information Order. Third World plans for such accreditation had been a significant cause for the two countries eventually to quit the organisation in the mid-1980s.

The purposes of the pools

The pooling system was used by the military not to provide access to the front but keep journalists away. Steve Anderson (op cit: 12) commented: 'Those who had schemed and scrapped their way on to the MRTs had been promised a grandstand view of the allied annihilation of Iraq. In the end, all they got to see was a few bombed-out tanks.' And US pool reporter Christopher Hanson (1991: 128) commented: 'Most of us never saw a battle and few of us even saw a dead Iraqi soldier but at least we got to be part of the big adventure.'

Robert Fox, with the Seventh Armoured Corps for the *Telegraph*, summed up the situation: 'Too few journalists were locked into the British armoured division for weeks on end with little to do.'[15] David Beresford, of the *Guardian*, suggested that journalists were supposed to be eye-witnesses to history but added: 'Recent US Defense Department estimates that as many as 200,000 Iraqis may have died suggests that much witnessing was left undone.'[16] The massacres were inflicted from the air primarily but only one journalist, ABC's Forrest Sawyer, flew with a fighter jet (unlike during the Second World War or Vietnam when journalists repeatedly witnessed bombing missions) and a few flew with tankers. (Woodward, Gary C. 1993: 14)

Those pool reporters confined to ships saw virtually nothing. No interviews were allowed with B52 pilots; no access was given to the US Army's Ist Cavalry Division; no ceremonies were held for the dead arriving at Dover Air Force base simply to avoid press coverage. US freelance Jonathan Franklin was hired

---

15 ibid p 13.
16 ibid p 16.

temporarily at Dover Air Base and described the mangled faces and bodies of dead soldiers – but his report only appeared in alternative newspapers like the *San Francisco Bay Guardian* and *Boston Phoenix*. Few stories were able to cover the enormous psychological stress facing the soldiers. Few stories covered the spate of desertions from the US army. Few stories covered the recruitment of Iraqi prisoners for rebel armies – totally in violation of the Geneva convention covering the treatment of PoWs. (Ray and Schaap 1991: 13) Most of the best reporting consequently came from those journalists outside the pools. Of the six pool journalists included in an IPI survey only two had any good words to say about them. Paul Majendie, of Reuters, with the American pools, went so far as to describe his assignment as 'a total disaster'.[17]

The pooling system gave the military considerable powers to determine the nature of coverage. The US Army's *Stars and Stripes* magazine, for instance, had many representatives in the pools while, in contrast, the *New York Times* for months was only able to get one journalist accredited. The US military also gave priority to local TV crews which they refer to as 'hometowners'. The Pentagon even arranged under the Hometown News Program for 960 reporters to travel to the Gulf at military expense and spend as long as four days with units from their regions. According to Howard Kurtz (1994: 226), the result was 'Hi mum' journalism, 'soft-focus picture postcards from the desert with reporters asking softball questions'. And Andersen (1991: 23) commented: 'The emphasis on local news has promoted coverage which is far more likely to be soft-morale-boosting, sending words and pictures of the boys in the field to the folks back home.'

The military also deliberately exploited the pooling system to cement the bonding between journalists and soldiers. Journalists, according to the 'free press myth', are supposed to be independent, neutral, sceptical observers of events. Yet, thrown together with soldiers facing possible death, the two groups are likely to share the same sentiments.[18] Don McKay, of the *Mirror*, commented: 'There was that very strange feeling of being in a hotel, drinking at a bar at night with a pilot, or playing snooker and all of a sudden you know subconsciously he'd started playing his wartape, preparing for his

---

17 ibid p 7.

18 Morrison, David and Tumber, Howard (1988): *Journalists at war*; Sage; London. They identify a similar phenomenon during the Falklands 'war': 'It was not just a question of sharing the moods of the troops through shared experiences but of actively beginning to identify with them by being part of the whole exercise. Consequently, although some of the journalists disagreed with the decision to send the task force, once it was likely there would be a battle they felt an affinity with the troops and a shared determination to see the venture through to the end.' p 97. Robert Fox, of the *Daily Telegraph*, speaking of the Gulf and recalling the Falklands 'war' (in *UK Press Gazette*, 3 February 1992) says: 'Anyone who thinks you can detach yourself is talking absolute nonsense. You rely on frontline troops to protect you mentally as well as physically.' See also Clarke, Genevieve (1991): 'Credibility at stakes', *Spectrum*; London; Summer. Quotes Hugh Colver, chief of public relations at the MoD: 'Our philosophy has always been to get the media living alongside the troops to get them into a situation where the security of the operation becomes indelibly linked to their own security.'

flight. And then sometimes they didn't come back which was even stranger. You get attached to them – that's the name of the game. And your attachment is more than professional.'

Keith Dovkants was very aware of the military's attempts to bond with journalists yet his sense of 'journalistic independence' made him resist. 'But at the same time, if there had been a big cock-up with lots of lives lost it would have been very difficult to turn around and say: "Look you guys you've gone and made a terrible hash of things'. Access is always crucial. The price you pay for being with those guys is a little freedom. There's a trade-off. And in the end, I think it was worth it.'

Colin Wills, of the *Sunday/Daily Mirror*, recorded how his seven-strong MRT slept for more than six weeks in a tent measuring 12ft by 12ft or in the open air close to Land Rovers. They were given first aid and chemical warfare training. 'We immersed ourselves totally in the day-to-day life of the front line. Once there, there was no way out.'[19] A major even told Robert Fox, of the *Telegraph*: 'My main intention was to teach the journalists how to live in the field like soldiers.'[20]

This resulted in many allegations of too many journalists becoming 'instant soldiers'. Robert Fisk also spoke of the relationship between journalist and soldier becoming 'almost fatally blurred' leading to the 'unquestioning nature of coverage'.[21] Christopher Walker, of the Times, said: 'My over-bearing memory of the war is of too many reporters trying to be soldiers.'[22] And Ben Fenton, of the *Telegraph* commented: 'The self-contained nature of the Bahrain RAF detachment did more than anything to encourage self censorship as well as any latent gung-ho militarism in some reporters.'[23] Journalists were not forced to wear uniforms (with epaulettes saying 'War correspondent'), according to the MoD's Hamish Lumsden, but happily did so. Thomson (op cit: 21) saw journalists 'locked into the military system' – 'the honorary rank [of major] was more than a quirk left over from a different age, it was part of the assimilation process'.

The pooling system was also used by the military to manipulate coverage by enforcing delays in the transmission of news. Five of the six pool journalists in the IPI survey complained of delays. Paul Majendie, of Reuters, with the Americans, commented: 'At best the copy took 72 hours to get back to the pool. At worst it just vanished.' And he added: 'To send 17 despatches, risk

---

19 Quoted in *Reporting the war* (op cit) p 5.

20 ibid p 12

21 Fisk, Robert; The *Independent*, 6 February 1991. The establishment loves its mavericks and Fisk was rightly much applauded for his reporting. A profile of him by Steve Clarke, 'In a class of his own', appeared in *UK Press Gazette*, London, 4 March 1991 p 10. Fisk also won a journalism award from City University, London Graduate Centre for Journalism, for his Gulf reports.

22 Quoted in *Reporting the war* (op cit) p 23.

23 ibid p 22.

all and then see virtually nothing on the wire is not my idea of a rewarding experience.'[24]

Martha Teichner, of CBS, had only four of her reports from 32 days in the frontline reach Dhahran; the rest were 'lost' by pool handlers. (Rosenblum 1992: 126-127) One AP reporter said he spent ten days with a unit without being able to file a story. According to AP's Edie Lederer: 'For veterans of the Vietnam War like myself, it appeared that the US military deliberately adopted a policy to do as little as possible to facilitate the delivery of pool products.'[25] Almost 80 per cent of the pool reports filed during the 'ground offensive' took more than 12 hours to reach Dhahran, by which time the news was often out-of-date. Some 10 per cent of reports took more than three days which, as Rick Atkinson comments, was 'far longer than the time needed for dispatches to reach New York from the battle of Bull Run in 1861'. (op cit: 160)

It was only after the conflict that 15 major news organisations in the States, including the *Los Angeles Times*, the *New York Times*, *Time*, *Newsweek*, the *Washington Post* and *Wall Street Journal*, complained to Dick Cheney, the Defense Secretary, in a letter that: '...the pools did not work. Stories and pictures were late or lost. Access to the men and women in the field was interfered with by a needless system of military escort and copy review. The pool system was used in the Persian Gulf war not to facilitate news coverage but to control it'. (Cohen and Gatti 1991: 269)

Resentments about exclusion from the pools were inevitable. Rodney Pinder, of Reuters, comments on how contempt was widespread for a representative of the US women's magazine *Mirabella* whose main quest appeared 'to determine whether female soldiers took their vibrators to the front'. All this meant that journalist was divided against journalist and thus a united press front against the military censorship regime was never a possibility. In any case, journalists' culture gives low priority to long-term planning. Brian McNair (1995: 183) blames journalists' acceptance of the military's management and control of their newsgathering on 'straightforward commercial criteria'. 'Media organisations accepted the pool system in the Gulf, and the restrictions which it entailed, in the knowledge that the alternative was exclusion.'

Emergence of the mavericks

A few journalists decided to have nothing to do with the official arrangements and so became 'unilaterals' (the military called them 'rovers' or 'mavericks', in France they were called *reportages sauvages*). They shared a mixed fate. They were tolerated (they clearly could have been kicked out at any time) but they were also closely watched and heavily intimidated.

---

24 ibid p 8.
25 From letter to Pete Williams by Edie Lederer, 27 August 1991.

In mid-February, new military guidelines placed a ban on non-pool reporters from wearing NBC (nuclear, biological, chemical protection) suits. And a memorandum from the military just before the close of the massacres put still further pressure on the unilaterals, stating that any who went within 63 miles of the Saudi-Kuwait border without a military minder risked being shot. As David Beresford comments, the unilaterals were left bribing or begging ground troops for equipment as basic as helmets, flak jackets and chemical gear.[26] Some even stole military uniforms, acquired standard four-wheel drive Jeeps and had military style haircuts.

Amongst the unilaterals were Bob Simon (a former Vietnam correspondent with considerable experience of reporting from the Middle East) and the other three members of his Columbia Broadcasting System (CBS) team – Peter Bluff, producer, Roberto Alvarez, cameraman, and Juan Caldera, soundman. They went missing on 21 January, were captured by Iraqis, beaten and released on 2 March.[27] Then there was CBS's Bob McKeown (who achieved world fame for being the first journalist into 'liberated' Kuwait City) and ABC's Forrest Sawyer, the *New York Times*'s Chris Hedges (who was detained and denied press credentials after interviewing Saudi shopkeepers on a road 50 miles from the Kuwait border), the Frenchman Patrice Dutertre, and AP reporter Mort Rosenblum (detained for three hours for operating without military escort).

Rosenblum later remarked: 'In 25 years of covering wars around the world, the first time I was held prisoner was by the Americans.' (op cit: 122) And Retired Army Col. David Hackworth, America's most decorated living veteran who became a unilateral while reporting for *Newsweek*, commented: 'I had more guns pointed at me by Americans and Saudis who were into controlling the press than in all my years of actual combat.'[28]

Peter Sharp, of ITN, broke the Gulf oil slick story but had his press pack removed for his pains. Sandy Gall, also of ITN, independently joined the Saudi advance into Kuwait and claimed 'a world scoop'. Gall later pronounced the media controls 'inoperable and so should be scrapped forthwith'.[29] A wire

---

26   Quoted in *Reporting the war* p 4.

27   An international campaign for the release of the CBS crew was launched by a group of international media organisations: the Committee to Protect Journalists, the International Federation of Journalists, the International Federation of Newspaper Publishers, the International Press Institute, the North American National Broadcasters Association, the Newspaper Guild, the Union of African Journalists and the World Press Freedom Committee, supported by Article 19, *Index on Censorship* and *Reporters sans frontières*.

28   Quoted in Gertler, Michael (1991): 'Do Americans really want to censor war coverage this way', *The media and the Gulf War*; (ed) Smith, Hedrick; Seven Locks Press; Washington DC p 166.

29   Quoted in *Reporting the war* p 21. See also Gall's *News from the front: A television reporter's life* (1994); William Heinemann; London. He relates (p 255) how during the 'ground war' *The Times* had invited him to write a 1,000-word article on the invasion. He declined because of pressures of time. 'Unknown to me, however, someone at ITN in London wrote instead under my name which I thought was a questionable practice although perhaps understandable in the circumstances. But his version was completely inaccurate on one point. My ghost writer had me saying it was the most nerve-racking experience of my life. On the contrary it was a piece of cake.'

service photographer was held for six hours by Marines who threatened to shoot him if he left his car. An officer told him: 'We have orders from above to make this pool system work.' AP photographer Wesley Bocxe was seized by a Saudi and handed over to the Alabama National Guard who held him overnight, blindfolded and driven to a base 60 miles away where he was lectured by a public affairs officer before being released.

Women unilaterals such as US National Public Radio's Deborah Amos faced special problems. Not only were they violating US military guidelines that prohibited venturing beyond certain areas but they were also violating Saudi religious laws that forbade women to travel with a man not her husband. (Woodward op cit: 18) Robert Fisk described how he had to be driven into the desert to avoid checkpoints specifically set up to prevent journalists travelling. On one occasion an American NBC pool reporter, Brad Willis, ordered him away from the scene during the massacre at Khafji in late January. He commented: 'For the US reporter, the privileges of the pool and the military rules attached to it were more important than the right of the journalist to do his job.'[30]

Breakdown of the pools

On 18 February, non-pool journalists threatened to storm to the combat zone *en masse*. 'We are claiming our right to free information,' said Perry Kretz, correspondent for Germany's *Stern* magazine.[31] By the time the 'ground offensive' was officially launched on 24 February, journalists' frustration at being denied access to the 'war zone' and getting their patriotic pieces over the wires was at bursting point. On 18 February, after TF1 broadcast an unauthorised interview with French troops in Saudi Arabia critical of the 'war', news crews were banned from the front by the Ministry of Defence. (Badsey 1992: 239) In protest, the French correspondents, *en masse*, took the extreme step of agreeing to boycott coverage. But immediately afterwards the 'ground offensive' was launched and the boycott was abandoned.[32]

Colin Bickler, a veteran Reuters correspondent with experience covering conflicts in Malaysia, Cyprus, the Philippines and Pakistan, explains the journalists' reactions this way: 'You can't blame the correspondents on the ground. Faced with the military controls, either they ask to come home and who knows how the editors are going to take this. Or they end up very frustrated. But the most committed are always trying to push the parameters. At the end of the day, they have to go with what they can get.' He was surprised the American news organisations did not do more to get the rules relaxed during the 'war'. 'The British were not in a position to do much. This was essentially a US/Saudi control system.'

---

30 The *Independent*, 6 February 1991.

31 See Reuters 'Journalists threaten to storm front', the *Guardian*, 19 February 1991.

32 See Marnham, Patrick (1991): 'Not quite as American as pomme tarte', the *Independent*; 26 February.

Inevitably more and more journalists, locked away in hotels in Riyadh and Dharhan, broke free and joined the ranks of the unilaterals. So in the end it was they who first covered the entry into Kuwait City and thus went away with all the major Gulf scoops. It was four days before the pools caught up with them. As Hodgson (op cit: 18) comments: 'If the war had gone on longer, if the coalition had sustained heavy casualties, if the morale of the Arab members of the coalition had ever been shaken (as many predicted it would be) it is plain that relations between the generals and the journalists would have deteriorated to a point where Vietnam would have seemed a love feast.'

Controlling the image

'The Gulf war is an important one in the history of censorship. It marks a deliberate attempt by the authorities to alter public perception of the nature of war itself, particularly the fact that civilians die in war.' These are the words of Phillip Knightley (1991: 5), author of the seminal history of war correspondents, *The first casualty: the war correspondent as hero, propagandist and myth maker*. The war was above all a media spectacle and thus the control over the visual image was of supreme importance to the authorities. As for print journalists, the pools functioned for photographers and broadcast crews to keep them away from the action. The invisible was always far more important than the visible.

Pictures of coalition dead were banned outright. Journalists were denied access to hospitals which further prevented coverage of casualties. Severe controls were placed on photographs of Iraqi dead. Only one photographer went to the front with a pool team (Mike Moore, of *Today*) and the Saudis granted visas to photographers from only three British papers, the *Mirror*, *Sun* and *Today* (though by the time the 'ground offensive' was launched there were 35 photographers in the American pools). Darkrooms were set up in a hotel miles away from the main media centre which further delayed transmission times. And if photographs were not censored by the authorities, journalists did this work for them. According to P.T.Benic, a unilateral for Reuters, photographers 'actually red-flagged their own films. This was absurd'. A similar process of self-censorship was at work in the Falklands. (Morrison and Tumber 1988: 97).

The US military also cleverly manipulated coverage by feeding the media shots from attacking aircraft or missile warheads. The head of the Defense Department information in the Gulf was, significantly, Michael Sherman, formerly responsible for 'Top Gun' – a dominant reference point throughout media coverage of the massacres – 'Hunt for Red October' and 'Flight of the Intruder'. Videos supplied by Sherman (such as the one of a missile hitting the Ministry of Defence in Baghdad) were repeated time after time on television and reproduced in the popular press, providing some of the dominant images of the 'war'. Such images were new and fascinating to the media which, hyped-up on their patriotic crusades, handled them unproblematically. Some film reports were used by the military for PR purposes before being released for media use. (Levinson 1991)

Jim Lederman, the longest serving US foreign correspondent in Jerusalem, argues that the lack of military experience among most of the journalists in Saudi Arabia meant they were particularly susceptible to manipulation. He says (1992: 318) the vast majority of reporters who covered the 'war' with Iraq were men and women 'who spoke no Arabic and who were ignorant of the area in which they were working. And with the end of military conscription in the United States, only a minuscule pool of reporters had even a passing acquaintance with the ways in which armies operate. Most were thus heavily reliant on their military briefers and extremely susceptible to manipulation'.

The subtle use of press conferences

The agenda-setting role for the massacres was monopolised by the military. One of the subtlest ways in which they did this was to promote the use of live press conferences. Despite evidence of considerable chaos behind the scenes journalists in Riyadh and Dharhan welcomed these conferences. There was little else to cover, after all. And Nahdi stressed how 'professional' the press releases provided by the US military were. They were full of the 'hard facts' (numbers of sorties flown, for instance) and quotable superlatives ('biggest raid in history', for instance) that journalists found irresistible. 'I sent 5,000 words every day. I would just need to change the first and last pars of the press releases, they were so good,' Nahdi commented. But in this way, too, the military were dictating the agenda over the heads of the journalists to the global community. They were building on precedents set by Reagan and Thatcher who used live television performances to promote the image of populist leadership over and above the heads even of representatives in the Commons and Senate.

In Washington, the Pentagon held a daily hour-long televised press briefing at 3 pm EST. They were usually introduced by Assistant Secretary of Defense for Public Affairs, Pete Williams, and given by Lt. Gen. Thomas W. Kelly and Rear Admiral Michael McConnell, Joint Chiefs of Staff Directors of Operations and Intelligence respectively. Defense Secretary Dick Cheney and Chair of the Joint Chiefs of Staff Gen. Colin Powell gave briefings for major events.

The Pentagon briefing was preceded at 10 am EST (6 pm in Saudi Arabia) by a half hour briefing from Riyadh, usually given by Brig Gen Richard ('Butch') Neal and Gen. Norman Schwarzkopf. It was at these press conferences where Gen. Schwarzkopf, leader of the coalition forces, acquired his enormous prestige during the massacres, and so too Britain's Group Captain Niall Irving, though to a lesser extent. Schwarzkopf's performances were above all theatrical, straight out of the Hollywood tradition. As Thomson commented: 'The whiff of entertainment, almost show business hung heavy in the air.' And the 'Stormin' Norman Show' was perfectly suited to the largely male-dominated, chauvinist environment of the press conferences. He helped make the massacres a merry affair for the media corps. He was straight talking, witty and the press clearly like him. Here was a man perfect for the media spectacle war.

For Hodgson, the most abiding image of the 'war' was a photograph of Gen. Schwarzkopf at a briefing. 'This is the conqueror in his late 20th century glory, not dominating a mettlesome horse, like Napoleon or Wellington, not poring over his maps and his order of battle like a Moltke or an Eisenhower but caught by the cameras is the quintessential of the modern commander.'[33] Yet, intriguingly, even Gen Schwarzkopf's body weight was declared a military secret.[34]

Censors' pen not the real issue

All this means that, having set the ground rules, the military did not impose overt censorship very often. There were a few cases but since most of the journalists identified with the army and its aims the censors had not a great deal to do. Keith Dovkants, of the British FTU, said he faced only 'odd quibbles' over copy from the two censors attached to his unit, Lt. Col John King and Lt. Chris Sexton. 'We had no sinister arguments. I certainly saw no attempt to manipulate media coverage.' And as Bahrain-based Don McKay, of the *Mirror*, commented: 'Some RAF academy lecturer looked at copy but he became superfluous because of all the "bonding" between reporters and pilots that was going on.'

He continued: 'We were always conscious we would never say anything that would annoy families back home. I did a couple of stories about Rapier missile batteries downing Scuds with a Bahrain by-line. I did not say the batteries were based in Bahrain but the implication was there. That was enough to annoy the Bahrain government who were aware that the re-opening of the base closed in the 1960s was a highly sensitive issue. The commander of the base told me there would be severe trouble if I repeated the story.'

During the crisis and massacres, the D Notices (a voluntary censorship system arranged between editors and the British government) were activated only once after the lap-top computer with the allied plans was stolen from a car in London. The *Irish Times*, not covered by the notices, subsequently mentioned the theft and so the embargo had to be lifted for all the other papers. Most of the censorship incidents were cases of media theatre turned farce – none of them involving sensitive operational intelligence. For instance, the MoD imposed a security blackout on weather reports and forecasts from the Gulf – even though Cable News Network continued providing them so making them accessible to the Iraqis (presuming they wanted such information anyway). The official war artist, John Keane, was refused permission to write a diary for the *Guardian*.[35] Robert Fox told of how he

---

33 Hodgson, Godfrey (op cit) p 20.

34 See Heibert, Ray Eldon (1995): 'Mass media as weapons of modern warfare', *Impact of mass media: current issues*; (ed) Heibert, Ray Eldon; Longman US; New York pp 327-334.

35 See Lawson, Mark (1995): *John Keane: Conflicts of interest*; Mainstream Publishing; Edinburgh/London (in conjunction with Angela Flowers Gallery) pp 61-76.

discovered that half a section of the Royal Scots he visited had been to jail but this was excised 'on grounds of tone and taste'.

Response of journalists to censorship regime

Many elite journalists were remarkably supportive of the government-imposed censorship ground rules. Some were positively enthusiastic. An editorial in *The Economist* of 19 January 1991 commended opposition politicians for suspending 'the normal play of democratic argument'. 'The truth about the Gulf war, no details expunged, must await the end of the fighting.' Ron Spark, chief *Sun* leader writer, said journalists had a responsibility to support the cause uncritically: 'Newspapers are in the business of telling news and freedom of information is a precious part of our democracy. Yet when we are fighting men and women are in peril, we have no choice but to accept some limitations.' Both he and Sir Peregrine Worsthorne, of the *Sunday Telegraph*, re-invented the archetypal 'vulnerable state' scenario with images of hordes of anti-war voices taking over the press. [36]

Max Hastings, in the *Telegraph* of 5 February 1991, remained 'unconvinced of the case for objectivity as between the US-led coalition forces and Saddam, when even the most moral assessment ... suggests he is an exceptionally evil man'. *The Times* said on 23 January 1991: 'The media should be able to cover the war without offering gratuitous oxygen in the relentless repetition of horrific images.' The *Independent*, on 8 January 1991, while broadly sympathetic over the government-imposed constraints, was critical of the pooling arrangements: 'Justifying these restrictions, officials cite the demands of the Saudi government. That sounds too convenient an explanation to be wholly credible. Coverage by experienced reporters is in the interests of the public and those in the front line alike.'

Views differed on the value of the London briefings. Peter Almond, of the *Telegraph*, argued that they were often better than those in Saudi Arabia, with defence intelligence providing some of the 'deepest' backgrounds. Michael Evans, defence correspondent of *The Times*, also considered the unattributable, off-the-record briefings he attended in London throughout the 'war' 'incredibly good' and 'right on the ball'. Every day he compiled an 800-word analytical commentary piece and found being based in London crucial for gaining the necessary overview. He was able to cross-check information with contacts in Israel, France and the Pentagon. 'It was not a scoopy kind of event for me. That was more for the chaps in Saudi Arabia. I was being told a hell of a lot of information on an unattributable basis. My time was taken up analysing it and writing it up.' Did he feel, in retrospect, he was fed any misinformation? 'It would be highly likely in a war.' Harvey Morris, of the *Independent*, claimed the censorship regime was not worth opposing since his newspaper had easily worked around it.

---

36 See the views of Spark, Worsthorne (and Peter Preston, editor of the *Guardian*) in 'The role of the press at war', *UK Press Gazette*, London, 18 February 1991 pp 2-3.

Yet a group of dissident journalists did form Media Workers Against the War which proved to be one of the most articulate groups to campaign against the massacres. Packed-out meetings were held in London venues such as Westminster Hall, newsletters were published, branches were formed throughout the country, and Fleet Street journalists such as Victoria Brittain and Edward Pearce, of the *Guardian*, John Pilger, and Paul Foot, of the *Mirror*, spoke from campaign platforms. It was almost totally ignored by the press. The National Union of Journalists, representing some 75 per cent of working journalists, also voted against supporting the 'war'. On 16 January, its executive issued an eight-point *Principles and guidelines for reporting the Gulf War* to counter censorship and government manipulation of information. Point No. 3 stressed: 'Journalists including editors should not succumb to self-censorship and suppress information or comment that might be embarrassing to military or political leaders.'

Journalists in the US were also mixed in their responses to the massacres coverage. In a survey published in the authoritative *Columbia Journalism Review* (March/April 1991) nine of the eleven were deeply critical of the media performance. William Broyles, former editor in chief of *Newsweek*, summed up their views: 'The sense of war as the massing of means of death and destruction and its application against an enemy is, I think, completely lacking.' A number of US journalists also quit the Gulf in protest at the restrictions. But most elite journalists backed the Pentagon.

Two major law suits challenged the legitimacy of the censorship regime. On 10 January 1991, the Center for Constitutional Rights, on behalf of a group of news organisations, journalists and writers (*Harpers, Mother Jones, In these times, Los Angeles Weekly*, the *Progressive, Texas Observer*, the *Guardian*, the *Nation*, the *Village Voice*, Pacifica Radio, Pacific News Service, E. Doctorow, William Styron, Michael Klare, Scott Armstrong and Sydney Schanberg) claimed the censorship regulations were in violation of the First and Fifth Amendments. The suit also accused the Pentagon of favouring 'hometowners'. Agence France Presse filed a companion suit at the same time in protest at being excluded from the pools.

Most of the mainstream press kept well clear of the case, claiming the suit was irresponsible since it could end up enshrining dangerous precedent in law. The case was finally thrown out of court after the end of the massacres, with Federal District Judge Leonard Sand declining to issue a sweeping declaratory judgment against future use of the pools. The case was almost totally ignored by the British and US press. On 22 February, the American Civil Liberties Union filed a complaint on behalf of several photographers, news media representatives, veteran groups and military family support groups over the banning of the public and press from the Dover Air Force Base. No verdict had been given before the ending of the massacres. This was also largely ignored by the press in both countries.

8 The making of the just war as media spectacle: the Atlantic consensus

As Desert Shield became Desert Storm with the launch of air strikes on Baghdad, Fleet Street spoke with one voice – this was going to be a 'just war'. New militarism's dream of unity had been achieved – in the crucial area of propaganda, at least. Reading between the lines of the heavily manipulated opinion polls it was clear the country was confused and ambivalent over the conflict. The Labour Party, while it had virtually no support in Fleet Street, was being dubbed at the time as the likely winners of the next general election – and it was calling for the continuation of sanctions.

The 'free press' notion is based on the idea that newspapers reflect the will of the people and somehow (through the workings of the market) articulate the democratic spirit of the nation. The Gulf massacres consensus showed, once again, that this notion, so central to the political and journalists' culture, is a myth serving to preserve the privileges of the already powerful and wealthy. But the consensus creation is not part of a grand conspiracy. Certainly conspiracies exist in new militarist societies (where secret services play such significant roles); but the creation of myths and consensus is an integral product of the underlying ideological, political and economic system.

Journalists did not find this consensus in any way problematic. For instance, one of the most prominent UK media commentators, Brian MacArthur, of the *Sunday Times*, presented an overview of Fleet Street attitudes on 13 January when the *Guardian* was still backing sanctions, and concluded: 'If Britain goes to war it will be with the united support of 21 national newspapers.' This is presented as a given fact. It is not analysed nor deemed worthy of concern. Out of all of Fleet Street just the relatively small-selling *Guardian* was calling for sanctions, not war. The one major daily supposedly backing the Labour Party, the *Mirror*, was heavily committed to the war option from early August. This is not worthy of critical analysis.

Silencing the media debate going for the 'good story'

One of the intriguing features of the August to January crisis period was the silence in the media about the media. There were very few articles (or indeed television programmes) exploring critically the coverage of the crisis. The trade press predictably carried lots of news and features about the logistics of press coverage. But the moral justice of the government's case went unquestioned. Thus MacArthur wrote as far back as 27 August 1990 in the *UK Press Gazette* of local press reporting on what he even then unproblematically called the Gulf War. The necessity for the military build-up was never questioned. MacArthur was more concerned to praise the regionals for grabbing at 'a good story'.[1]

Editors for War pronounce – in Britain

The pro-war consensus held firm in the mainstream media on both sides of the Atlantic. Only the *Guardian*, in Britain, made any shift from pro-diplomacy views promoted since August, finally accepting the dominant frame of good versus evil just before hostilities commenced. (On 9 December 1990, the *Sunday Times* had said of the *Guardian* that it was 'to appeasement in the Gulf what *The Times* was to Munich'.) Finally, on 17 January, the *Guardian*'s editorial commented: 'The simple cause – at the end – is just. An evil regime instigated an evil and brutal invasion. Our soldiers and airmen are there at the UN's behest to set that evil to rights.' But some later editorials continued to call for negotiations.

For the rest the cause always had been just, Saddam had been evil, the allies had travelled that extra mile for peace, war was inevitable to save the world. Now nothing could stop the bloodbath. The new militarist machine was hyped up for war – and that it must have. It never was a war to force the removal of the Iraqis from Kuwait. Now, parts of the press were coming clean. It was war simply for the sake of war, for reasons which lay too deep in the political culture to be articulated.

---

1 Tripp, Charles (1991): 'How the medium dictates the message', the *Independent*; 9 January. One of the rare overviews of media coverage of the crisis, it argues that television as a medium encouraged concentration on military build-up. 'It can present a vivid image of military forces rehearsing for action. It cannot easily sum up a tortuous series of negotiations.' In fact, the media were rather uncritically pursuing the Bush agenda. Had Bush promoted negotiations then so, too, would the media. The Reagan/Gorbachev summits show how the media can dwell on negotiations when the dominant agenda requires. This view of the inherent unattractiveness of diplomacy for television is reproduced in Taylor, Phillip (1992): *War and the media: Propaganda and persuasion in the Gulf War*; Manchester University Press p 163.

See also Pilger, John (1991): 'Mythmakers of the Gulf war'; the *Guardian* 7 January. A rare critical overview of media coverage of the crisis. 'If war breaks out in the Gulf the British media – which unlike Iraq's is said to be free – will bear much responsibility for a patriotic and culpable silence that has ensured that people don't know – and can't know.'

As *Today* said on 14 January: 'It hardly matters about the outcome of any last-minute peace initiative. War with Saddam is inevitable sooner or later as long as he rules Iraq. Perhaps his troops will start to withdraw from Kuwait. They may even pull out. Regrettably none of that will stop there being a war.' Saddam Hussein by now had out-Hitlered Hitler: 'The damage inflicted on the world could be far greater than Hitler achieved.' War for war's sake was now inevitable (as the press had made it appear since August): 'To fail to accept the inevitability of war would be to condemn the world to years of misery and devastation.'

The *Independent* took the over-simplified 'Saddam guilty' line with as much ferocity as the patriotic pops: 'With the deadline for Iraqi withdrawal expiring this midnight war looks unavoidable. Its sole progenitor is President Saddam.' The *News of the World* said the same thing: 'Saddam is the name to blame.' This was to be a 'cool, calm', rational war. The mistake of the peace lobby was to let their 'hearts rule their heads at the wrong time'. There was going to be no place for compassion as the massacres went on and on.

For *The Times*, war was 'inevitable and right'. Under the headline 'No choice but war' the leading article read: 'Not since 1939 has an aggression left so clear a choice to those seeking a just international order.' The *Telegraph* attacked the last-minute attempt at mediation by Francois Mitterrand, the French President, as 'an act of vanity and an irresponsible attempt to usurp the Western leadership'. The *Mail* of 13 January seemed to forget that only 26 (deeply divided) countries were in the coalition and of these only a small minority were to fight. It still proclaimed: 'The whole world is right to take on Saddam Hussein.'

The *Express* pushed a predictable Labour-attacking line: 'How strange to see the Labour left once more wanting us to bend the knee to a brutal, fascistic tyrant.' Saddam was the megalomanic Hitler. (Indeed, how constantly this imagery was to appear over the following days – it was as if the press was afraid it was not convincing its readers and so needed to reiterate constantly the same clichés). The 'global threat' argument was developed intriguingly by raising the spectre of Saddam's missiles reaching European cities. 'Those who claim Kuwait is not our fight should know that a nuclear armed Saddam leading the Arab world would constitute a global threat.'

Editors for War US-style

In the US the elite split on the crisis brought some intriguing responses from the press. During the week before the UN deadline there was a flurry of diplomatic activity and the Congress vote had only narrowly backed the military option (so much for 'the world' opposed to Saddam). Many newspapers were ambivalent. The *Los Angeles Times* (10 January) saw the Congress vote as being important part of bluffing 'Saddam'. 'But at what time does bluff become real war?' it asked. The *Washington Post*, indulging in Orwellian doublespeak, suggested that authorising war improved the chances of peace. The *Atlanta Constitution* (10 January) and the *Chicago*

Tribune (11 January) both backed a congressional vote approving the use of force. The *New York Times*, uniquely, opposed the military option. (10 January)

Once Desert Storm was launched the doubts dissolved and all backed the President blaming the war primarily on Saddam Hussein. The *New York Times* did a kind of *Guardian* U-turn. Under the title 'What the bombs said' (this humanising of weapons of death was to be a constant feature of press coverage throughout the massacres), it editorialised on 17 January: 'It is a powerful message on behalf of honorable goals.' The *Atlanta Constitution* followed the predictable course: 'It is no wartime bluster to say that we fight for a just cause against evil personified.'

The invention of the credible 'enemy'

Central to the mythology of the massacres as a 'heroic' media spectacle was the representation of the Iraqis as a credible fighting army. This project was not without its problems. The most obvious one was the refusal of the Iraqis to fight in any major contest. Here was supposedly the fourth largest army in the world, with 1m battle-hardened troops, led by a power-mad megalomaniac, going as lambs to the slaughter. The role of propaganda to resolve these contradictions and silence the reality was crucial.

On 16 January, the *Sun* carried an assessment of the opposing forces by resident 'military specialist' Major Gen. Ken Perkins. Yet the final totals bore no relation to any credible military analysis,. They failed, for instance, to take into account the crucial possession by the US-led coalition of space-based weapons systems, night-fighting jets and the factor of morale, logistical support services, and provision of water and food of which the Iraqis had virtually none. The 'assessment' was, rather, a sort of fantasy serving to reinforce the 'war' myth being perpetuated by the paper and the media in general.

Under the section 'command' it said: 'Saddam has a simplified command structure which has been proven in battle' so the Iraqis were awarded seven points out of ten! The allies on the other hand were 'brimming with top brass' which could become a problem. They too were awarded seven points (a sort of macabre variation on the Eurovision Song Contest theme). From a military standpoint this, it could be argued, was nonsense. The Iraqi army, for instance, had distinguished itself by not winning its long war with Iran despite its massive military expenditure. In the 'tactics' section Iraq was awarded eight points simply because it was 'easier to defend in the desert'. The allies faced the more difficult job of attacking (!) and so won only seven points. In fact, the very opposite applied. As Air Vice-Marshal R.A. Mason (1991) commented: 'The sparsely occupied desert terrain was ideally suited to air attack. Iraqi ground forces, most of which were located away from towns would either be dug in and static, or mobile, visible and vulnerable.'

All talk of casualties was silenced. The final totals, Iraq 45, the 'allies' 65, gave exactly the right picture: war would be fought but there was to be no doubt which side would eventually win on points. The picture the *Sun* produced here was to be repeated in different guises throughout the press. Though British troops were to form only a relatively small contingency within the overall coalition forces (32,000 compared to the United States' 500,000) the patriotic imperative of the coverage meant that the Brits' role was exaggerated out of all proportion. Contingents from Saudi Arabia (45,000), Egypt (38,500) and Syria (21,000) were very large but almost totally ignored by the press. Efraim Karsh (1993: 41) puts the total number of Arab ground troops in the anti-Iraq coalition as 100,000.

The 'inevitable' unfolding drama of war

On 16 January, the *Express* gave a foretaste of the massacrespeak, which was to serve to silence the massacres, in its overview of the coming war. The details of the coming slaughters were detailed in fine print, the controllers of the conflict were revealing to the world the secrets of the stage plan for the bloody theatre of battle. But the language used merely silenced the horror of the atrocities that were to come.

Phase One of the war was to involve the RAF Tornado GR1s screaming into Iraq at low level to destroy Saddam's airforce and airbases. In Phase Two US Stealth fighters and Tomahawk cruise missiles launched from the sea would pound Iraq. In Phase Three, to stop 'Saddam' showering Israel with poison gas and germ warfare, bombers would attack Soviet-made Scud missiles. In the next phase, coalition forces would 'soften up' Saddam's forces and 'carpet bomb' his massed troops. So with such euphemisms, it could be argued, the horror of the allies' atrocities was to be hidden. Finally the coalition forces would send in their ground troops for 'one of the biggest land battles since 1945'. Here, then, was to be articulated one of the most significant features of the Gulf war imagery. When all around, Iraqi troops were being slaughtered from the air, there always continued the constant references to 'the biggest land battle since 1945' to reinforce the war myth. It never came.

The various stages of warfare were represented as being part of an inevitably unfolding drama. As Jay Rosen argues (1991), the coverage of the massacres was 'lifted out of the realm of the real and into the plain of the theatre'. The idea that the atrocities/hostilities could be halted by a ceasefire at any time was never envisaged by any of the press's overviews of the conflict. In this way, too, the diplomatic option, largely silenced since August, was silenced during the massacres.

After the war it became known that the figures for the Iraqi forces had been grossly exaggerated and the allied figures significantly reduced. A report by the House of Representatives' armed services committee in April 1992[2] said coalition troops numbered as many as 700,000 at the same time. By the time the 'ground assault' began, following mass desertions and aerial bombardment, the Iraqi forces numbered no more than 183,000 – so the allies grossly

---

2 The *Guardian*; 24 April 1991.

outnumbered the 'enemy' at all times. Some 63,000 were taken prisoner, the rest either escaped or died.[3] Similarly the fighting abilities of the 'elite' Republican Guard were always exaggerated – as was quickly admitted after the massacres. John Simpson (1991: 334-335) records: 'When the ground offensive came the Republican Guard showed little more inclination to fight than the regular army divisions and reservists.'

Silencing the casualties: first moves

The central feature of the war was to be the merciless ongoing slaughter of Iraqi troops and civilians. But the media spectacle war could not cope with that reality – and so silenced it. There was understandable concern for possible 'allied casualties', particularly those in Israel: there was virtually no concern for Iraqi deaths. Thus pre-war overviews set the tone for later coverage hiding the likelihood of mass deaths behind the shroud of massacres-peak ('carpet bombing', 'soften up') or speaking of them in sensationalist terms as the inevitable consequence of modern warfare.

The *Star* of 14 January used the title of a war film 'Apocalypse Now' to headline its overview and a reference to Space Invaders in its opening paragraph, thus framing its coverage within the stereotypes of the Hollywood entertainment genre. Indeed, when war is essentially a new militarist media spectacle it is logical that the dominant representational frames should be drawn from the entertainment industry. But such framing compounding fiction with 'fact' serves to distance the reader from the reality of horror.

'Experts predict massive casualties as Space Invader technology unleashes the deadliest firepower yet developed,' the *Star* reported. The future massacres were shrouded in these vague, sensational generalities and euphemisms: 'On the ground, the modern battlefield will make World War Two look like a picnic.' As E.P.Thompson writes (1980: 51): 'We can kill thousands because we have first learned to call them "enemy". Wars commence in the culture first of all and we kill each other in euphemisms and abstractions long before the first missiles have been launched.'

The *Star* goes on to examine forecasts for possible casualties, but no mention is made of the Iraqis. Their deaths are not part of the equation. All the focus is on the coalition forces. 'The Department of Defense expects 4,000 killed and 16,000 wounded if fighting lasts two months.'

Pictorial representations of the likely war scenario usually accompanied newspapers' coverage – but they were like *Boy's Own* comic versions full of

---

3   Bellamy, Christopher (1991): 'Arithmetic of death in wake of Gulf conflict', the *Independent*; 20 March 1991. 'Before the air war the British estimated the total number of Iraqi troops in the Kuwait theatre of operations as 590,000. The American estimate was 540,000. At one point in the conflict, the coalition estimate went up to 630,000 but by this week the Pentagon had revised its estimate downwards to 'over half a million'. However this may still be too high...The starting number could be as low as 350,000.' Lumsden, Hamish, chief press officer, Ministry of Defence, interviewed September 1992, argued that the error over the numbers of Iraqi soldiers was due to the failures of human intelligence and the limitations of satellite intelligence.

pictures of jets swooping down creating craters and explosions. Peter Almond, defence correspondent of the *Telegraph*, argued that a lot of the war coverage was 'graphics-driven'. It was, therefore, crucial for him to be based in London during the war so that he could liaise closely with the sub-editors and graphics people. 'Is the F15 or F16 involved? It's important to get that kind of information right. If you get it wrong people will ring up.' But to what extent can a graphic convey a picture of battle? Soldiers never died in these illustrations. Were they, then, the newspaper equivalent of Peter Snow's bloodless sandpit over which he regularly pored on BBC2's *Newsnight* – perpetuating the same myths of 'deathless' war?

The Great Deception Strategy mystery

Central to the representation of the 'brilliant' campaign was the deception strategy supposedly adopted by General Schwarzkopf. It was yet another myth since it became one of the most publicised deception strategies in history.[4] It could be argued it was more an attempt to dignify the atrocities with some sort of credible military strategy. After all, great generals adopt cunning battle strategies against formidable enemies; they don't inflict atrocities on fleeing conscripts. Perhaps it was part of the allied attempts to recreate the atmosphere, rhetoric and imagery of the Second World War when a deception strategy, code-named Bodyguard, was said to have been of crucial significance before the allied invasion of Normandy in June 1945. It also symbolised the military's new power over the media – so necessary to assert as part of the process of 'kicking the Vietnam syndrome'. Polls suggested Pentagon restrictions on the press were popular; co-opting the press so intimately into the military strategy could only reinforce the military's power and popularity.

Colin Wills, a pool reporter for the *Mirror*, recounts how privileged he felt to be given the entire battle plan a week before the land war started. 'To be in the know and not to be able to file a word was like being given the secret of alchemy and at the same time being struck dumb.' But unknown to him in London journalists openly before the launch of Desert Storm spoke of the crucial elements of the deception strategy. The *Express*, for instance, wrote of the Americans outflanking the Iraqi defences and sweeping into Kuwait from the west. On 14 January, the *Star* predicted the war almost exactly as it was to unravel – complete with the 'deception strategy'. 'Allied commanders could also try to envelop the Iraqis in Kuwait by moving troops. tanks and artillery round the west end of Kuwait behind the enemy. This would also cut off reinforcements from Iraq. The entire operation could take six weeks to drive Iraqi forces from Kuwait.' No mention of the Marine

---

4   Thomson, Alex (ITN pool correspondent) (1992): *Smokescreen – The media, censors and the Gulf*; Laburnham and Spellmount; Tunbridge Wells. Highlights the *Newsweek* issue just before the start of hostilities which mapped out the war (complete with 'deception strategy') in full. All the pool reports knew of the plan – but they were sworn to secrecy. Being party to a 'secret' helped in the media/military bonding process. pp 22-23.

invasion from the sea which was supposedly so crucial to the deception. Peter Almond, at the *Telegraph*, described the 'Great Deception Strategy' as 'bullshit'. 'I never took it seriously,' he said. He had described the allied westward thrust in December, based on information from his defence intelligence sources. 'I was, in fact, a little surprised MoD people didn't come back to me on the "Great Left Hook" thing.'

As the massacres went on the supposed 'Great Deception Strategy' was being revealed to the world. Both Edward Luttwak and Michael Evans explored the speculation surrounding it in detail in *The Times*. Michael Evans wrote on 7 February: 'Take for example, the speculation that American and British forces might be involved in a flanking manoeuvre to the far west, across the Saudi-Iraq border, by-passing the "Maginot Line" in southern Kuwait and advancing into Iraq to cut off the Republican Guard divisions from the rear. Although no-one in authority has outlined such a strategy, enough information has been given to add credence to the reports.' Evans later commented that the only occasion the MoD approached his newspaper over coverage was after a national newspaper reported on the 'left hook' strategy in the week before the hostilities began and they were advised not to follow it up. Yet by mid-February discussion of the strategy was becoming 'widespread' in the press. (Taylor 1992: 234)

A similar open debate of the Great Deception Strategy was happening in the US. For instance, on 19 February Col. Harry G. Summers Jr. (Ret.), in the *Los Angeles Times*, summed up the situation: 'Most analysts believe the main allied ground attack in the Gulf will be an envelopment or turning attack. This is the tactic most discussed in the media. Strike deep with armoured columns through the desert around and behind Saddam Hussein's western flank.' Gen. Schwarzkopf even records in his autobiography (1992: 440) how in the middle of February, *Newsweek* 'showed up with a map almost exactly depicting our flanking plan'. He continues: 'I called Powell. "This stinks! *Newsweek* just printed our entire battle plan. Now the Iraqis could put chemical weapons in that area and completely reorient their defenses." "Don't over-react," Powell cautioned.'

Towards the end of February 1991 most papers resurrected the 'deception ploy' as part of the 'brilliant', 'cerebral' coalition strategy. At his victory press conference on 27 February, Gen. Schwarzkopf described it as the 'Hail Mary' tactic (thus managing to delight the press corps with the sporting metaphor and offend his Arab allies at the same time). In the *Los Angeles Times* of 28 February, John M Broder's report of the press conference was headlined 'Schwarzkopf plan based on deception'. BBC reporters Ben Brown and David Shukman (1991: 115) add a further dimension to the 'Hail Mary' mystery. They report that the Marine invasion from the Gulf was actually part of Gen. Schwarzkopf's original plan and only dropped after the British complained that their minehunters were likely to suffer unacceptable losses in the action.

The myth of the chemical threat

A central feature of the demonisation of Saddam Hussein throughout the crisis period was the stress on 'his' chemical weapons threat. Such a focus served a number of ideological/political purposes. It helped to distract attention from coalition's possession of similar weapons, from the use of such weapons by the British against the Kurds in 1920 and the reluctance of the US to negotiate a worldwide ban on chemical weapons. (Chomsky 1992: 182) It also served to downplay the West's role in building up Iraq's chemical arsenal. (Darwish and Alexander 1991: 101-114)

David Beresford, of the *Guardian*, suggested after the massacres that he had been fed deliberate misinformation by field intelligence officers. They had convinced him that the Iraqis intended to use chemical weapons. But no evidence of chemical capability was ever found by coalition forces. (Yant 1991: 110-111) Beresford discovered that some Iraqis were wearing chemical protection equipment not against 'blow-backs' but because they were convinced the allies were going to use them. Significantly, Gen. Schwarzkopf's biographers, Cohen and Gotti (1991: 273), comment: 'Schwarzkopf was, in fact, never seriously worried that the Scuds might be fitted with chemical warheads. Since becoming Centcom's commander-in-chief in November 1988, US intelligence had briefed him that Iraq was many years away from mastering the relatively complicated technology for adding a chemical warhead to the missile.'

In the run-up to the launch of Desert Storm most of newspapers suggested that the Iraqis were 'likely' to use chemical weapons. On 14 January 1991, David Fairhall and Jasper Becker reported on Iraqi missiles in the *Guardian*: 'It is assumed that such missiles will by now have been fuelled with chemical warheads – nerve gas, mustard or a mixture of both.' The *Sun* said the Scud missiles 'have been modified to take chemical warheads'. The *Star* of 14 January said: 'Madman Saddam Hussein has a massive stockpile of chemical weapons to unleash against our troops in the desert. And he will have no qualms about using the terrible nerve gases and germ strains against his enemies – he has already used them against Iran.'

Fears of chemical attack were to continue throughout the massacres, and as the Iraqi troops were slaughtered, grow in prominence. The *Express* of 29 January headlined: 'World's worst poison 'in Saddam's arsenal'.' Here was fear-mongering at its most blatant: 'Saddam may have armed himself with the deadliest poison known to man – botulin toxin. Less than four ounces could kill hundreds of millions of people and a strike on storage containers could have world-wide consequences.' After the end of the massacres, the chemical threat was suddenly downplayed. The *Sun* of 1 March 1991, under the headline 'Why no chemical show' quoted Frank Brenchley, of the Research Institute for the Study of Conflict and Terrorism: 'He [Saddam Hussein] did not have the technology to put a chemical warhead into the Scuds.'

The myth of the nuclear monster

The myth of the chemical threat was closely linked to representations of Saddam's supposed nuclear threat at the opening of hostilities. On 16 December 1990, for instance, the *Sunday Times* quoted an American Defence Intelligence Agency report to the effect that Iraq was just two months away from producing a bomb. Such coverage served to downplay Western responsibility in helping Iraq launch its nuclear industry. (Darwish and Alexander op cit: 115-134) Secretly the US and Israeli administrations discounted Iraq as a nuclear threat.[5] Before the crisis exploded, British intelligence estimated Iraq was 10 years away from producing a viable nuclear weapon. (Dorril 1993: 413) And after the massacres, UN investigations into Iraq's nuclear programme found it had managed to extract three grams of plutonium, though eight kilograms were needed to make a successful nuclear device. (Macarthur 1993: 241)

The public rhetoric was very different. Bush administration references to the alleged nuclear threat had intensified after a *New York Times*/CBS poll (13-15 November 1990) found 54 per cent of respondents thought there was one good reason to act against Iraq – to prevent it from obtaining nuclear weapons. (Niva 1992: 64) The *Sun*'s front page splash (lead story) of 17 January read simply: 'Saddam 'has nuke'.' But the paper is keen to stress this is a 'dirty nuke' (presumably in comparison with the coalition's clean nukes) and 'primitive' and 'DIY' (compared to the highly sophisticated allied versions). 'It is likely to be more primitive than the atomic bombs dropped in Japan at the end of World War Two. But a crude "dirty nuke" – killing by radiation fallout rather than by massive blast – would still be a fearsome weapon in the Gulf.'

Emphasis on Saddam Hussein's supposed nuclear threat to the world ignored Iraqi attempts to negotiate a nuclear free zone in the Middle East. It also served also to legitimise talk of the possible use of nuclear weapons by the US-led coalition or indeed Israel, strengthening the positions of the nuclear lobbies in these countries. On 10 August, the *Sun* reported: 'Military sources said that nuclear weapons would provide the necessary "massive retaliation" if Hussein unleashes his huge arsenal of chemical weapons.' And on 30 September, the *Observer* quoted a senior army officer attached to the 7th

---

5   Cockburn, Alexander and Cockburn, Leslie (1992): *Dangerous liaison: The inside story of US Israeli covert relationship and the international activities it has served to conceal*; Bodley Head; London, quote Shlomo Gazit, former head of military intelligence during the US-Iraq war: 'We did not have any expectation that he might reach a nuclear capability soon.' p 351.

A new twist to the 'nuclear monster' saga emerged in August 1995 when Saddam Hussein's son-in-law, Gen. Hussein Kamil al-Majid, who had just sought refuge in Jordan, claimed that Iraq was on the point of testing an atomic bomb just before the outbreak of hostilities in January 1991. It was impossible to know whether he was telling the truth or merely trying to ingratiate himself with his US handlers by telling them exactly what they wanted to hear. But, significantly, the claims were reported uncritically in the press. See Bhatia, Shyam (1995): 'Lion of Iraq fears song of 'canary", the *Observer*; 20 August. (Mystery surrounded al-Majid's death in February 1996 after he had found no support in Jordan and returned to Iraq.)

Armoured Brigade, which had begun to leave for the Gulf the previous day, confirming that an Iraqi chemical attack on British forces would be answered with a tactical nuclear response. The coverage reflected no outrage over this suggestion; no questioning even.

Paul Rogers (1994: 7-8) has since suggested that the Royal Fleet Auxiliary Argus, though portrayed to the media as a hospital ship, was, in fact, equipped with tactical nuclear weapons. 'Even without Argus, Britain would have had a small nuclear capability in the Mediterranean, and could have moved nuclear bombs for Tornado strike aircraft from Britain or Germany at short notice.' This suggests that the British government, while in public committed to controlling nuclear proliferation, had shifted from a policy of massive nuclear targeting in the Cold War to selective nuclear targeting – without any media debate at all.

Two mass-selling papers, the *Sun* and *Star*, actually advocated the use of the nuclear bomb against Iraq. (For instance, on 10 January 1991, the *Sun* headlined: 'Let's nuke them'.) Public opinion polls were on hand to add further legitimacy to this talk. Shaw and Carr-Hill found that among *Sun* readers, no fewer than 21 per cent favoured nuking Iraq. (Shaw and Carr-Hill 1991: 13) Some 15 million people are said to read the *Sun* every day. Thus, in promoting the 'nuking' option, talk of the unthinkable (the nuclear holocaust) and the blunt crudities of nukespeak ('Let's nuke Saddam') are introduced as part of the legitimate political discourse.

9 The myth of the clean war: the casualties cover-up

Crucial to the mythology of the new militarist war is the representation of military technology as clean, surgical, modern, 'super'. New militarism is premised on the notion of 'modern' violence as being of a totally different kind from the 'primitive' form of Iraqi violence. It was smart violence in defence of global order – which actually saved civilian lives. In contrast, Iraqi violence was indiscriminate and anarchic. (Aksoy and Robins 1991) Yet the myths on which the clean war can be fought are highly vulnerable. How long can the reality of slaughter be hidden? The new militarist elite know that the myths and constructs on which they base their military adventures, even given a pliant media, cannot be sustained for long – hence the need for quickie wars.

Before the end of Desert Storm it had become a cliché to talk of the video game, micro-chip war. Yet behind the media blitz, appalling secret atrocities were being inflicted. As Robins and Levidow argue (1991: 324): 'The remote technology served to portray as heroic "combat" what was mainly a series of massacres.' Media consumers during the massacres saw warfare more closely than ever before. Shots from video cameras on missiles heading towards their targets (shown on television and reproduced in the press) meant that spectators actually 'became' the weapons. These images, constantly repeated, came to dominate perceptions of the conflict. Yet, paradoxically, the media spectacle war, while offering such openness, in fact kept secret the reality.

On a basic level such stress on 'pinpoint' weaponry eliminated the existence of non-precision, though utterly devastating bombs. After the war it was reported by the US Air Force that 'smart bombs' had constituted only 7 per cent of all US explosive dropped on Iraq and Kuwait but accounted for 84 per cent of the cost of the munitions in the war. (Weiner 1996) Moreover, 70 per cent of the 88,500 tons of bombs dropped on the two countries during the massacres had missed their targets. Such figures, in fact, represent a military disaster.

In 1993, the armed services committee of Congress reported that the US military command had estimated that 388 of the 846 tanks of the Iraqi Republican Guard divisions were destroyed from the air. In fact, only 166 were destroyed. Moreover, during the early 1980s massive peace movements had grown in Europe and north America against the deployment of cruise and Tomahawk. The glorification of those same incredibly expensive weapons during the massacres sought to eliminate those popular protests from the historical record as well as any debate over the redistribution of weapons expenditure (at a time of mass poverty and famine in Africa, South America and Eastern Europe) to more socially useful purposes.

But on a deeper level such representation providing hyper-real proximity between killer and victim desensitised the media consumer. As Robins and Levidow comment: 'It was the ultimate voyeurism: to see the target hit from the vantage point of the weapon. An inhumane perspective. Yet this remote-intimate kind of watching could sustain the moral detachment of earlier military technologies. Seeing was split off from feeling; the visible was separated from the sense of pain and death. Through the long lens the enemy remained a faceless alien.' (op cit: 325) Similarly Bauman and Kovel have pointed to the dehumanising tendencies of technocratic societies. (Bauman 1990; Kovel 1983) And Steiner has identified the inhumanity lying at the root of modern culture and 'civilisation'. (Steiner 1971: 478)

The new militarist media spectacle, then, provided a way of seeing and not seeing. A study of pictures in the *Sun*, *Mirror* and *Express* from 17 January 1991 to 4 March shows clearly the emphasis on technology to the virtual exclusion of the reality of the death. Some 206 images focused on technology compared to 75 which related to human suffering and just nine relating to death.[2] Over the same period, the *Guardian*, *Times*, *Telegraph* and *Independent* carried 279 images of technology, 144 relating to human suffering and just 13 to death. In the *Sunday Times*, *Observer*, *Independent on Sunday* and *Sunday Telegraph* there were 112 images of technology, 43 relating to human suffering and only four dealing with death. The press did not show close-up pictures of Iraqi soldiers being blown to bits as they fled the onslaught with an accompanying commentary condemning them as morally outrageous. Instead, there was Gen. Schwarzkopf drawing laughs from attendant journalists with the quip: 'I am going to show you the luckiest man in Iraq on this particular day.' as an Iraqi vehicle was videoed passing through the crosshairs of a bomb site just before the bomb 'took out' a bridge.

---

1   The *Guardian*; 17 August 1993.

2   Figures drawn from unpublished University College, London, MSc dissertation by Collis, Eli (1992): *A war without death*.

The post-heroism of new militarism

Modern war-fighting strategies have virtualy eliminated the possibilities of heroic action. Technology has taken the place of men. Men now largely press buttons and watch the consequences on a video. Electronics and space-based technologies are all important. Luckham comments (1984: 2): 'We are now entering a new stage in which the manufacture of warfare is overtaking man and expropriating his culture. Automated warfare and the nuclear bomb have deprived man of this capacity to strive for glory, recognition or safety through combat.'

Alvin and Heidi Toffler (1993: 116) quote Col. Alan Campen, former director of Command and Control Policy at the Pentagon, to the effect that the Gulf war was the 'first instance where combat forces largely were deployed, sustained, commanded and controlled through satellite communications'. In all, the coalition was said to have used some 60 satellites (such as the KH-11s and Lacrosse satellites). The Tofflers report on how robotic weapons (such as Pioneer RPVs – small, pilotless planes under the control of teleoperators sitting at computer consoles miles away) were secretly used in the conflict. (ibid: 133)

The massacres represented a desperate attempt to resolve the contradictions posed by the destruction of a distinctly masculine heroism in this new militarist, post-heroic age. Hostages became the instant media heroes. British Tornado fighter pilots were constantly dubbed 'Top Gun' heroes in the patriotic pops. Don McKay, based in Bahrain for the *Mirror*, explained the use of the reference in this way: 'They were "Top Gun" heroes. They were the high echelon of pilots. It's a generic term, a form of shorthand. It's not implying they were gung-ho. They were not fools. They were not cowboys. It's like in the First World War they were called "Biggles". It's a suggestion of bravery.'

Yet in sending thousands of soldiers to the Gulf, there was an attempt to revive the heroic images of the Second World War. From a military standpoint many soldiers were largely irrelevant, massively outnumbering their enemy. For the symbolic assertion of the heroic possibilities of warfare, they were essential. Yet, on the other hand, the 'fire and forget' technologies, as Zygmunt Bauman (op cit: 30) has argued, 'eliminated face-to-face contact between the actors and the objects of their actions, and with that neutralised their morally constraining impact'. The press made constant efforts to revive the image of major hand-to-hand heroic combat (through cartoon representations and photographs of troops in training); but it was never to come.

Kicking the Vietnam syndrome – again

Since the Vietnam debacle military strategy had tended to concentrate on Low Intensity Conflicts prioritising the use of small, elite or proxy, secret forces. The Gulf was to provide the opportunity for America's much larger, complex, tightly integrated, highly specialised, high-technology military organisation (the focus of so much investment during the 1980s) to get a 'piece of the action'. Here was the chance to relegate the trauma of Vietnam to the dustbin of history. Moreover, a central myth of the Vietnam War was that American super-firepower had been constrained by a sceptical Congress, peacefreaks and the media – and other elements of the 'democratic' state. The US had gone into the war 'with one hand tied behind its back'.

Young (1991: 24) has demonstrated how, in fact, the US military fought the Vietnam war with both hands and both feet and all its teeth. Half a million US troops and an equal number of Republic of South Vietnam troops and more than 60,000 allied soldiers were involved. During the war, Vietnam, Laos and Cambodia were hit by 15 million tons of explosives, about half dropped from the air (the equivalent of 7,000 atomic bombs). This included 400,000 tons of napalm and 19,114,000 gallons of herbicides. 'President Bush and the military insist that what they learned from Vietnam is how to fight a war: fast, hard and massive. But the major lessons have been not so much how to fight as how to market it.'

Yet the myth of the massive constraints on the US military persisted, constantly repeated in the media. For instance, the *Sunday Times* of 13 January 1991 wrote: 'The allied planners have recognised from the start that the key to the conflict lies in the air. In the last two major wars fought by the Americans in Korea and Vietnam, the military were restrained from crossing into enemy territory. Bush has ordered. however, that there would be no such constraint this time.' Now had come the time for the secret state to unleash its 'overwhelming force'.

America's complex military organisation was essentially the child of the Cold War when the American elite prepared to face the supposedly massive forces of the Soviets. Against such armies as the Vietnamese, even though they were much less equipped in terms of modern military technology, such military organisation was useless. The Soviets were to experience the same in Afghanistan against highly motivated, technologically less advanced rebels. Kaldor has highlighted the growth of 'baroque' superpower arsenals of ever increasing technological sophistication yet too complex for use in battle. (Kaldor 1982) The glorification of the allied technology was ultimately done in the self-serving interests of the military/industrial complex and the secret state.

Since the Iraqis, in any case, offered hardly any opposition, virtually all military assessments drawn (despite all the media hype to the contrary) were of only limited value. Military equipment assessors and defence/offence planners really required a more credible 'war' scenario in which to test their products effectively and observe the performance of Soviet and French weapons. While 'victory' was claimed, if anything, the massacres pointed to the vulnerability of the American war machine. (Rochlin and Demchak 1991)

The emphasis on the technicalities of warfare was a feature running through all the media through crisis to Desert Storm and built on the basic ideological frameworks and consensual attitudes towards the military established in times of 'peace'. This served to marginalise the broader political, moral and historical factors (such as the responsibility of the major powers in supplying Iraq with such arms) and the horrible death-dealing potentials of such weapons. Harvey Morris, of the *Independent*, conceded that his newspaper's coverage of the military hardware was 'too gung-ho'. But his editor and deputy editor were committed to it and he accepted that.

Such representation was built around some deeply entrenched frames which all the media reproduced.

- There was the rhetorical assertion that the allies were defending civilisation and fighting a just cause. As the *News of the World* editorial of 20 January 1991 commented: 'If Saddam has to be stopped by a bullet from his own side, the civilised world will be grateful.' Allied warriors were, in fact, portrayed as pacifists at heart. Kovel comments astutely: 'There is a tendency for technocracy to stay clear of gross violence and even to appear as the antithesis of violence.' (op cit: 149) In contrast the enemy were brutal, barbaric and evil monsters.

One of the reports that fitted this stereotype in the run-up to the massacres was of Iraqi soldiers grabbing babies from incubators at a Kuwaiti hospital. First reported by the *Telegraph* on 5 September 1990, two days later the *Los Angeles Times* published a Reuters account reproducing the atrocity story. The Citizens for a Free Kuwait (95 per cent of its funding coming directly from the Kuwaiti government in exile) hired the public relations firm, Hill and Knowlton (HK), at a cost of $10.8 million to promote its image and campaign for military intervention. HK arranged for a 15-year-old girl, identified as 'Nayirah', to reproduce the babies horror story at a meeting of the Human Rights Caucus of Congress on October. It later emerged that 'Nayirah' was, in fact, the daughter of Saud al-Sabah, Kuwait's ambassador to the United States. President Bush referred to the dead babies story first on 15 October and then five more times in the following five weeks. It was even reproduced in an Amnesty International report on human rights violations in occupied Kuwait, published on 19 December 1990. But after the massacres, it emerged that the atrocity story had been fabricated. (Macarthur 1993: 51-77)

The *Sunday Times* of 13 January highlighted the story, quoting a 'Dr Ali Al-Huwail, 36, a Kuwaiti traced to a secret address in the United Arab Emirates' who 'said he could vouch for only 92 deaths'. A large drawing accompanying the story reinforced the message showing 'devilish'-looking Iraqis seizing the babies from the incubators. But the report ended with quotes from a 'Franco-Jordanian doctor' who was sceptical of the baby atrocity stories.

Macarthur claims that the dead babies story was a defining moment in the disinformation campaign to prepare the American public for the need to go to war. Jowett and O'Donnell comment: '... in the Senate debate on whether to approve military action, seven senators specifically focused on the story. The final margin of victory in favor of military intervention was five votes.' (Jowett and O'Donnell 1992: 262)

- The allies were rational and cool; the enemy were irrational, fanatical, mad, out of touch with reality. An editorial in the *Independent* of 2 February 1991 said that President Saddam's actions had proved one of Israel's central contentions, namely 'the failure of its Arab neighbours to come to terms with the realities of the modern world'. And Martin Woollacott wrote in the *Guardian* of 4 March 1991 that Iraq was 'simply a case of Arab sickness'.

- The allies were most commonly identified with Christianity. A lot of editorials, for instance, ended up with a prayer for the allies. The Pope's fervent opposition to the military option was significantly marginalised by the press. In contrast, the Iraqis were identified with Islam which was portrayed negatively as backward, primitive, sick and irrational. Saddam was often identified in copy and in cartoons as the devil.

- An underlying frame tapped the belief running deep in Western culture that the movement of science was a progressive one. As history moved, science advanced and thus high-technology, as the product of advancing science, could only be good. Luckham comments: '... weapons more than almost any other human product, embody scientific progress. Like modern culture, they are the fruit of the Enlightenment (albeit in mis-shapen form) and they are readily legitimised by it.' (op cit: 5)

Modern military science could be seen as people-friendly and politically uncontroversial. Thus, allied weapons (such as the positively sounding Patriot) saved lives; enemy weapons (such as the ugly sounding Scud) were indiscriminate. Louise Cainkar (1992: 351) reported a post-massacres advertisement in the *New York Times* for Northrop Corporation, the makers of the Stealth plane (that dropped the two bombs on the Baghdad shelter on 13 February 1991 that caused so many deaths): 'Stealth saves lives.'

- The coalition forces were always humans with human feelings; the enemy were reduced to the level of animals – to be slaughtered. They became non-human targets.

These basic frames had a crucial moral foundation: the US-led coalition were always good, they were not to blame – all fault lay with Saddam. Along with technological supremacy went moral superiority. According to Aksoy and Robins (op cit: 28) : 'The Gulf War demonstrated that the power and the dominance of the technological order had become so well secured that it is now the criterion of what is moral.' In this way the massacres (a definition which is ultimately grounded in a moral response of outrage at the perpetrator and compassion for the victim) were silenced – just as the barbarism civilisation carries was hidden. The dominant ideological frames simply excluded such a perspective. John Bulloch, of the *Independent*, after the massacres suggested that a lot of reporters were 'happy to go along' with their military briefers on the advanced technology of warfare since they were largely unfamiliar with the esoteric and complex subject.

The precision myth

Central to the representation of the massacres was the myth of the 'precision' weapons. The media never lost its commitment to this kind of representation – even when the evidence was conspiring to contradict it. It was almost an article of faith. Yet an assessment by the US House of Representatives committee on armed services reported in August 1993: 'The body count given by General Schwarzkopf on Iraqi tanks destroyed during the air campaign was, in all likelihood, exaggerated. A careful analyis of 22 per cent of claimed kills shows an over-estimation of tanks killed by 100 per cent and perhaps by as much as 134 per cent.' (Adams 1994: 50)

One of the military 'stars' of the conflict was the F117 Stealth fighter jet which reportedly had an 80 per cent success rate on bombing runs. But in July 1996, a report from the Congressional General Accounting Office concluded that the success rate was closer to 40 per cent. (Weiner op cit) Furthermore, the much-touted laser technology had done little to liberate pilots from age-old weather problems. The multi-million-dollar sensor system failed to 'see' through fog, rain, clouds, smoke or humidity, the report concluded. (Robinson 1996) Roy Greenslade, editor of the *Mirror*, has since admitted: 'I was not at all sceptical of the American claims over the success of the "smart" bombs. We treated the war in a comic-book style: how "we" shot down "their" Scud with our Patriot. I was not aware the Americans were lying. I was never aware of the toll of human life in Iraq.' He added: 'If I have an excuse it would be that I was a prisoner of the job. I just didn't think enough about it all.'

He said he was in an extremely difficult situation. 'I forbade the use of the phrase "our boys" and tried not to be jingoistic. But then I had a Jewish proprietor who was exceedingly anti-Arab. You had to work round him.' Representations of 'precision' warfare on television and the press reinforced each other constantly – the primary aim being to ensure continuing public support for the 'war'. Descriptions applied to allied weaponry were always positive: sophisticated, super, spectacular, awesome, stunning, brilliant, smart, precise, accurate, amazing, incredible. For the enemy the descriptions were the opposite: dirty, crude, primitive (the Iraqi 'supergun' was an exception – but that was being constructed by British firms). Allied onslaughts always provoked superlatives (such as the 'greatest aerial bombardment in history') behind which the human suffering was hidden. Throughout the crisis and massacres the military monopolised the agenda and the language in which it was articulated – the glorification of military technology was the inevitable consequence and a crucial ingredient of the propaganda project. The habitual soundbite nukespeak of the military (and their fellow travelling 'experts' and politicians), which has been identified by Paul Chilton (1982; 1983), became the unproblematic massacrespeak of the media in 1991.

The *Sun* on 18 January said: 'The Allied blitz on Baghdad and other Iraqi targets – the biggest air raid in history – was also a victory for the state of the art technology packed into the Tornados and American F15E bombers... The cruisers aimed at Saddam Hussein's key installations are believed to have landed exactly where intended. Again sophisticated technology gave the missiles their fantastic precision.' Next day US Flight Leader Col. Al Whitley was quoted as saying the Stealth was so accurate and sophisticated 'you could choose to take out the men's room or the ladies' room'. US Air Force commander was 'delighted' with the 'pinpoint accuracy of the raids'. Mad dog Saddam's palace was shattered after a 'pinpoint blitz' by allied missiles. The paper's resident 'military expert' said the 'amazing accuracy of the Allies air power held the key to victory'.

After the Second World War the effects of the fire bombing of thousands of civilians in Dresden by the allies was kept secret for years. Only then was the military forced to respond to allegations of 'indiscriminate bombing'. (Best 1980) Such a phrase was totally absent from the Gulf coverage. High technology had supposedly cleansed warfare strategies. As the Falklands War leader Marshall Lord Bramall commented in the *Express* on 18 January: 'In the Second World War we indulged in massive area bombing because we could not make the planes more accurate. But now they can locate targets with infra-red which allows you to get your weapons right on target.' He said such 'pin-point accuracy' was vital to 'allow the Allies to keep the high moral ground'. On 19 January, the *Express* carried photographs across two pages showing a bomb hitting its target, thus complementing the television coverage of this same event. Under the headline 'Bombing so precise even experts gasped', the copy ran: 'The spectacular surgical precision of allied bombing against Iraq was displayed to the world yesterday. The first combat video of the war showed laser controlled smart missile blowing the airforce headquarters in Baghdad to smithereens... The display had even defence experts gasping in amazement.' An RAF air chief is quoted: 'It is amazing. In this case hi-tech weapons are real war winners.'

An emphasis on 'precision' warfare was also evident in the US press. Robert C. Toth, in the *Los Angeles Times* of 20 February, for instance, in assessing the lessons learnt by the US for any future conflict with the Soviet Union, claimed US tactical intelligence had 'precisely pinpointed targets, even in downtown Baghdad'. And the paper's 'victory celebration' editorial of 28 February, following the 100-hour rout, persisted with the precision myth (and the myth of the credible enemy): 'Iraq was a formidable fighting force. But that army utterly crumbled in the face of a well-conceived, well-planned and rather precisely executed campaign of coalition forces.'

Brian Easlea (1983) has tracked the psychological origins of militarism in the imagery of distorted sexuality, rooting it in male, sexist fears and hatreds. Traditionally men have transferred their emotional 'deadness' into the creation of death. Significantly, during a exultant profile of the B52 bombers in the *Sun* of 24 January, a Major Cole is quoted as saying: 'The devastation underneath these babies is incredible.' In other words, the mass deaths to be inflicted by these bombers is to be a source of celebration, wonder even. Men have given birth to massacres. A major general is quoted: 'The B52 has a mystique about it. Because of its destructive power it has a sense of awesomeness.'

The *Los Angeles Times* B52 profile of 16 February 1991 also described the bomber in typically glowing terms: 'The great airborne Cold Warrior has taken on a new mission blasting away at Saddam Hussein's vaunted Republican Guard. Although the planes are older than most of their pilots they bring to this latest conflict a package of state-of-the-art electronics and smart weaponry.' And while the B52 is used for 'carpet-bombing' an area indiscriminately, the paper managed to link the myths of precision, clean, smart warfare to it: 'Even when its bombs are dropped from miles in the air the B52 is surprisingly accurate. The addition of sophisticated electronic defence systems and 'smart' weapons enables the huge planes to fly low-level missions with complete safety.' Moreover, this glorification of advanced military technology is part of what Luckham identifies as the 'fetishism' of the weapon which permeates all levels of the culture. (op cit: 2-3) Accordingly, weapons are given human attributes and names being absorbed into the general technology of modern popular cultures in which war is 'a particularly extreme example of the belief that any problem can be solved if technology and capital are applied to it in large enough doses'.

Indiscrimate: precisely

The stress on precision warfare served to detract attention not only from the majority of bombs which missed their targets but also from the most commonly used bombs which were the opposite of precise. They were part of the secret war. As Paul Rogers has argued (1991: 26): 'Alongside the "precision war" of laser-guided bombs and pinpoint missiles, there was a second type of war. It was fought with munitions specifically designed to kill and injure people on the widest possible scale ... Their use was largely censored during the war – sometimes by and sometimes from the media.'

Like napalm and the early cluster bombs, modern area impact munitions (as they are called) are intended to devastate a wide area rather than confine their destruction to a precise target. They do this by creating a mist or cloud of explosives which is then detonated such as the fuel air explosive, or by sending out a large number of bomblets, as with the cluster bomb. The most commonly used area impact bombs used were cluster bombs and multiple launch rocket systems. The death and destruction they cause is colossal. While 297 Tomahawks were fired during the massacres and were so central to the 'precision' myth, most coverage failed to mention that some of them used such non-precision weapons as the cluster bombs. Ralph Vartabedian, in his *Los Angeles Times* report of 24 February 1991 ('Ordnance: high-tech's gory side'), even managed to link the 'precision' myth to his coverage of cluster bombs, nicknamed 'Adam', 'Beehive' and 'Bouncing Betty'. He reported that the 'Beehive' spewed out 8,800 tiny flechettes of razor sharp darts but then went on to say that it killed troops 'with deadly precision'.

One of the main purposes of the massacres was to vindicate the enormous expenditure placed on such weaponry in the previous decades. Moreover, a report by the American human rights group, Middle East Watch, *Needless deaths in the Gulf War* (1991: 120-121), criticised the use of enormous numbers of 'dumb weapons', with 25 per cent accuracy, in built-up areas in total contravention of Article 57 of the First Protocol of the Geneva Convention. The report commented: 'Public statements by Bush Administration and Pentagon officials during the war suggested that the choice of weaponry took into account the need to minimize civilian casualties. But this claim is yet to be squared with the Pentagon's public admission that less than 9 per cent of the total tonnage of ordnance dropped during the air war was precision-guided bombs.'

Myth of the technological success

No weapon achieved more fame during the massacres than the Patriots which were quickly deployed in Israel after Iraq launched Scud missiles on Tel Aviv. Gen. Schwarzkopf told reporters that 'the Patriot's success, of course, is known to everyone. It's 100 per cent'. After the ceasefire, President Bush went in person to the Raytheon plant where they were made to congratulate the company whose orders suddenly soared. The *Sun* on 28 February described it as 'the most famous weapon in the world'. As late as 10 September 1992, the *Independent* reported: 'Patriot missiles, as every American schooolboy knows, were the ones that shot down Iraqi Scuds in the Gulf war.'

But evidence released subsequently suggests the media were pushing yet another myth, reproducing military/government lies. On 18 January 1991, the Patriot, rapidly deployed to Israel in face of the Scud threat, appeared to achieve a historic 'knockout' – being the first defensive missile to destroy an offensive missile. As Sherwood says (1992), that first shot 'remains a defining moment embedded in the country's consciousness'. Yet that famous first shot hit at nothing. Satellite information suggested the target had come from two improbable places – the Gulf or Iran. The army ruled out these possibilities. Sherwood concludes: 'Most probably, the "Scud" was a Patriot computer glitch.'

Further evidence debunked the Patriot myth. A US armed services committee report, quoted in the *Guardian* of 17 August 1993, concluded: 'A post-war review of photographs cannot produce even a single confirmed kill of a Scud missile.' And on 22 November 1993, the *Guardian* reported Moshe Arens, Israeli defence minister during the Gulf conflict, Dan Shomron, Israeli chief of staff at the time, and Haim Asa, a member of an Israeli technical team dealing with Patriot missiles, saying that Patriots intercepted just one, or possibly none of the Scuds.

According to Alexander Cockburn (1991a), '158 Patriots were fired at 47 Scuds within Patriot coverage. Very few of the successfully intercepted Scud warheads were prevented from hitting either a structure or the ground and exploding. Moreover, large numbers of Patriots, some fired at real Scuds and some at radar false alarms, came down and exploded themselves, contributing substantially to the casualties and damage'. Miller reports (1991) that before Patriots were used 13 Scuds damaged 2,698 apartments and injured 115 people. With Patriots in use 11 Scud attacks damaged 7,778 apartments, wounded 168 people and killed at least one person. During the 'war', US military briefers claimed 81 Scud launchers had been destroyed. But afterwards former Marine Corps analyst Scott Ritter claimed no mobile Scud launchers were destroyed and only 12 of the 28 fixed launchers were eliminated. (Macarthur 1993: 250)

The myth of the Stealth and Tomahawk successes

Robert C. Toth, reporting in the *Los Angeles Times* of 20 February 1991, was typical in his comments on the weapons systems deliberately tested in the conflict for the first time: 'The first performances of new weapons such as Stealth F117s, Tomahawk cruise missiles and the Patriot anti-Scud defence system have been a success.' But following the massacres it was revealed that two of the most celebrated weapons, the US airforce Stealth jet and the navy's Tomahawk cruise missile struck considerably fewer targets than was claimed at the time. Edward Luttwak commented (1991): 'The cruise missiles much celebrated in the press and costing a million dollars each were least useful. A very great help during the first hours when they could be launched without risking a pilot against the then unknown dangers of Iraq, they simply could not compete against cheaper weapons when those could be used with impunity.'

Air force officers estimated just after the massacres that the Stealth's laser-guided bombs hit 90 per cent of their targets. But in a classified analysis, reported in the *Washington Post*/the *Guardian* (11 April 1992) it was said that targets in only 60 per cent of missions were hit, while the Tomahawk hit targets only slightly more than half the time. In any case assessment at all times can only be tentative being based on the subjective interpretation of bomb damage. Many targets were hit many times by a variety of planes, such as F16s, FA18s or A6 attack jets so it is virtually impossible to determine which aircraft inflicted what damage. Claims of Stealth and Tomahawk successes during and immediately after the massacres were mere propaganda stunts – which the press gladly lapped up.

Silencing the horror: the casualties cover-up

The ideological frame in which the necessary new militarist adventure in the Middle East was presented in the dominant media remained remarkably consistent throughout the August 1990 to March 1991 period – and at root was extremely simple. Hence its strength and seductive qualities. Saddam was the monster threatening the world; the allies were fighting a clean war for a just cause. Integral to this frame was the denial of the reality of the horror in the fog of war. As Claude Le Borgne argues, the war was, in fact, a series of 'discreet massacres'. (Le Borgne 1992)

The new militarist media machine attempts to revolutionise the image of war. This is to be, essentially, a non-war war. A war with all the blood and butchery and death drained out of it. It has to be quick, clean, cool and victorious. A harmless, heroic spectacle. So it has to be a war fought in secret. Journalists were kept away from virtually all the slaughter. Out of sight – out of mind. Most newspapers carried only one picture of a dead Iraqi – following the massacres at Khafji at the end of February 1991. In contrast, coverage constantly focused on the image of the dead cormorant, a victim, supposedly, of Saddam the 'eco terrorist' who had caused the oil slick disaster in the Gulf. Yet it became known afterwards that the images had been drawn from another Gulf oil slick disaster and that some of the firing of Kuwaiti oil wells resulted from allied bombing. (Seager 1992: 25; Pilger 1992: 127)

Gen. Schwarzkopf constantly refused to be drawn on the issue of casualties. This was nothing new. The military had been reticent over casualty figures (defined in militaryspeak as 'collateral damage') during the slaughters of new militarist adventures in Grenada and Panama. Schwarzkopf tried to legitimise the strategy, describing talk of the dead as the 'pornography' of war. The US military were determined to have no repeat of Vietnam when they had tried to explain the complex war in the simple language of body counts, BDAs (bomb damage assessments) and KIA (killed in action). The Vietnam conflict appeared to have no clear beginning or end, no clearly marked goals. The 'body counts', it could be argued, were an attempt to bring order to the anarchy, to establish a quantifiable assessment of the military's performance. Susan Jeffords comments (1989: 7): 'That false numbers were reported, that anything counted as a body – an arm, leg, torso – and that non-enemy bodies were included in the count confirm the extent to which the technology of performance became ascendant.'

By the time of the Gulf conflict, the propaganda rhetoric had changed. On February 5, the *Mirror* reported Gen. Schwarzkopf as saying the allies were at pains to avoid hitting innocent people. 'We are not, not, not, not, not deliberately targeting civilian casualties and we never will. We are a moral, ethical people.'

Silencing strategies

Most of the press followed a similar line to the military's, silencing the horror in a variety of ways:

- behind the crass 'go get 'em boys' gung-ho massacrespeak of the military sound-bites;
- through the cold, technical jargon of the constantly quoted military 'experts';
- through exultant warmongering;

- through smearing Iraqi talk of casualties as propaganda; (Glasgow University Media Group 1991: 1)
- through the elimination of Iraqis with the demonisation of Saddam Hussein and the simple equation Saddam = Iraq;
- through the representation of the 'enemy' as animals and so exonerating the perpetrators of the atrocities from any guilt. Much of this discourse reproduced the traditional rhetoric of Victorian imperialism in which the enemy were dismissed as 'savages' in need of suppression by the 'civilising hand' of the British (Featherstone 1993);
- through the emphasis on precision, clean warfare.

Victoria Brittain, assistant foreign editor of the *Guardian*, argued that journalists were forced, as during the Vietnam war, to 'switch off' from all the horror. 'The experts and most of the Western journalists reporting the Gulf war today, have switched off too and are reporting a monstrous and needless human and ecological tragedy with detached earnestness and close attention to technological detail.' Terry McCarthy, in the *Independent* of 12 February 1991, however, highlighted the devastation caused by the B52s in Vietnam. The caption to the photograph comments: 'In Vietnam, the Americans flew fewer than 400 sorties a day. Iraq has been subjected to 2,000.' The inferences were easily drawn. But even the *Independent* was trapped within an ideological frame which ultimately placed blame on 'Saddam'.

The construction of the merry massacres

Another way in which the press hid the horror of the massacres was to hype them into a fun event. Barbarism became a big joke; a Hollywood-style media extravaganza complete with dramatic action, 'heroic' endeavour, the noble struggle against an evil, global threat – and laughter. The press faced an enormous dilemma resulting from the contradictions of new militarist adventures. The military strategy prioritised the use of air power (it was safer and kept the enemy at a distance, for instance). But with the absence of any credible 'enemy' fighting force, and the dull repetitiveness of the allied attacks, the war rapidly became 'boring'.

This was all the more paradoxical since war reporting traditionally represents the summit achievement for the reporter. As Don McKay of the *Mirror* commented: 'It's every reporter's wish to cover a war. It's the ultimate news story.' Or as George Esper, of Associated Press, wrote (somewhat overcome by idealism) in the *Los Angeles Times* of 17 February 1991: 'We are seduced by its glamour and romance ... We take pride in staying the course and pursuing the truth. We are driven by belief in the people's right to know. We treasure the competition among us as well as the camaraderie.'

But, reporting from Bahrain, McKay summed up the problem of Gulf war boredom in this way: 'With the loss of the Tornados in the early days of the conflict there were ten days of "wonderful stuff". After that even the war became a doorstep. I kept sending over copy – a couple of marriages, a murder scoop even. But little of it was used. It became exceedingly boring. On the launch of the ground war I returned to London hoping to go to Kuwait to cover the attack. But it was over so quickly. So I was left thinking: How dare you finish this war when I'm back in London feeling a mixture of jealousy and frustration.'

Not every one felt the same. Michael Evans, London-based defence correspondent of *The Times*, said: 'I never once found it boring. I was zinging from the beginning to the end.' Yet Martin Woollacott, who filed reports from Baghdad, Amman, Syria and Kurdistan during the crisis, massacres and aftermath for the *Guardian*, also remarked on how the war became 'deeply boring'. 'During the air war there were meaningless daily packages of statistics telling us nothing about anything in military or human terms.'

The populars solved the problem of the 'dull war' by concentrating on celebrities (the royals, pop stars and television personalities) and human interest angles, making it all a bit of a giggle. As Roy Greenslade, *Mirror* editor, remarked, the war after a while got boring and so his paper was obliged to 'mix it up' with 'razzamatazz and entertainment'.

He explained: 'Tabloids are both a contributing factor and a response to the alienation of the working class from political life, social relationships and their old traditions of solidarity. In fact, tabloid newspapers have had on their agenda since the early 1970s the debunking and lampooning of the political process. Trade unionists have helped in this process. People have turned their backs on the political system and industrial organisation and sought a kind of leisure. Thus a serious subject, if it is not to lose their attention, has to be covered in a way to feed their diet of fun. This even includes war.'

One of the longest running stories in the paper was archetypally mediacentric – being over a leader in the *Sunday Times* which criticised the performance of the royals during the 'war'. 'Kilroy in telly punch up' (13 February, page one); 'What a right royal fuss' (Anne Robinson comment; 14 February); 'You can't take her anywhere' (on Sarah Ferguson, then wife of Prince Andrew and known commonly in the tabloids as 'Fergie'; 16 February) and 'Fergie father in jibe fury' (19 February) were among the follow-up stories. Hardly any other story received such treatment.

Following a similar agenda, the *Sun* tried to encourage its women readers to 'Flash your knickers for our brave boys: Go give 'em a frill', accompanying the story with a picture of a woman bending over and showing her knickers. 'Who bares wins', the paper added. Pushing puns to the limit, it said: 'Our boys know all about military briefings, but if you look racy in lacies we want you to give em a cheeky low-down briefing of your own.' Later the paper reported: 'Wives say knickers to Iraq'. Lovesick army wives were supposedly bombarding 'fellas' with their favourite lingerie.

And when Harlow Council supposedly ordered workers to tear down a Union Jack 'backing our Gulf heroes', the *Sun* (reporters and Page Three girls etc), continuing its well-established strategy of attacking 'loony left' authorities,[3] staged its own mock invasion of the town hall in protest. Thus on 31 January, it gave more coverage to its story '*Sun* sends Patriots into Harlow' than to the massacre at Khafji. 'The *Sun*'s Patriots stormed into the shamed town of Harlow yesterday to give the town hall lefties a rocket ... We flew a Union Jack, the size of a bus, cheered on by citizens who are disgusted at the council's ban on flags supporting Our Boys in the Gulf.'

On 29 January, it carried Gulf 'war' jokes under the headline 'Giggle at the Gulf'. For example: 'Iraqi soldiers are changing their socks every day – because they smell de-feet.' On 2 February, the paper invited its readers to learn the 'hilarious new slang used by US troops in the Saudi desert.' For instance: BAM (Big Assed Marine: women officers); BMD (Black Moving Object: Iraqi woman dressed in Arabic robes). Even the military hardware was transformed into a merry massacring machine. A 'profile of the B52 bombers' (famed for its 'carpet bombing' of Iraqi conscripts) described them as the 'Jolly Green Giants'.

Behind the merry myths: the massacres

Yet following the 42-day round-the-clock bombardment of Iraq by 'the greatest power ever assembled' the devastation caused what a March 1991 UN survey described as a 'near apocalyptic' tragedy. The survey warned that it threatened to reduce 'a highly urbanised and mechanised society to a pre-industrial age'. Saeed Khanum spoke of the 'post nuclear holocaust' landscape of Basra during the January/February period. (Khanum 1991; see also Cainkar 1991)

In September 1992, an international team of researchers from Harvard estimated that 46,900 children under five died in Iraq between January and August 1991 as an indirect result of the bombing, civilian uprisings and UN economic embargo. Those suffering the most were Kurds, the very people the coalition sought to support in their conflict with the Iraqi regime. The *Independent* of 24 September 1992 carried these details under the headline 'War tripled child deaths in Iraq'. The report was worth only ten lines and was buried in an inside page. Focusing just on civilians and soldiers still minimises the enormity of the tragedy. The conflict, it could be argued, involved the deliberate destruction of the Iraqi social and economic infrastracture. Louise Cainkar (1992) commented: 'The decimation of the infrastructure of Iraq was the aim of coalition bombing, a goal achievable only with good intelligence and highly sophisticated technology and weaponry. It naturally follows that most of the civilan casualties of this war would result from this destruction and not from direct hits on civilian areas.'

---

3 See Curran, James (1987): *Media coverage of London councils*; Goldsmiths' College; London; reprinted as (1987): 'The boomerang effect: the press and the battle for London', *Impacts and influences: essays on media power in the twentieth century*; Methuen; London/New York pp 113-140.

The massacres created 1.8 million refugees, of whom 30,000 were estimated to have died. Moreover, the Overseas Development Institute estimated that at least 40 low and low-middle income countries faced the economic equivalent of a natural disaster as a result of the massacres. (Pilger 1991a and b) Many ancient and valuable archaeological sites in cities such as Nineveh and Babylon (the cradle of civilisation) were bombed. No one will ever know how many Iraqis were killed. To the elites of both sides they were irrelevant. Such silence is represented as 'inevitable'. And yet casualties in less well observed conflicts have been known more precisely. Moreover, while little attempt was made to count bodies considerable precision was applied to Iraqi military equipment losses.

Bulldozed and burnt out of existence

Many Iraqi bodies were bulldozed both dead and alive into mass graves. (Rosenfeld 1991) News of this activity only emerged after the end of the massacres. Three Labour MEPs Coates, Crampton and McCubbin pointed out in a letter to the *Guardian* on 12 March, 1991, that such mass burials were contrary to Articles 16 and 17 the Geneva Convention 1945. But this view is strongly challenged by US journalist Rick Atkinson. He expresses surprise at the 'hue and cry' which arose over the strategy, 'as if burying the enemy was less humane than eviscerating them with tank fire or eleven thousand artillery rounds'. (Atkinson 1994: 397) He concludes: 'In truth, similar tactics had been used since the advent of armored warfare in World War 1; against the Japanese, beginning with the bloody fight for Tulagi in the South Pacific, US Marines had buried the enemy in their caves and bunkers whenever possible rather than dig them out. The tactic had been reviewed by a United Nations conference on conventional weaponry during the late 1970s and left unregulated as a "common, longstanding tactic entirely consistent with the law of war".'

Many Iraqi victims were also burnt to ashes making identification more difficult. As Robert Fox, of the *Telegraph*, who spent two days after the massacres travelling 235 kilometres along the front line, commented: 'They were consumed in the most terrible way: there is so much fire there is so much fissile capacity in these weapons now, I don't mean to be disgusting but they are just incinerated ... A terrifying, novel aspect of this campaign is that not even the bones remain.'

A Saudi military source quoted on 1 March radio news bulletin a figure of 65,000 to 100,000 Iraqi casualties. Julie Flint, in the *Observer* of 3 March said 100,000 were killed and injured. By mid-March the figures were being revised upwards with the *Christian Science Monitor* reporting estimates of 100,000 to 200,000 while on March 20 the *Independent* reported that up to 190,000 Iraqi soldiers had not been accounted for. Gen. Colin L. Powell, chairman of the US Joint Chiefs of Staff, suggests in his autobiography (1995: 525-526) that half of Iraq's 1 million-strong army were based in the Kuwait theatre, and that half of them were eliminated during the conflict.

Three months after the slaughter the US Defense Department estimated that 100,000 Iraqi troops had been killed. (Cohen and Gotti 1991: 270) Dr Sa'adoun Hammadi, deputy prime minister of Iraq, said that 22,000 civilians had been killed in air raids on Baghdad alone. (Heikal 1992: 316) But the *Telegraph*'s defence editor and eminent military historian John Keegan (1993: 384) went so far as to say that there were no civilian casualties at all.

Christopher Lee, a defence analyst of Emmanuel College, Cambridge, who acted as the BBC Radio 4's military expert through the Gulf 'war', monitored all the allied briefings and was convinced journalists had failed to press the military hard enough over the casualties issue. Their relationship with the military was far 'too cosy'. 'They gave the impression of just re-writing what the spokesmen said and they didn't publicly press home questions day after day. For example, what are Iraqi casualties even if they knew what the answer was going to be so that they could say to people at home we are asking on your behalf.' [4]

Mark Laity, of the BBC, in contrast, argued that journalists should not get involved in the 'morality of war'. 'I think a lot of criticism comes from people who seem to think that the only story was whether bombs killed people. Well, of course they do. The big story was were the allies going to win the war.' [5]

The silencing role of massacrespeak

Central to the dominant new militarist ideological frame was the denial of the humanity of the Iraqi conscripts. This draws on a tradition of war propaganda. Phillip Knightley has recorded the racist way in which the German enemy in the two world wars and Vietnamese were similarly dehumanised. (Knightley 1982) During the massacres, the Iraqis were constantly described as 'animals', 'beasts'. The military called them 'turkeys', 'rats', 'ducks', 'ants', 'fish'. The military destroyed 'targets' not people. Kuwait was described as a 'target-rich environment'. Indeed, Luckham (op cit: 18) has identified how strategic discourse borrows 'heavily from the rhetoric of theatre, organised sport and the capitalist market place'. Thus the slaughter never once drew any outrage from any of the press.

The Iraqi conscripts were, in any case, always enveloped and eliminated in the demonisation of Saddam Hussein. The military were never slaughtering thousands, they were, instead 'kicking Saddam's arse'. As Paul Johnson described the Americans in the *Mail* of 19 January: 'They are giving Saddam hell and they love it. It's as much as they can do to stop themselves telling you they are bombing Iraq back into the Stone Age.' But that's alright. God's on our side. 'A markedly high proportion of British pilots are regular churchgoers,' Johnson continued.

---

4   Lee, Christopher quoted in transcript of BBC Radio Radio Four 'File on Four' programme 9 April 1991.pp 11-12.

5   Laity, Mark quoted in transcript of BBC Radio Four 'File on Four' programme 9 April 1991 pp 12-13.

When civilian casualties were reported more widely the dominant view focused on the inevitability of such horrors. Joe Haines, writing in the *Mirror* of 9 February, summed up this view: 'I don't want to appear unfeeling but the constant harping on civilian deaths in Iraq verges on hysteria. Those who support the war but turn every civilian death into an occasion for breast beating are refusing to face up to the reality of what they have chosen to do. Civilians get killed in wars. They always did and always will.' Another strategy, implicit in all the coverage but often stated overtly, was to place all blame on Saddam. Or the focus was shifted almost exclusively to the 'atrocities' committed by Iraqis in Kuwait, Israel or Saudi Arabia. There was also the suspicion always that casualty figures were part of Saddam's propaganda project.

Post-war perceptions

Two years after the end of the massacres a new version of the 'precision, clean war' myth emerged to reinforce the original ones. The *Independent* reported on its front page of 10 March 1993, a former analyst in the US Defense Intelligence Agency, John Heiderich, as saying that as few as 1,500 Iraqi soldiers may have been killed by allied forces. Christopher Bellamy, defence correspondent, reported: 'Mr Heiderich calculates an absolute maximum of 6,500 dead and 19,500 wounded but only if all Iraqi vehicles struck had full crews. In fact, they did not and the number of Iraqi dead is estimated at 0.5 per cent of those in theatre, or 1,500.'

David Fairhall, who covered the 'war' from Riyadh for the *Guardian*, said that journalists had tried very hard to secure more information on casualty figures but they had generally met 'a brick wall'. But then after the war, the casualties 'were far less than we feared'. He continued: 'We assumed very high numbers of casualties, basing that on worst case intelligence assessments. In fact, a lot of Iraqis were never there. They had left before it all started.' He did not believe that talk of the Iraqi army as being the fourth largest in the world by his intelligence sources involved a deliberate attempt to deceive. 'People usually do make errors in wars. They tend to look at wars through very prejudiced lenses and everyone tends to exaggerate the situation.' He also expected more allied casualties. 'If the Iraqis had met inexperienced Western troops in a straightforward ground battle they would have given a good account of themselves. British military chiefs warned people back home that we should realise we could be taking heavy casualties. That was my conditioning.'

Coalition contrasts

In contrast to the silence over the Iraqi casualties the press predictably gave massive coverage to the relatively few allied deaths. But it remained unclear after the massacres exactly how many allied soldiers were killed in and out of combat and by 'friendly fire'. Arab countries in the coalition have failed to provide casualty figures; Palestinians were often counted as non-persons. Indeed, Chris Buckland, in his report in the *Express* of 7 March 1991, throws into doubt the figures of war dead. He wrote: 'Saudi Arabia claimed only one person in Riyadh was killed by Scuds. Hospital staff however say 54 were killed in one attack but as 53 were Third World workers they didn't count.' The 'miraculously low' allied figures may, in fact, be not so low. Official Ministry of Defence figures issued after the war gave 23 Britons killed between 23 August 1990 and January 16 and 24 killed during the 'war' (plus four special forces soldiers). Certainly, fewer British soldiers died in the Gulf than during normal 'peacetime' periods.

During the blitz of Iraq the focus was directed at their potential threat to captured allied airmen; Iraqi civilians were completely ignored. Thus the *Mirror* headlined on 29 January: 'Allied blitz 'hits captive air crews'.' When the British Tornados were lost or the crews went missing there was enormous coverage. Relations, pen pals were interviewed; brave mums of hero pilots said their patriotic pieces: 'If he has died I hope he has done so to make a better world for our children' (*Mirror*, January 22). Fellow pilots were shown weeping for their comrades. Deaths always occurred during heroic battle.

On 23 February, the *Mirror* reported the first British soldier lost in action as a 'heroic squaddie lost during a fierce gun battle'. He was involved in a 'fearsome battle' against 'overwhelming odds'. But alongside the one British death the report buries the fact that 'scores of Iraqis were believed killed or wounded' in the 'battle'. Great emphasis was given in the run-up to the massacres on the capabilities of the RAF Tornados' JP233 'runway denial system'. But, in fact, the Americans had pulled out of the programme early on because of justifiable fears that it would cause unnecessary casualties forcing pilots to fly extremely low. According to Michael Spaven, the RAF was flying to win its political battles in Whitehall. It needed to justify 20 years of concentrated effort on low-level bombing and its specialised 'offensive counterair' role in attacking enemy airfields. Such coverage during the 'war' would have questioned the patriotic endeavour of 'our' brave pilots – and so rarely appeared. (Spaven 1991)

Israel and the myth of vulnerability

When Israel came under attack from Scud missiles coverage reached hysterical levels. Only one person was to die from these attacks yet constant reports focused on the enormity of the threat facing the country. As so often happens in media coverage, fears are translated in the heat of the moment into reality. Thus, when a Scud missile first hit Tel Aviv on January 17, it was reported on the midnight news on Channel 4. By 1.38 am the BBC was reporting falsely that Israel was retaliating; soon afterwards Channel 4 reported that the missiles had chemical warheads. The *Mirror* of 18 January reported falsely in its front page lead: 'Pentagon sources were reported as saying Israel is poised to make a 'massive retaliatory strike' and the Israelis immediately launched an air counter attack.'

Next day, the paper was saying, wrongly again, that the Israelis would definitely launch revenge attacks on Iraq. Such falsehoods were willed on by accompanying comment. For instance, the editorial of the *Mirror* of 19 January was rhetoric of a kind never directed at the allied bombardments: 'The Iraqi missile onslaught on Israel was an act of barbarous treachery. In its half century of life this brave little country has always followed the Biblical precept of eye for an eye. If the Israelis now strike back at Saddam who under God's heaven can blame them?' *Mirror* editor Roy Greenslade has since revealed that all the editorials at the time were compiled by the newspaper's proprietor Robert Maxwell, a fervent supporter of Israel. 'I was prepared to go along with this. It left me free to run the rest of the editorial operation as I wanted.'

Iraq's attacks were certainly designed to spread terror among civilians and thus contrary to Article 51 of the Geneva Conventions. But they were symbolic rather than militarily significant; attempting to actualise the claimed linkage between the Israeli occupation of the West Bank, Golan Hights and Gaza with the invasion of Kuwait. Thus it was important for the media to deny this link and responsibility for any casualties ensuing.

Richard Littlejohn, in the *Sun* of 19 January, was on hand to comment: 'Israel seized the West Bank, Gaza and the Golan Heights in a pre-emptive strike in self-defence against hostile armies massing on her borders. Iraq's invasion was straightforward theft motivated by the greed and megolomania of a deranged dictator. ... The crisis has been provoked by one man. He must not live to fight another day.' Accompanying these accounts were dramatic pictures of Israelis (usually women and children) injured in the attacks with captions highlighting the horror. The *News of the World* commented on 20 January: ''We badly need Israel to continue displaying the superhuman self-restraint it has exercised for two days in the face of outrageous provocation from Saddam's Scud missile terrorism.'

John Bulloch, Middle East expert of the *Independent*, remarked on how Israel was constantly represented as if it was facing Armageddon. This was 'total rubbish', he claimed. 'The Israelis received huge kudos for doing nothing in response to the Scud attacks. But what else could they do?' He believed the Jewish lobby was extremely powerful and that the 'whole pervading atmosphere in dominant circles' meant that the 'Israelis were seen as the good guys, the Arabs the bad guys'. And Stephen Badsey (1992: 230) suggests that Israel manipulated the international media with its 'customary sophistication' to secure a major military and political victory without firing a shot. 'Like Saudi Arabia, Israel blocked direct coverage of Scud attacks and accurate reporting of target locations after 23 January but thereafter played brilliantly on the major media weaknesses by personalising the event. The world's press was allowed within hours of a Scud attack to interview survivors in the wreckage of their homes.'

Friendly fire storms

Despite all media attempts to represent the conflict as 'heroic warfare' the facts conspired against this. Very few allied deaths occurred as a result of actual combat; while the massacres were going on the greatest threat to coalition forces was posed by allied soldiers themselves. Out of those 353 allied deaths, Lt Gen. John Yeosock, commander of all troops, said that only 46 were killed in active service. And of those 24 (52 per cent) were caused by so-called 'friendly fire' (military jargon that slipped effortlessly into the lexicon of the massacres). (Sloyan 1991) Macarthur reports that of the 467 US troops injured, 72 were injured by their own side. (Macarthur op cit: 148) Some 144 US service men and six women died during Operation Desert Storm compared with 108 deaths from early August 1990 to 16 January 1991. (Allen, Berry and Polmar 1991: 219-220).

Of the British deaths, nine were from so-called friendly fire and only one of those killed by incoming fire. The rest died as a result of 'malfunctioning equipment'. (Sackur 1991) A number of deaths originally said by the military to be the result of enemy fire were later found to be 'friendly fire' deaths. Those British 'friendly fire' casualties became the focus of massive publicity in Britain in 1992 after relatives tried, unsuccessfuly, to force the pilots responsible to attend a coroner's inquiry.

To a large extent, 'friendly fire' accidents were regarded as inevitable by the US military. A number of press reports in the run-up to the launch of the 'ground offensive' stressed this 'inevitability'. As Alan C. Miller (under the headline 'Friendly fire lurks on the front lines') wrote in the *Los Angeles Times* of 17 February 1991: 'The spectre of friendly fire, a cruel reality in every previous war – particularly modern wars – is likely to continue, perhaps even intensify.' But such a focus served to reduce the responsibility and guilt for 'friendly fire' deaths and psychologically prepare the public for any such casualties. Miller, in fact, managed to use the 'friendly fire' threat to manufacture the myth of the 'credible enemy': 'With US forces controlling the sky, an analyst says that the closer the fighting became on the ground the better for the Iraqis – given the problems this will cause for bombers trying to distinguish between the two sides from the air.'

10 Mediating massacres: The illusion of war

The myth of the Khafji battle

The 'battle' at Khafji, 12 miles inside Saudi Arabia, at the end of January 1991 came at a crucial time for both sides. The massacres were continuing. Allied forces had complete control over the air and space. As Lambakis (1995: 418) wrote: 'The battle over the control and use of space in the Persian Gulf war was as impressively one-sided on paper as it was in the theatre – simply no contest.' Kuwait had become a 'target-rich environment'. So far there had been no evidence of anything more than token resistance from the Iraqis – supposedly the fourth largest army in the world and a threat to the new global order.

Then, in the midst of the fog of war, the 'battle' of Khafji, when the Iraqis allegedly held a deserted town (though Gen. Schwarzkopf persisted in calling it a 'village') for 36 hours, provided both sides with ammunition in the propaganda war. Iraq could claim a victory. Some 11 Marines were killed, according to Gen. Thomas Kelly at a 30 January Pentagon briefing in Washington. But it later emerged they had been killed through 'friendly fire' along with 18 Saudis – not at Khafji but 150 miles to the west. (Thomson 1992: 199) Equally it was also in the interest of the US-led coalition commanders to represent Iraq as a credible threat at this stage – and the Khafji confrontation provided just that scenario.

In particular, in order to legitimise the participation in the coalition's ground assault on Kuwait of the Arab forces, an attack was necessary. In September 1990, King Fahd of Saudi Arabia had stressed at the Cairo summit that Arab forces would never join in an attack on Iraqi forces unless attacked themselves. (Heikal 1992: 232) The Khafji 'battle' provided them with just the excuse they needed. Indeed, allied commanders stressed (for PR purposes) the role of Saudi and Qatari troops in the 'battle' though it later emerged that US Marines and, for the Arabs, Pakistanis played far more significant roles.

For the allied military there were two competing imperatives: to stress: 'victory in battle' against a credible enemy and at the same time their role as victims of a dangerous, ruthless enemy poised for mass attack. Press representations dutifully helped the military in their crucial propaganda war. In fact, the reporting, tightly controlled by the US military, served to hide the reality of massacres both at Khafji and to the west. Despite all the chaos and confusion, Thomson concludes: 'In most cases the reporting of Khafji, as the allied command wanted, simply mirrored the information being put out by the briefers in Riyadh and around the world.' (op cit: 205) *Independent* maverick reporter Robert Fisk recounted afterwards how pool reporters came to do the military's work of controlling the media. As he headed to the town to investigate, an NBC reporter told him: 'You asshole; you'll prevent us from working. You are not allowed here. Get out. Go back to Dhahran.'[1]

Origins shrouded in the fog of war

The main source for the origins of the massacre was Marine Major Craig Huddleston whose words were uncritically reported by virtually all the press in Britain. Apparently, on the night of 29-30 January an Iraqi column of about 80 armoured vehicles advanced on Khafji, their turrets reversed to indicate they wanted to defect. But then, according to the official line, they suddenly turned on the Saudi forces and 'battle' commenced. Gen. Sir Peter de la Billière (1993: 250), commander of the British forces in the Gulf, in his best-selling personal account of the massacres, added a new twist to this angle saying that the Iraqis produced white flags before firing on Saudi troops.

Huddleston's comments were certainly useful in putting the blame for the massacre on the Iraqis. The *Mirror* headlined the story 'Cowards'. But the editor, Roy Greenslade, was later to regret using that headline. He said: 'I believe that was a wrong assessment of the situation. The one thing were not was cowardly. It was also what I was trying to avoid ... labelling the other side as the worthless, no-good enemy.' There was no military sense to the Iraqi attack – as all the papers were keen to stress. Without any air cover, it was simply a suicide mission. In such a situation the entry by the Iraqis into the deserted town of Khafji was more a desperate defensive action to seek the cover of buildings more than an attacking move, as it was represented in the press.

A possible scenario is that the Iraqi troops were drifting in no-man's land along the southern Kuwait/Saudi Arabian border (deliberately left deserted by the allies and recently cleared of journalists) without any communication with their military headquarters. By accident they ended up heading for Khafji where they planned to surrender. (Or, according to the *Sun*, they 'sneaked over the Saudi border'.) They could do nothing else.

---

1   Fisk, Robert recounts this in 'Tales from the Gulf', 'The Late Show'; BBC2; 20 June 1991.

Gen. de la Billière, in his later account, discounted the element of surprise in the Iraqi move: 'It was exactly what we had expected and hoped for, as it brought enemy vehicles, weapons and men out of their prepared positions and into the open where our pilots were able to see them and pick them off.' (ibid: 250) And reporting from Hafaral-Batin, to the west of Khafji, for the *Independent* on 31 January, Richard Dowden spoke of the 'first major engagement of ground forces in this area, an artillery duel started shortly after dusk'. He added: 'It appeared to have been started by the Americans. The US troops appeared to be trying to provoke the Iraqis into giving away their positions in preparation for a full-scale frontal attack.'

The US press failed to highlight the 'fake surrender' angle over the Khafji 'invasion'. John Balzar, in the *Los Angeles Times* of 1 February, focused on the role of the special forces – Navy Seals and reconnaissance Marines – who spotted the Iraqi advance on Khafji from behind enemy lines and radioed information to the army. 'By the time they determined they were surrounded it was too late,' said one Marine. In the ensuing massacre planes were said to queue up for 20 minutes to bomb their targets. 'My biggest danger was running into another US aircraft,' Lt Col. Dick White was quoted. The *New York Times*, similarly, made no reference to the 'fake surrender'.

But for the both the British and US press, determined to report the massacres in the traditional language of warfare, Khafji was represented as the launch of Iraq's 'ground war' (the *Guardian*, January 31). The *Sun*, of 2 February, spoke of an 'enemy attempt to invade Saudi Arabia'. The *Star*, of 31 February, headlined their report: 'Battle for a ghost town'; a number of papers spoke of 'fierce fighting', of a 'bloody battle'. Martin Woollacott wrote in the *Guardian* of 31 January: 'The Iraqis have struck their first blow in the ground war, that mother of all battles which Saddam Hussein professes he can win.' The next day, the *Guardian*'s front page headlined: 'Iraqis mass for surge south' and the editorial commented: 'Khafji demonstrates again what every infantryman knows. Fighting with tanks and air supremacy in open country is one thing. Street fighting in towns is bloody, quite another thing. There man, not machines, count.' The *Sunday Times* of 3 February reported: 'The Iraqis fought much harder than expected' and this had 'led to a fundamental reassessment of the morale of Iraqi troops by the Pentagon'. This is the traditional language of military strategy. Little mention of the slaughter of terrified conscripts.

Reports from Baghdad fed this interpretation where broadcasts claimed Iraqi troops had routed allied forces. In the States, the *Los Angeles Times* quoted Christopher Foss, editor of *Jane's Armour and Artillery*, praising Iraq's artillery as being superior to America's: 'When it comes to range and accuracy Iraq's 155mm howitzer will out-perform anything the US army possesses ... It will give our boys bloody hell.' Yet there was a necessary ambivalence about the overall coverage. It was necessary to show the Iraqis to be 'a better fighting force than expected'. At the same time it was impossible to deny the fact that they faced impossible odds against the coalition forces. Thus the *Sunday Times* summed up this ambivalence on 3 February. While the soldiers were preparing for the 'greatest land battle since the Second World War, they knew they faced a demoralised, starving and lice-ridden army reduced to scavenging for food among the ruins of Kuwait'. The Kuwaiti 'battlefield' was now left open for 'the biggest turkey shoot of all time'.

Massacrespeak shrouds the horror

The popular press openly spoke of massacres. 'Iraqis are massacred in bloody battle of Khafji', headlined the *Express*. 'Massacre in the desert' was the *Sun* headline of 2 February. But there was no moral condemnation involved in this definition – rather it was a dramatic, emotive word to denote merely the massive casualties suffered by the enemy. Khafji was to prove a prelude to the final allied onslaught in late February – when Iraqi casualties were to be shrouded in the endlessly repeated, deadening language of massacrespeak.

From the beginning to the end, the agenda and language of the conflict were set by the military. At Khafji, the coalition forces were fighting Iraqi soldiers (in reality, innocent conscripts) so no mercy was spared. They became non-people, animals, mere cannon fodder. In fact, it was a merry massacre. The *Guardian* of 31 January quoted a Marine: 'It felt really good. We kicked their asses.' The *Star* of the same day quoted US Captain Bill Wainwright: 'It is a joint operation and it is working like clockwork. It feels good. We're kicking their asses.' The *Express* headlined with the words of Gen. Schwarzkopf: 'We are in the business of shooting them, not counting them.'

The *Sun* of 31 January spoke of 'hundreds of Iraqis frying in their tanks'. As the massacres to the west of Khafji continued, with 'up to 60,000 men trapped in a 15-mile convoy of carnage', on 2 February the paper quoted a US pilot: 'They were virtually defenceless, sitting right on their tails waiting to be hit.' A US spokesman in Dharhan is quoted: 'Our pilots are telling us there is absolute carnage down there and that the Iraqis are sitting ducks.' On 1 February, the *Independent* and the *Star* quoted Col. Dick White as saying there were almost too many targets to choose from. 'It's almost like you flipped on the light in the kitchen and the cockroaches start scurrying and we're killing them.' The *Mail on Sunday* quoted a 'delighted marine': 'They are all over the place like headless chickens.'

This was battle against a credible enemy and so the morality was never questioned. The editorial in the *Star* of 31 January showed the extent to which the press had been so sucked in to the new militarist mindset that it had unproblematically adopted the language of massacrespeak: 'Saddam Hussein hopes that people in allied countries will be sickened by a long, bloody war. But he should not delude himnself. This is a war we are going to win. We are going to kick his ass so hard he's going to scream for mercy. We won't give him any.' There is no humanity in that language.

At the official level, there was complete confusion over the number of casualties. The Americans saw the event in public relations terms – and largely messed it up, even though they kept pool reporters away from the scene for 18 hours. First they claimed no US Marines were involved. This was to be symbolically significant in being a Saudi, Qatari 'defensive' action. But non-pool journalists on the scene saw some US Marines in action and the Americans were eventually forced to admit Marines were present.

The British first said 300 Iraqis had died: this was then amended to 30 (perhaps the first sounded too much like a massacre). According to the *Sunday Times* of 3 February, an extra '0' had been added by a typing clerk. Confusions over casualty figures continued well after the massacres. In his account, Gen. de la Billière said the Iraqis suffered 800 casualties. (op cit: 250) But Rick Atkinson, in his semi-official report of the massacres, concluded (1994: 211-212): '... thirty Iraqis had been killed and 466 captured, thirty seven wounded among them. Nineteen Saudis and Qataris had died and thirty six were wounded; an uncertain number of these had fallen to friendly fire. American losses, including those in the fighting out west were twenty five dead, nearly half from fratricide.'

Inventing the victim syndrome

While the coalition forces were inflicting a series of massacres, it was still important to represent them as victims – how else could the representation of the Iraqis as a credible enemy be maintained? Here the mediacentrism of new militarism serves a unique role for the elite. For when all is crumbling around the Iraqi leadership, Saddam Hussein can still be represented as having won a propaganda coup. John Cassidy, in the *Sunday Times* of 3 February, spoke of a propaganda victory for Saddam, despite heavy losses. The *Sun* of 1 February wrote under the headline 'Stormin' mad': 'Stormin' Norman is seething over the Iraqi propaganda coup' after 'cheeky Iraqis caught the Yanks with their pants down'.

It also highlighted the case of a woman Marine (Army specialist Melissa Rathbun-Nealy) captured by the Iraqis in a way which merely served to fuel the demonistaion of Saddam Hussein and tar all Iraqi men with a racist slur. Under the headline: 'At the mercy of the beast' the paper wrote: 'A US girl marine was at the mercy of brutish Iraqi troops last night after being captured in the Battle of Khafji'. And it continued: 'Allied military chiefs think the Iraqis, who treat their own women appallingly, might abuse or even rape their captive.' Ms Rathbun-Nealy was, in fact, released unharmed after the end of the massacres. The Iraqis had done everything to make her imprisonment comfortable. She was told by her captors that she was a hero, as brave as Sylvester Stallone and as beautiful as Brooke Shields.[2] Her greatest fear was not of Iraqi rapists but, ironically, of allied bombers hitting the place where she was being held. (Johnston, Anne 1993: 205)

---

2   See Walsh, Edward (1991): 'As brave as Stallone...Beautiful as Brooke Shields', *Washington Post*; 6 March.

Rape was to feature prominently in the demonisation of Saddam and the Iraqis in general. Yet, in fact, as became known after the end of the massacres, rapes were running at epidemic levels in the US army. These were never reported at the time. A Senate committee report estimated that 60,000 women had been sexually assaulted or raped while serving in the US armed services. And Senator Dennis DeConcini commented; 'American women serving in the Gulf were in greater danger of being assaulted by our own troops than by the enemy.'

Kate Muir (1992: 156-160) reports that on just one American ship during the 'war' 36 women became pregnant but the US navy said no fraternisation whatsoever took place on board. She quotes a Pentagon survey of 1990 which found that two-thirds of women in the forces claimed they had been sexually harassed. There was a 55 per cent increase in reported rapes and sexual assaults over the three years 1987-1990. There are no equivalent statistics for the British army but Muir says sexual harassment is a 'growing problem'. The US navy secretary was also forced to resign in 1992 over reports of sexual harassment of women in the navy. Significantly, the British media's obsession with the rape angle at Khafji meant that they missed a far more interesting point. Ms Rathbun-Nealy was the first US woman soldier captured in action, as the *New York Times* of 1 February pointed out.

Mediating a massacre: how the press covered the bombing of the Ameriyya shelter

On 13 March, the *Sun* reported, *en passant*, that a bunker in Kuwait City, housing 400 Iraqis had been blown to smithereens by one-ton shells from USS Missouri in the Gulf. No Western journalists or camera crew were on hand so this outrage went unrecorded during the massacres. But how many other such incidents occurred during the biggest bombardment in history? We will never know.

However, on 13 February, two bombs dropped from a Stealth plane (which had become a technological 'star' of the massacres) on to a shelter in the Ameriyya district of Baghdad killing as many as 1,600 people.[3] Television shots of appalling carnage were distributed around the world, though journalists at the BBC and ITN censored the worst on grounds of taste. (Glasgow University Media Group 1991: 9) The allied military first claimed it was a military bunker; the people had been put there by Saddam Hussein so that

---

3   Most reports said there were hundreds of casualties. The *Guardian* (14 February) reported 'hundreds of civilian corpses'; the *Independent* (14 February) said 'At least 400 civilians' died in the attack; the *Sun* said 'hundreds of women and children died' but that the figure of 400 was 'plucked out of the air' by the Iraqis; the *Star* said: 'While the Iraqis claimed that 500 women, children and old men had died in the bunker fewer than 40 bodies were seen being removed on stretchers'. But Cainkar, Louise (1992): 'Desert sin: A post-war journey through Iraq', *Beyond the Storm: A Gulf crisis reader*; (eds) Bennis, Phyllis and Moushabeck, Michel; Canongate; Edinburgh suggests that these figures grossly underestimate the actual casualty figures. Her on-the-spot survey immediately after the massacres showed that men had been excluded from the shelter by the time of the bombing. Local residents said the shelter could take in 2,000 when it was bombed. There were few survivors.

he could gain a propaganda victory if they were hit. In Tunisia headlines screamed: 'Shame on them' and 'Barbaric butchery'. The *Jordanian Times* said the bombing was 'living testimony to the US-led alliance's cruelty, cynicism and total disregard for human life in conducting this ugly and pointless war against Iraq'.

In a wide-ranging report published after the massacres, Middle East Watch (1991: 7) accused the US of breaking the rules of law in times of war in attacking the shelter without adequate warning. 'The Pentagon concedes that it knew the Ameriyya facility had been used as a civil defence shelter during the Iran-Iraq war but US officials gave no warning that they considered its protected status as a civilian shelter to have ended. Article 65 of Protocol 1 added in 1977 to the 1949 Geneva Conventions provides that special protection afforded civil defence structures ceases in the event that a shelter is used for military purposes "only after a warning has been given setting, whenever appropriate, a reasonable time limit and after such warning has remained unheeded".'

In Britain and the United States the ideological frame established so firmly in August 1990 provided all the tools necessary for the crisis to be resolved in the interests of the elite. Mediacentrism was exploited to deflect away the main moral dimension of the atrocity; most of the emotion provoked by the outrage was redirected away from the allies and on to either the demonic figure of Saddam Hussein or (fuelled by the myth of the 'adversary media') British television. The response of the military and political elite was prioritised; the views of the victims of the bombing and anti-war voices were either marginalised or non-existent.

Yet the nervousness with which the elite responded to images of horror confirmed the vulnerability of new militarist myths. A massive, in parts hysterical, propaganda campaign was required to shroud the reality of horror and thus ensure the public's supposed support for the massacres continued. The *Express*, summed up this jittery feeling saying 'weeping over inevitable and unavoidable enemy casualties' would 'undermine public support for the war'. No newspaper suggested that the bombing constituted an outrage, an atrocity. Such a focus would have disturbed the moral consensus so faithfully pursued by Fleet Street. The Iraqis committed murder and atrocities. Never the coalition forces.

Manipulating mediacentrism

As Steve Platt (1991) observed, the only occasion on which Fleet Street expressed 'outrage' during the massacres was over BBC coverage of the shelter disaster. 'Outrage over BBC bias' headlined one edition of the *Express*. In other words, the mediacentrism of new militarism is unproblematic – so long as events are proceeding roughly according to the wishes of the elite. But once a major crisis emerges, the myth of the 'free, adversary press' and 'independent media' is resurrected – to serve various ends. The controversy is redirected to focus on the messenger of the bad news and thus its political and moral dimensions are marginalised. The major follow-up angle in all the newspapers focused on the media coverage, though different attitudes were taken here. The plight of the victims and their families, any debate about the necessity for the continuing bombardment of Iraq, were ignored or marginalised.

The bombing came after a considerable campaign by certain sections of the British press to damn the BBC and those organisations with correspondents based in Baghdad. Columnists such as Peregrine Worsthorne in the *Sunday Telegraph* argued that they could only become propaganda mouthpieces for Saddam Hussein. Woodrow Wyatt, in the *News of the World* of 20 January, had even taken exception to a 'Panorama' programme which he claimed 'was an unbalanced and prolonged onslaught against fighting against Saddam'. The BBC was full of 'left-wing, trendy programme makers and commentators'.

The shelter bombing seemed to conform all the worst fears of those who opposed the Baghdad press pack. The overall coverage of the bombing by television predictably prioritised the elite's response. But Jeremy Bowen, of the BBC, looked distinctly distressed as he consistently refused to be drawn by anchorman Michael Buerk to say the shelter appeared to have a dual military purpose. (Some of his distress must have been due to his awareness he could not speak, in all conscience, his master's voice.) Brent Sadler, on ITN, gave a similar version. 'Ameriyya is a middle class residential area. I could see no military or strategic targets in the vicinity.'

Such eye-witness reporting could only provoke the anger of the gung-ho editors safe in their Fleet Street bunkers. *Today*, of 15 February, said the broadcasters were 'a disgrace to their country'. The *Mail on Sunday* said the coverage, not the bombing, was 'truly disgusting' and 'deplorable'. The *Express* (following up the bombing with two stories on the media controversy) criticised the broadcasters' 'insistence that they are right to report from the enemy' which demonstrated 'the degree to which they have lost touch with the very people they purport to serve'. The BBC was dubbed the 'Baghdad Broadcasting Corporation' by Conservative critics while Brent Sadler, of ITN, was accused of being manipulated by Iraqi propaganda. (Shaw 1996: 76) But the *Sunday Times* backed the journalists and said their critics should stop 'carpet bombing' them.

Transform the perpetrators of the atrocity into a victim of a propaganda coup

Here the mediacentrism of the new militarist 'vulnerable' state is exploited to mediate the massacre in the interests of the allied elite. Accordingly the coalition forces, having committed an atrocity, deflect attention from their guilt by assuming the role of victim themselves. So they become the victims of a 'propaganda coup'. The 'propaganda war' supposedly fought between Saddam Hussein and the allies was, in large part, a grotesque invention serving to legitimise the military ambitions of the allies – as the Ameriyya coverage shows.

Today, of 14 February, spoke of Saddam's 'propaganda coup'. 'With sickening haste he ordered TV crews and journalists to the scene. As bodies were still being removed Saddam has his pictures.' The editorial commented on Saddam's 'sick but skillful propaganda armoury'. According to the *Star*, of the same day, Saddam stage-managed a TV circus to convince the world there had been an allied atrocity. 'He even arranged for "grief stricken" relatives to be on hand when foreign news teams were brought to the bunker by Iraqi publicity officers. The "relatives" all spoke English and screamed and wailed into the cameras and microphones – but none of them wept.'

The *Sun*, under the headline '10 facts to damn Saddam' made a number of extraordinary claims: that Saddam's men had started fires after the initial blast and before TV crews arrived on the scene; that the civilian casualties may have been military dead, stripped of their uniforms and dumped at the scene. Saddam was a 'master of propaganda' and so would realise that 'scenes of devastation and reports of hundreds of civilian deaths could damage the allied coalition and give ammunition to anti-war campaigners'. The *Sunday Times*, of 17 February, said it was 'a propaganda victory for Saddam'.

A similar response was followed in the States. The Los Angeles Times, of 15 February, described the bombing as a 'propaganda coup for Baghdad'. In his television column the previous day, Rick de Brow said Saddam was 'clearly using it as a powerful propaganda weapon'. The paper's news story managed to transform victim into aggressor this way: 'Iraq on Wednesday delivered the equivalent of a fuel air explosive through images of charred Iraqi women and children.'

Meekly follow the military

Virtually all the press followed the military/elite line. The *Express* headlined an editorial on 14 February: 'It WAS a military bunker'. Hence the precision myth remains unscathed. Marlin Fitzwater, the US spokesman, is quoted: 'This was a military bunker which fed instructions directly into the Iraqi war machine, painted and camouflaged to avoid detection. We did not know civilians were in it.' Similarly, the *Telegraph* headlined its report: 'Military HQ was in bombed bunker, says Washington' while the *Times*' main headline ran: 'Hundreds of Iraqis killed in shelter', with a subordinate headline: 'Allied leaders claim bombed bunker was a legitimate military target'. The *Independent* headlined 'Shelter 'a military target'' and began: 'At least 400 civilians died in an attack on a Baghdad bunker described by the allies as a command and control centre.' The *Star* quoted a US spokesman in Riyadh: 'We felt comfortable that the attack was a legitimate target.'

Today said the innocent had died 'in the same camouflaged bunker in which the Iraqi military directed operations'. The *New York Times*, in its main front page story, did not direct blame at any one side but its coverage elsewhere highlighted the military justifications. In contrast, the *Mirror* led with a photograph of a victim accompanied by the headline 'Whose fault? Slaughter, says Iraq. Military target, says US' As Shaw (op cit: 102) points out, alone among the tabloids it corroborated television journalists' accounts. 'Whatever the truth, there was no disguising the horrific scenes of civilians incinerated in the worst incident yet of the Gulf War ... Correspondents said they could see no evidence of any military presence inside the wreckage.' But Shaw adds that the *Mirror* failed to follow-up the story in any way; nor did columnist Paul Foot, strongly opposed to the war, deal with it.

The *Guardian* also challenged the military line on the atrocity though it significantly highlighted the propaganda 'disaster' for the US administration. Under the headline 'US insists it hit army bunker', it reported: 'An unrepentant Bush administration courted a propaganda disaster yesterday insisting in the face of television evidence of hundreds of civilian corpses that the US precision-guided weapons had struck "the legitimate military target of a command bunker" in Baghdad.'

Blame Saddam

The demonisation of Saddam, begun in earnest on 3 August 1990, had always sought, on an ideological level, to deflect any responsibility for the crisis and later massacres away from the allies. They were morally pure. It was all so seductively simple. Whatever happened – from massacre to possible nuclear holocaust – was the fault of one man: Saddam. That was the message that was constantly drummed out. Repeat an absurdity constantly enough and people will eventually believe you. That could be the only rationale for the press's tedious and constant focus on Saddam the monster, madman etc.

Over the Ameriyya atrocity, most of the press followed the line taken by US spokesman Marlin Fitzwater and blamed Saddam – in hysterical terms. The *Star*, under the headline 'Sacrificed: Saddam herds his people to die in military bunker' wrote: 'Saddam Hussein pulled the cruellest contrick of the Gulf War yesterday. He let his own innocent people die in a military bunker ... Women and children went into the Baghdad bunker because he told them it was an air-raid shelter. But he knew the bunker was a top priority military target and due to be hit by American Stealth bombers.' *Today* wrote, under the headline 'Entombed by Saddam': 'Once again the evil tyrant has set up a human shield to protect a key military site – only this time the victims were his own people.' The *Sun* said the victims had been sent to their deaths by the Iraqi leader himself. On 15 February, the *Independent* refocused attention on the crimes of Saddam Hussein. Its editorial argued that 'horrible and tragic though the deaths in the shelter at Ameriyya were, they should not obscure the untelevised horrors of murder, mutilation and torture that President Saddam inflicted on Kurds and Kuwaitis'.

The *Sunday Times*, of 17 February, quoted a *Washington Post*/ABC poll which showed 81 per cent of Americans believed the shelter was a legitimate target while 79 per cent blamed Saddam for the deaths. The *Express* said: 'Saddam Hussein was last night accused of deliberately sacrificing hundreds of women and children in a military bunker he knew was a target for allied bombers.' Woodrow Wyatt, writing in the *News of the World* on 17 February, said it was all Saddam's fault. An editorial in the *Mirror* of 15 February commented: 'If there were innocent victims we grieve for them. But the real guilt belongs to Saddam Hussein.'

Stress the inevitability

Until the Almeriyya bombing, the media image of the massacres had been dominated by the emphasis on precision bombing, high-tech, clean warfare. Almeriyya represented the first serious threat to that imagery. The US elite resolved the dilemma by ignoring it. The bombing had merely reinforced the precision image. As the *Sun* commented: 'Allied pilots show that the bombs were delivered with pin-point accuracy and entered the building through a ventilator shaft.' The *Express* editorialised: 'Alas, the awesome precision of the allied bombing cannot guarantee that all escape.'

Another way in which the allies absolved themselves of guilt was to stress the inevitability of the carnage. First the war was clean, then it became, inevitably, dirty. Simple. Guilt implies some measure of human responsibility; inevitability, on the other hand, implies humans are victims of forces beyond their control and so not entirely to blame. Yet the atrocities could have been stopped had the will been there, they were not 'inevitable'. According to the *Guardian* of 14 February, it was 'absolutely inevitable' that civilians would be killed along the way. Such a stress on the inevitability helped the newspaper rationalise its lack of emotional outrage: 'Yesterday in Baghdad may be horrifying but it is not shocking because utterly predictable.' It suggested that the bombing may have pushed the allies faster into the ground war 'because air bombardment has lost its glossy allure'.

Columnist Robert Harris wrote in the *Sunday Times* of 17 February: 'There is a great reservoir amongst the general public most of whom reluctantly accept that dead children, burning homes and dying soldiers are a fact of war.' In the *Telegraph* of 14 February, editor Max Hastings took a similar approach: 'The tragic truth is that it is probably impossible to bring this war to a reasonably swift conclusion, at a tolerable cost in both allied and Iraqi lives, without accepting such episodes as that which took place in Baghdad yesterday as part of the price.' And Patrick Cockburn wrote in emotionally low-key terms in the *Independent*: 'The development of the allied air offensive over Iraq in the past three weeks made an incident like the bombing of the Baghdad shelter almost inevitable.' In the States, the *Los Angeles Times* sought to remind its readers of the inevitable horrors of war: 'The American people must understand that for better or worse this war will continue to horrify.'

Admit it was a 'mistake'

A number of reports immediately after the atrocity implied or admitted it was a 'mistake'. For instance, implicit in the reporting of Jeremy Bowen, of the BBC, who had stressed that he could not find any evidence of the shelter being used for military purposes, was the conclusion that the coalition forces had made a mistake. Dr David Manley, civil defence adviser to the Home Office, said on BBC2's 'Newsnight' that the shelter was definitely only used by civilians. On 15 February, Robert Fisk, in the *Independent*, quoted a somewhat ambivalent anonymous US military source. On the one hand the source was prepared to say the raid was a serious error. 'There's not a soul who believes it was a command and control bunker.' But at the same time, the source managed to blame Saddam for it. 'Saddam Hussein does put civilians in military bunkers and he is to blame for this irresponsibility. But we were wrong too.'

By 17 February even the gung-ho *Sunday Times* was ready to admit it was a mistake. And on 27 February, the US National Security Adviser Brent Scowcroft told Foreign Secretary Douglas Hurd (who had added his voice to the criticisms of the broadcasters over their coverage of the bombing) that US intelligence had been at fault over the bombing. But a mistake is morally neutral. It focuses attention on the technology of warfare and on the failure of military intelligence. Everyone makes mistakes – even heroic soldiers. There is nothing morally condemnatory about that. The bombing sparked no outrage from Fleet Street – the ideological consensus held firm in the crisis.

Show no regret for the loss of life

Most striking about the coverage in both Fleet Street and in the United States was the lack of concern for the victims of the attack. The *Guardian* did carry a moving 'Eyewitness' account under the headline 'Bodies shrunk by heat of fire' by Alfonso Rojo, of the Spanish daily *El Mundo*, who, with Peter Arnett of CNN, was one of only two Western journalists in the Iraqi capital throughout the coalition air attacks. Occasionally tokenistic regret was rapidly expressed; usually there was nothing.

An editorial in the *Mirror* of 15 February even sought to question the existence of any casualties. Iraqi civilians were only 'alleged' to have died in the bombing. Most papers followed up the atrocity with the news that opinion polls suggested the public still backed the bombing campaign. The *Sunday Times* was pleased to report that television pictures 'filmed under official Iraqi guidance' of burned babies had had little effect on their continuing support for the 'war'. Seven out of ten said the coalition forces should continue bombing.

Not giving peace a chance

The new militarist ideological framework was simple, consistent and seductive. The prioritising of the military option from 2 August 1990 was accompanied by the marginalisation of the diplomatic track; anti-war voices were marginalised, eliminated or demonised; peace moves were similarly marginalised or silenced. Peace was never really given a chance. The elite media in

Britain represented war as inevitable; during the massacres the surge to the 'greatest land battle since 1945' was represented as a sort of natural force (rather like a desert storm, in fact) flowing to an inevitable conclusion.

Demonisation of anti-war voices

Attacks on anti-war voices during the massacres reached vitriolic levels, perhaps suggesting a nervousness among the elite about the vulnerability of the lies and myths on which their strategy was based. Every possible form of abuse and stereotypical denigration was levelled at those who called for a halt to the massacres – they were 'mad', 'nutty', 'devils', 'hypocrites', 'animals', 'violent', 'traitors', 'ranters', 'unpatriotic', 'friends of terrorists', 'apologists for Saddam Hussein', 'barbarians' and so on. Virtually all the prominent Fleet Street columnists added their gunshots to the volley of invective.

Richard Littlejohn in the *Sun* of 17 January dismissed opponents of the massacres as 'pathetic posturing' protesters. 'They drive Citroen 2CVs to the wine warehouse but take their Volvos to the Dordogne in France every summer. Most of them have never done a proper day's work in their lives.' Their hero was 'Nelson Mandela, a convicted terrorist' [though a few years later he was to become the first black president of South Africa]. Similarly, Woodrow Wyatt (dubbed 'The voice of reason') commented in his 20 January column in the *News of the World* on peace protesters: 'They're the heirs of the appeasers of Hitler. They're the people who protest and demonstrate at the drop of a hat ... In our democratic society we have a fixed proportion of nutters. They just love demonstrating and protesting.'

A typical device of the press is to label people who voice views beyond the narrow limits of consensual acceptability as mad. Of anti-war campaigner Tony Benn MP, the *Sun* on 18 January 1991 said he did not need a psychiatrist, he needed 'a hospital full of shrinks'. They called him 'batty Benn'. Columnist Robert Kilroy-Silk in the *Express* of 11 February asked if former Conservative Prime Minister Ted Heath, who opposed the massacres, was 'unhinged or something'. After pop singer Sinead O'Connor objected to the massacres, the *Sun* on 15 February dubbed her a 'she devil' and dragged in their resident 'top psychologist' (a typical *Sun* ploy) who suggested 'her warped outbursts betray a tortured, troubled background'. He continued: she was seeking attention like a small child, her blood lust was common in people who think they are intellectuals, she appeared to believe she had a divine right to tell people how to behave, she was very badly emotionally abused, and so on.

Labour MPs who opposed or abstained on a motion backing the use of force were called 'treacherous misfits' who 'shame the whole nation' in the *Star* of 22 January. Brian Hitchen, in his *Star* personal column of the same day, did not mince his words in attacking the peace demonstration in London the previous Saturday. He said they were the 'usual treacherous misfits trying to knife our boys in the back' and were 'mainly made up of assorted rat-droppings, together with misguided contingents from the clergy and fringe show business'.

In a similar vein, the *Sun* of 23 January reported that 'Leftie Labour MPs who voted against Our Boys in the Gulf were blasted by *Sun* readers yesterday. Our switchboard was jammed by hundreds who said the 34 were traitors'. The *Star* returned to this same emotive theme on 1 February when, under a headline 'Traitors', it editorialised: 'How childish of Islington Council to ban kids from playing soldiers in the schoolyard. Whose side are these traitors on? If they feel so strongly about Saddam and his butchers they can go and join him in Baghdad.' This echoes Cold War rhetoric when peace campaigners were alleged to be 'commie backers' and told to go to Moscow.

After some Labour MPs protested over the bombing of the Ameriyya shelter, the *Mirror* directed its anger, not at the Stealth fighter pilots, but at the 'enemy within'. Its editorial of 15 February thundered: 'We cannot allow ourselves to be deflected by misguided, twisted individuals always eager to comfort and support any country but their own. They are a danger to us all – the enemy within.' In a similar vein, the *News of the World* of 20 January reported under the headline 'Commies hijack march': 'Extreme left-wing supporters of Saddam Hussein tried to hijack an anti-war march in London yesterday.' And the *Sunday Telegraph* of 24 February claimed criticism of the war was being led by communist-controlled front organisations.

Nailing rogue nations: the enemy abroad

Anyone or any group/nation which the press felt did not support the massacres with sufficient vigour were similarly tainted. As Traber and Davies comment: 'The media denounced such countries as virtual enemies. This was particularly the case of Jordan and the Palestinian leadership whose efforts for peace were hardly acknowledged.' (Traber and Davies 1991: 9) Thus Jordan's King Hussein, whose public stance was to appeal constantly for peace, was accused by Kilroy-Silk in the *Express* on 11 February of lining up with the barbarians – the supporters of terrorists, the hostage takers, the women and child murderers, the practitioners of chemical warfare. Richard Littlejohn, in the *Sun* on 14 February, attacked 'curiously named' Queen Nor, wife of the 'odious little weasel, King Hussein' for expressing concern for the casualties in Iraq.

In fact, King Hussein was playing a typically ambivalent game (missed by the mass-selling media which represented the conflict in simple black-and-white terms). For many years, the King, according to a number of sources, was a highly-prized CIA asset, though this is hardly ever mentioned in mainstream profiles.[4] Now, his public rhetoric was in support of Iraq, the large Palestinian majority in his country forcing him in this direction. But secret-

4 See, for instance Woollacott, Martin (1990): 'King Hussein: Peacemaker or appeaser?', the *Guardian Collection*, a 68-page magazine drawing together 13 features on the first 60 days of the crisis following the Iraqi invasion of Kuwait, in which no mention is made of his CIA links. pp 41-42.

ly, he was continuing his role developed since the early 1980s of covertly allowing Western arms to be moved through his country to Iraq. Friedman reports: '... despite the assurance to Congress that military aid to Jordan had been cut off, the flow of weapons from the US in fact continued. Bush and Baker's policy on Jordan was cynical enough to ignore even Jordan's violations of the UN embargo after the invasion of Kuwait. Between 2 August and 4 October, 1991, the State Department approved twelve new military equipment orders worth five million dollars, including items such as spare parts and components for TOW missiles, helicopter components for AH-1S Cobra, 105-mm cartridges for artillery shells and conversion kits for the M-16 rifle.' (Friedman 1993: 172)

On 31 August, Premier Margaret Thatcher met King Hussein at Downing Street for what were described as 'very frosty' talks. The *Mirror* of 1 September spoke of Mrs Thatcher giving the King 'an ear bashing'. 'Furious Premier Margaret Thatcher gave Jordan's King Hussein a dressing down yesterday. Mrs Thatcher is angry with the King for proposing deals which would reward the aggressor.' But Friedman suggests that on 14 September 1990, the Department of Trade was still continuing its normal approach to Jordan approving the sale of large quantities of British artillery shells. 'These were shells, the British knew, that were liable to be diverted to Iraq.' (ibid: 173)

Xenophobia and racism merged in many of the attacks on anti-war campaigners. Julie Burchill, describing supporters of the Campaign for Nuclear Disarmament as 'merely marginal, moaning muesli munchers' in the *Mail on Sunday* of 10 February, said of CND chairwoman Marjorie Thompson: 'Every time she speaks a battered British subconscious registers yet again some bossy Yank telling us what to do with our own country – and we don't like it. Yankee go home.'

Making peace moves a non-event

Taylor highlights the way in which, following the Ameriyya shelter bombing, 'more and more stories about the treatment of Kuwaitis by the Iraqi occupiers began to emerge from various coalition forces'. (op cit: 227) There were clearly atrocities committed by the Iraqis in Kuwait, but as ITN journalist Alex Thomson, who travelled with the soldiers, commented: 'We had been told of the killing grounds, the mass hangings and executions, we had been assured that the city's ice-rink (the ice long-since gone along with the electricity) was full of bodies. Most of the horror stories were either nonsense (like the ice rink) or exaggerated.' (op cit: 253) But the outrage over the invented atrocities took attention away from the massacres being inflicted by the allies.

Yallop, David (1994): *To the ends of the earth: The hunt for the jackal*; Corgi; London comments: 'King Hussein had been a CIA asset since 1957, the year after the Suez war. Since that time he had been paid three hundred and fifty million dollars every year by the CIA. In return, the King provided intelligence information, allowed American intelligence agencies to operate freely in Jordan and distributed part of his twice-yearly payments from the agency to Jordanian government officials who also furnished intelligence information and co-operated with the CIA.' p 47.

Reports of these Kuwait 'atrocities' also served a powerful political and ideological purpose of further marginalising the crucially important diplomatic dimension of the conflict (on-going since August 1990). The logic was clear – how could the allies talk to such barbarians? The press were in any case hyped up on the inevitability of the ground war – nothing could stop them getting it. Even the *Guardian*, most sceptical of all, was caught up in this mood. It editorialised on 31 January: 'As the ground war approaches we must expect more intensive attacks upon Iraq's infrastructure and inevitably, higher casualties.' The logic of battle had taken over. The military and political leaders (supported by an all-party consensus in Parliament) thought similarly.

Peace always did constitute the 'nightmare scenario' for the coalition. It was something to be feared rather than sought; it caused problems for the US-led coalition rather than offer any solutions. Thus when on 31 January, Fleet Street reported the peace moves by American Secretary of State James Baker and Soviet Foreign Minister Alexander Bessmertnykh (according to which hostilities would end if Iraq made an unequivocal commitment to pull out of Kuwait and make immediate steps to comply with all 12 UN resolutions) the focus was directed at the impact it had on the White House. 'Baker's peace offer rattles White House' said the *Guardian*. 'Disarray in Washington follows offer of ceasefire' was the *Independent* angle.

'Red faces at White House over Baker peace blunder' said the *Express*. Talk of peace, according to Derrick Hall, was 'shabby', 'worrying' and 'bizarre'. The following day the paper suggested 'fears were growing that France was planning another underhand peace initiative'. Its leader that day welcomed as 'reassuring' Mr Major's 'unequicoval opposition to any pause in the hostilities'. When later in February both Iran and the Soviet Union made strenuous efforts to negotiate a ceasefire the negative responses of the US and UK elites were similarly always prioritised. On February 5, for instance, the *Mirror* devoted two paragraphs to a story on an Iranian initiative headlined: 'Bush cool over peace bid'.

On 15 February, following the intervention of Soviet envoy Yevgeny Primakov, the Iraqis offered to withdraw from Kuwait (though attached a number of conditions) but President Bush quickly dismissed it as a hoax and this view dominated the press coverage. In fact, the peace move was seen as an invitation to step up the 'war' effort. The *Sun* of 16 February headlined its story 'Saddam the Sham' and editorialised: 'No amount of twisting and turning, lying and stalling can alter the fact that his latest statement shows he is a beaten man... So unfortunately the bombing must go on. It must continually until he finally recognises the futility of his war.' The *Mirror* of the same day followed the predictable line: 'Cruel hoax' was its headline. *The Times* linked its response to the mad Hussein angle: 'Saddam must be truly divorced from reality if he believed these terms would be accepted.' The *Sunday Times* of 17 February dismissed Saddam's display of 'crude political deceit and preposterous diplomatic dissembling'.

The *Los Angeles Times* also highlighted the 'hoax' angle. Its front page lead headline of 16 February ran: 'Bush rejects Iraqis' offer to leave Kuwait as 'cruel hoax''. A 'news analysis' piece by Robin Wright merely reinforced this view, using unattributed sources to promote the 'prefered approach': 'US officials and Middle East analysts believe that his government's offer – Friday to withdraw from Kuwait hedged with conditions Hussein knew Washington would instantly reject – was designed to entice the Soviet Union into serving as a wedge to split the coalition arrayed against Baghdad in the Persian Gulf.'

Indeed, prominent in some of the responses to the Soviet peace initative were echoes of old Cold War fears and stereotypes. Recent violence by Soviet troops in the Baltic states merely added fuel to these fears and the *Sunday Times* of 17 February expressed concern that a 'second Cold War' was about to begin. Thus 'any Soviet attempt to persuade Mr Bush to delay the final push in the Gulf while the Kremlin talks to Iraq must be resisted'. The offer was, however, welcomed in a number of places: King Hassan of Morocco, a coalition member, described the Iraqi move as a 'positive step along the path to peace in the region' while Tunisian, Algerian, Iranian and Jordanian leaders also reponded positively. (Hiro 1992: 366) But these views were either ignored or marginalised. On 16 February, the *Mirror* ran a story on the President of the Council for Mosques in Bradford welcoming the offer – but it covered only two paragraphs.

Moreover, President Bush coupled his denunciation of the offer with a call to the Iraqi military and the Iraqi people to take matters in their own hands to force Saddam Hussein, the dictator, to step aside. Not only had the President responded swiftly and unilaterally, without consulting coalition members, but this call represented a blatant attempt to interfere in the affairs of a foreign country – and thus, in theory, contrary to international law. Debates over these issues were virtually non-existent.

Making the Soviet deal a 'non-event'

Following the failure of the 15 February offer, the Soviets renewed their efforts to bring a ceasefire. But irrespective of the contents of any such deal, Fleet Street was busy preparing its readers for the 'inevitable' ground war with only the *Guardian* giving any support to the Russian peace moves. On 18 February, the *Mirror* reported that 'no one in London or Riyadh believes Gorbachev can deliver the peace'. Prominence was given to a statement by French Foreign Minister Roland Dumas (not usually given such a billing) that the land offensive would start 'within 48 hours'. That's exactly what the press wanted to hear.

The *Los Angeles Times* also highlighted administration doubts about the Soviet diplomacy. 'Soviet peace proposal falls short – Bush says', it headlined on 20 February while Robin Wright's 'news analysis' reinforced administration concern over the 'nightmare scenario' by constructing a neatly consensual view from his unattributed sources: 'An Iraqi withdrawal that permits

Hussein to survive as head of a still powerful military machine could leave the US and its allies with a more difficult, even more volatile situation in the Persian Gulf than it faced before the war began, according to US officials, foreign envoys and Middle East specialists.'

The eight-point peace plan agreed between Moscow and Baghdad was finally rejected by President Bush on 22 February. Frantic new negotiations were held so that next day Iraq pledged to withdraw 'immediately and unconditionally from Kuwait'. The ground offensive was officially launched. Over this period a massive disinformation campaign was launched to accompany the rejection of the peace moves and further demonise the Iraqis. The *Mirror* of 22 February reported: 'American intelligence sources said they suspected Iraq had already launched chemical weapons at allied positions.' It continued: 'Reconnaisance teams spotted tell-tale puffs of grey smoke from exploding grenades on Saudi Arabia's border with Kuwait. US commanders are convinced Saddam will order a full-scale gas attack within the first hour of the ground war.' Such reporting also drew attention away from the coalition's decision to use napalm (notorious since its widespread use in Vietnam) against Iraqi positions.

The *Sunday Times* of 24 February dismissed the peace initative with these words: 'Saddam's continued defiance in the last hours before the land offensive showed his refusal to accept the realities of his position and his contempt for Iraqi life. By holding fast to Kuwait and hurling abuse at the allies he left them no choice.' War was, in any case, all Saddam's fault and inevitable. And all the atrocities were being committed by the Iraqis: 'Yesterday's news that Iraqis are systematically executing Kuwaitis follows sickening reports of other atrocities.'

Brian MacArthur (1991: 114-115) describes the gloom that descended on the *Sunday Times*'s editorial staff just before the launch of the ground war. 'There was no land war; no statement from Bush – merely some opaque discussion in the UN about the Gorbachev plan. It was a depressed group that trooped off to Orso's that night.' But once the land war began at 1am the excitement returned. In contrast, the *Guardian* said Mr Gorbachev had 'performed a service' removing the need for a land war, while the next day the newspaper criticised Bush's speech as 'an ultimatum, not a reply to the Moscow peace plan'.[5]

Veteran US reporter Jim Lederman (1992: 320) suggests that the media's coverage of the Soviet peace attempts was distorted by 'old fashioned' Cold War stereotyping. Many reports cast doubt on Soviet motives and highlighted suggestions that it was only positioning itself for the post-war period. Bernard C. Toth, in the *Los Angeles Times* of 23 February, for instance, reported that US analysts were 'puzzled' over Gorbachev's 'attempts to play peacemaker in the Persian Gulf'. He highlighted suggestions that

---

5 Brittain, Victoria and Gittings, John highlighted these aspects of the *Guardian* coverage in a letter to the *New Statesman and Society*, 31 January 1992.

Gorbachev's 'ego may have been a factor'. Lederman comments: 'Moscow was undoubtedly trying to create a post-war role for itself. But the diplomatic effort may also have been a genuine effort to avert more bloodshed and to assist in the building of the new world order of which President Bush constantly spoke. In any case, every other country involved in the war was also positioning itself to try to grab some of the political and economic spoils so the Soviet Union was not unique in this regard.'

Bloodfest on the Basra Road: silencing the slaughter

One of the central myths about the massacres is that the 'war' had two distinct phases – first in the air, then on the ground. Such a myth accompanies the dominant view of the separation of peace and war. In both cases the simplification involved serves to marginalise certain 'subversive' views. In the first case, the myth hides the reality that most of the killing from day one went on the ground, that all the arms of the army (intelligence, special forces, navy, army, logistical support services etc) were involved from day one and before. It also marginalises the fact that crucially important in the coalition strategy were the space-based electronic systems. Moreover, the separation of war and peace marginalises the notion of the state as being at permanent (though, usually, secret) war. Military activities, in any case (particularly by special forces), began well before the air assault that launched Desert Storm. It could be argued that Desert Storm was the culmination of an 'offensive' US strategy in the region beginning as far back as 1980 with the setting up of the Rapid Reaction Forces to deal with any crisis in the region.

Even during the 'ground offensive' most of the deaths were inflicted on Iraqi conscripts by air bombers and helicopters. The main army job was collecting prisoners of war. And more importantly the myth of war obscures the reality of barbaric slaughter. As the *New Statesman and Society* commented on 21 July 1991, the evidence of the final slaughter 'is of an armed force out of rational control; an excessive and disproportionate use of force where it was not necessary'.

The myth of the credible enemy

All the 'war' scenarios carried in the press in early 1991 saw as inevitable the shift through the various stages to ultimate victory. For the dominant new militarist states this was the necessary 'war'. By early February details of the supposedly massive defences erected by the Iraqis were being featured prominently. The *Mirror*, for instance, on 1 February carried an illustration of this defensive system – including sand walls, anti-tank ditches, razor wire, anti-tank minefields, camouflaged tanks, artillery batteries, missile batteries.

But the Iraqis' massive defences were an invention of the coalition's disinformation specialists. Or did the forecasts result from intelligence failures? Richard Kay (1992: 128), who covered the massacres for the *Mail* and later wrote a short book describing his experiences, blamed faulty intelligence: 'Minefields meant to be 2,000 yards deep turned out to be only 140 yards.

Oil and napalm-filled trenches, talked of as huge reservoirs were only a couple of yards wide. The sand berms were pathetic and underground bunkers miserable holes in the ground, lined with corrugated plastic and a few sandbags, inadequate to prevent any explosion while the Iraqi soldiers themselves did not measure up to the menacing warriors they had been built up to be.' Elsewhere Kay describes the Iraqi army as 'closer to a rabble' while much of their equipment was 'useless and old'. (ibid: 107) Michael Kelly (1993: 156), who covered the massacres for two American magazines and a newspaper, described the Iraqi bunkers as 'hardly better than the slit-trench works of the First World War'.

But while the massacres were going on and starving Iraqi conscripts were deserting in droves, it was still necessary to maintain the myth of the credible threat. Thus the *Mirror* showed the coalition with 605,000 troops, 3,650 armoured personel carriers, 1,000 artillery pieces, 3,800 tanks facing a credible enemy with supposedly 545,000 troops, 2,800 armoured personnel carriers, 160 helicopters, 3,100 artillery pieces and 4,200 tanks. The only conclusion to be drawn from such figures is that the coalition forces would win – but they would be given a good fight.

Press coverage of the massacres, then, was always ambivalent. By 6 February, the *Mirror* was reporting starving Iraqi soldiers begging for food and 'pinpoint' bombing by the allies shattering the Iraqi oil industry. Yet on the same day it was stressing coalition commanders believing Saddam Hussein's crack Republican Guard to be still 'a formidable fighting force'. 'These men are being kept well fed so they are fit to strike back at the allies when the land war begins.' By 21 February, the *Mirror* was headlining 'Mass surrender by 500 battered Iraqis'. Mark Dowdney, in London, wrote: 'Four US Apache helicopters pounded the underground bunkers with laser-guided rockets and hellfire missiles. And not a shot was fired in reply.' A pilot is quoted: 'They made no attempt to defend themselves but fell on their knees facing Mecca and began to pray.'

Coverage by the *Los Angeles Times* was similarly ambivalent. On 25 February, it carried on page seven a graphic showing various devices the US forces could use in dealing with the 'network of anti-tank ditches, minefields, 10ft-high berms and other impediments to slow down the allies'. But elsewhere in the paper, its resident military expert, Col. Harry G. Summers Jr (Ret.) commented: 'Before the land campaign there was report after report of how formidable the Iraqi fortifications were. They were so well protected by mines, so well entrenched, so well guarded that they were virtually impregnable.' Now, just one day after the official launch of the ground war: 'No word of the many booby traps, field fortifications, trenches and the like that were supposed to have stopped such an attack.'

Slaughter of a helpless enemy can hardly be dignified with the language of battle. Yet most newspapers urged it on. On 25 February, the *Mirror* editorialised, still pounding away at the 'Saddam alone is guilty' line: 'Let victory be swift' and commented: 'Saddam Hussein brought the land war, the defeat of his army and the destruction of his country down on himself.' On 22 February (and again three days later), the *Mirror* reported Saddam Hussein as intending to use a crippling nerve gas and was planning to fit chemical weapons to his missiles. This was intelligence disinformation – but it helped create the image of the frightening, credible enemy.

Troops began advancing in earnest on 24 February for what had been billed by all the press as 'the largest land battle since 1945'. A three-day news blackout was unilaterally broken by the US government hours later. There was simply no enemy in sight – just conscripts desperate to give themselves up. As the Iraqis withdrew the merciless killing went on. Just 100 hours later a stop was called to the slaughter. Throughout this period the press desperately sought to maintain the fiction that the 'real battle' the elite had been wanting all along was just around the corner. Christopher Bellamy, in the *Independent* of 25 February, suggested the Gulf War was 'the biggest armoured battle since the Battle of Kursk in 1943 when the Russains halted the German advance into the Soviet Union'. Next day, the paper reported: 'Pentagon officials emphasised the real battle has not yet occurred'. Robert Fisk reported a brigadier as saying the 'real battle' lay ahead. An article on the Republican Guard quoted an intelligence 'expert': 'These are very capable troops. They have never known what it is to be beaten.'

Military 'expert' Lawrence Freedman was on hand to add to the 'war' myth. He commented on the same day that the allies were going to find it difficult to cope with the 'heavily armoured Republican Guard'. The guard were planning to counter attack, he said, for the 'decisive battle'. Yet Richard Dowden with the troops in Kuwait was reporting that one crucial thing was missing from this 'mother of battles' – enemy fire. 'Mother of surrenders' was the headline in the *Mirror* accompanying a story from Ramsey Smith in Kuwait telling of coalition forces being overwhelmed by prisoners. But this time the 'war' myth was given an added patriotic touch: 'British Challenger tanks are in the forefront of the battle and will come up against the Iraqi's powerful Russian-made T-72s.' Next day the same reporter profiled a 'bedraggled' Iraqi prisoner, without any shoes or socks, and desperately pleased to have survived. But he went on: 'Don't let anyone kid you that Saddam's battered army has already given up the fight.' Next day the paper reported the Desert Rats' victory in an 'epic desert battle'; they now expected to 'polish off with relative ease' the remaining Iraqis before they met their final trophy, the Republican Guard.

Ramsay Smith, accompanying the allies as they advanced, reported: 'Most of the Iraqi troops manning the front-line trenches surrendered as soon as they saw our tanks coming. In less than an hour more than 1,000 prisoners had been taken.' Yet still the myth of war was to survive. He added: 'And Britain's Desert Rats and other Allied troops slugged it out in fierce fighting in southern Iraq.' But there was no battle at all. The *Independent* reported Gen. Schwarzkopf as saying on 28 February the coalition's troops had stormed virtually untouched into southern Iraq and could have seized the capital 'unopposed at that time'. 'A few skirmishes and isolated incidents' was how Hamish Lumsden at the Ministry of Defence described the advance of British troops.

Alex Thomson reports the experiences of American pool correspondents John Kifner and Rick Davis who flew on two low-level helicopter missions in Iraq. '...not only did they encounter no incoming fire but, astonishingly, they saw little sign at all of the supposedly colossal Iraqi force which Western commanders insisted had been dug in for months along this region'. (op cit: 249) And Keith Dovkants, who was travelling with the UK pool Forward Transmission Unit behind the British troops as they advanced into Iraq, commented: 'There was no action at all; just surrendering all the time. This was not what a lot of people had hoped for.'

AP veteran war correspondent Mort Rosenblum (1993: 117) later described how, together with a Reuters colleague, he slipped away from the pack and sped up from Khafji to Kuwait City as the Iraqi defences were collapsing. 'Almost without noticing it, we passed the dreaded Saddam Line, the belt of steel and inflammable oil we had described to our nervous readers time and time again.' And he concludes: 'For its own purposes, the government exaggerated the threat. And rather than providing question marks, we [the press] chose exclamation points.' Also on 28 February, the *Independent* editorial was praising the performance of the coalition's weaponry and blaming Saddam Hussein for having taken the 'thuggish option'.

Eliminating the animals – through mindless massacrespeak

The whole of the 'ground assault' was mediated through the mindless massacrespeak of the US military. Not only were the US military constantly quoted but journalists, as throughout the war, adopted the same language. On 1 February 1991, Alan Hall, in the *Sun*, under the headline 'I've just flown a reamer in the KZ' provided an 'A-Z of Gulf warspeak'. Such military jargon, he said, was 'set to come tripping off everyone's tongue'. In this way, the euphemisms and crudities of massacrespeak enter and corrupt the popular culture. ITN journalist Alex Thomson commented: 'The urge to look like a soldier rather than whatever a journalist is supposed to look like was a little unnerving. Things became outright spooky when such people began to speak like soldiers.' Significantly, Richard Kay, of the *Mail*, titled his account of as front line reporter *Desert warrior*.

As the slaughtering went on, the US military time after time talked of their enemy as an animal, as a non-person. The *Independent*, for instance, on 25 February quoted one US soldier: 'By God, I thought we had shot into a damn farm; it looked like somebody had opened the sheep pen.' Another, in a unit stalking a truck convoy: 'We engaged it and took it out.' And another, who couldn't wait to attack: 'It will be a duck hunt.' A front page story in the same edition reported on the first high-tech video of ground fighting showing 'terrified Iraqis shot to pieces in the dark by US attack helicopters'. But in reporting it, the *Los Angeles Times* pool reporter slipped easily into massacrespeak. Iraqi soldiers, he said, were like 'ghostly sheep flushed from a pen. Some were literally blown to bits by bursts of 30mm exploding cannon shells ... The Iraqi soldiers as big as football players on a TV screen, ran with nowhere to hide'. Two days later the paper quoted Western military sources describing Iraqis as 'sitting ducks'. An American major, describing the 'bold, audacious action', comments: 'Don't worry about Kuwait, it's a piece of dirt. We're going after the Iraqi army. Once we destroy them Kuwait will be free.' Next day Iranian pilots described the slaughter as a 'rat shoot'.

This utter contempt for human life was similarly expressed by journalists – but in less crude language. The *Independent* editorial of 27 February, while thousands of Iraqis were being slaughtered, said: 'It has been a famous victory with astonishing light casualties.' While the *Star*, on 25 February, expressed the relief of the 'civilised world' at the 'extremely light casualties' – amongst coalition forces, of course. Mass Iraqi deaths did not count in the civilised world. On 1 March, reporter Martin Woollacott descended into massacrespeak in the *Guardian* commenting: 'The Iraqi army resembled nothing so much in its last days as a worm which is chopped by a spade – the segments wriggle but the creature is already dead.'

Celebrating the slaughter

The *Independent* sought to dignify the carnage with superlatives. Christopher Bellamy claimed on 25 February that 'this most cerebral of campaigns' was the result of a 'concentrated programme of intellectual self-improvement throughout the 1980s' in the US army. Bellamy, on 27 February, described the massacres as a 'perfect victory'. The battle for Kuwait was 'awe-inspiring and brilliant'. This is exactly what the military wanted to hear. But there was no battle – the coalition forces met no resistance. It was a merciless walkover. Bellamy was not having any of this. The battle for Kuwait, he argued, combined classical 'geometrical simplicity of conception' with a 'complexity of execution'. The paper's editorial of 27 February dismissed the Kremlin's 'ill-considered calls for a ceasefire' and praised the 'brilliant allied strategy'. Air power was the key to the 'spectacular two-day collapse of the fourth largest army in the world'. The *Star*, of 25 February, described the British soldiers as the 'finest fighting force in the world'. Next day, the paper was celebrating the technology of slaughter. 'The power of America's £6.3m Apache helicopters was impossible to fight off. It is the most sophisticated killer copter in the world.'

Highway to Hell and the ultimate myth of battle

The contradictions in the press coverage – maintaining to the very end the necessary new militarist myth of the credible enemy while reporting evidence of mass, unopposed slaughter – were most clearly evident over the massacres on the 'Highway to Hell'. Gen. Colin Powell told journalists just before the launch of the 'ground assault': 'We're going to cut it off and kill it.' At Mutla Ridge, that is precisely what the coalition forces did.

On 25 February hundreds of Iraqi men, with their families and some Kuwaiti prisoners, began fleeing north from Kuwait City. Encircled by coalition forces, trucks, cars, ambulances and a few tanks ended up jammed on three roads. For 40 hours the area became a 'kill zone' for the coalition forces. B-52s, FA-18 jets, Apache helicopters unleashed wave after wave of bombs. Virtually everything that moved was wiped out. Planes queued to drop their bombs on the 'targets' below. Army sources later estimated that 25,000 people were slaughtered on the highway. (Arkin, Durrant, Cherni 1991: 108)

According to the report of the Commission of Inquiry for the International War Crimes Tribunal: 'US forces left open only two roads out of Kuwait City. All retreating soldiers were forced onto these roads and it was made known that soldiers moving north would not be attacked. Later, the US military feigned ignorance of the troops' intentions and floated the possibility that they sought to reinforce the Republican Guards just over the border in Iraq. Thus, the Pentagon argued, the possibility of a serious threat from this retreating force left the Coalition no choice but to attack its adversary. However, the Coalition did not merely attack its foe; it massacred them.' (Clark 1991: 50)

There was little evidence of resistance by the Iraqis. Thomson, who visited the site of carnage, said: 'In the wreckage by Mutla Ridge, tanks, artillery or armoured vehicles were conspicuous by their absence.' (op cit: 256) Keith Dovkants, of the London *Evening Standard*, who arrived at the scene with the British pool, commented: 'I saw a pretty horrific scene of what looked like deliberate carnage, a massacre. I sent in a piece on the awful scene which would have been the first British account. But then the paper suddenly got a report that Saddam Hussein had fled to Mauritania and my piece didn't make it. The Mauritania story turned out to be wrong. I spoke to a military chap as the Americans were going after the retreating troops and he said "This is not a war as I understand it – bombing the hell out of van drivers and conscripted bank clerks."'

Yet still the 'war' myth survived. Philip Taylor, describing it as a 'battle', (op cit: 256) relies totally on a quote of Major Bob Williams: 'They fought harder than we have seen before.' Later Stephen Sackur, of BBC Radio, spoke to Williams again. He could find no military justification for the carnage. This time, Williams changed his story saying they were slaughtered simply because they were thieves. 'As you look at the vehicles down there you'll find they are all filled with booty...these were thieves, not professional soldiers...our cause was just.' (Sackur 1991: 266)

The military focus on the stolen goods amongst the debris of slaughter was also picked up by the press. As Taylor comments: 'The whole framing of the story by all the news organisations became such that any sympathy which reporters may have felt for the massacred army evoked by the shocking scenes they had witnessed was more than counterbalanced by the sheer scale of the plundering which the Iraqis had clearly undertaken. To consolidate this impression still further came the footage of the burning oil wells which Saddam's escaping army had set ablaze.' (op cit: 256) The *Mail*, for instance, on 2 March headlined a report on the slaughter by focusing on the looting in this way: 'On the highway to horror: a bottleneck of carnage as looters fled into ambush.'

The media/military agenda

Most of the first reports were based on military comments and thus the enormity of the carnage was shrouded in the predictable, inhuman soundbites of massacrespeak. When journalists arrived at the scene they saw a site of almost indescribable horror. Yet never once did any journalist condemn this as an atrocity. Most sought to legitimise it. Most sought to blame Saddam Hussein, once again. Outrage was directed, instead, at the alleged Iraqi atrocities in Kuwait. It will never be known how many Iraqis died in the slaughter. How many other Iraqis died in how many other unseen massacres?

A woman and two children were among those who somehow survived. The US lost just one man, hit by a sniper. Yet, even in the face of this slaughter still the myth of battle survived. The *Independent* reported on 27 February that Iraqis fleeing north presented a 'bounty of targets'. Next day it reported: 'The biggest armoured battle of the war developed further north near Basra. Iraqi forces were said to be offering determined resistance.' The *Star* of 27 February described the Iraqis as 'easy prey'. A pilot was quoted: 'And we toasted them, we hit here and hit there and circled round and hit here again'. But other pilots are quoted as saying the Iraqis could 'simply be regrouping for an attack'.

On 28 February, the *Independent* carried just six paragraphs under the headline "Slaughter' of fleeing Iraqis draws protests'. Elsewhere, in a lengthy feature Colin Hughes sought to legitimise the massacre. After 42 days of non-stop bombardment and slaughter, he suggested that the 'duck shoot risked straining the allies' clean fighting war record right at the last moment'. It was reported later that many Iraqis tried to surrender but even those who waved white flags were cut to pieces. Yet Hughes directs blame at the helpless Iraqis. 'The simple answer is that the Iraqis, if they wanted to avoid being bombed and strafed by allied aircraft should have surrendered rather than attempt to escape with their army and weapons intact. Properly trained soldiers would know that even in retreat they remain a wholly legitimate target.' Adam Roberts, professor of international law at Oxford University, adds academic respectability to this view. He said the allies 'were well within the rules of international conduct in continuing to attack a retreating force'.

Outrage at Iraqis

Stories about Iraqi atrocities in Kuwait had been gathering for a number of weeks before the final coalition onslaught. Then they reached a crescendo point. The *Los Angeles Times* of 24 February, for instance, carried prominently allegations by coalition spokesmen that Iraqis had been conducting an 'execution campaign' in Kuwait. David Lamb and John Broder quoted Marine Brig. Gen. Richard I. Neal, the US military spokesman in Riyadh, saying: 'This is terrorism at its finest hour.' Undoubtedly, appalling atrocities had been committed. Robert Fisk, who had written consistently against the 'war', wrote in the *Independent* of 2 March that the scenes witnessed by journalists when they arrived in Kuwait made them lose any sympathy they might have ever had for the Iraqis. But, at the same time, the press used these reports of Iraqi atrocities to deflect attention away from the slaughters being committed by the coalition and, in part, to legitimise them. The press never even displayed their much trumpeted commitment to 'balance'. They might have expressed horror at the Iraqi atrocities and equally at the coalition slaughters. They never did. Our side was blameless.

For example, the *Mirror* of 27 February said the Iraqis were 'brutes' for having seized Kuwaitis, Syrians and Egyptians. 'It was the last act of a brutal occupying force which left behind it a legacy of murder, torture and rape.' Thus they deserved all they got. The 'rag-tag army' was 'being cut to pieces by allied jets'. No outrage at the massacre; no thought even if it was necessary. 'A-6 Intruders and overhead jets swooped overhead picking off the Iraqis with cluster bombs. Giant B-52s were plastering the highway with 1,000lb bombs. A US pilot said: "They were like sitting ducks. It was like the road to Daytona Beach on a holiday just bumper to bumper."' The *Los Angeles Times* of the same day highlighted on its front page the views of 'Lt Armando Segarro, 26, a bombardier of Floral Park, New York': 'We hit the jackpot.'

On 28 February, the *Independent* reported Gen. Schwarzkopf as saying 'very, very large numbers' of Iraqis had been killed in the onslaught. But those described as 'evil' by the paper were the Iraqis, never the coalition forces. While the allies were indulging in their 'rat shoot', Robert Fisk reported that 'Something evil has visited Kuwait City'. 'What kind of men had raped Kuwait?' he asked, implying that they were, in fact, non-men. The *Express* on 1 March also managed to invert responsibility for the slaughter. Under the headline 'Slaughter of the innocent: Victims litter valley of death' it reported: 'Iraqi troops slaughtered civilians in a last act of wanton destruction as they scurried from Kuwait. Horrific evidence of their atrocities lies along the main route from Kuwait to Iraq where the destruction and human cost of war can be seen at its most shocking.'

The *Guardian* came nearest to blaming both sides for the atrocity. On 2 March, it commented: 'A combination of allied cluster bombing and Iraqi attacks has turned the main road between Kuwait City and the Iraqi city of Basra into a slaughterhouse.' A retrospective on the slaughter in *The Times* of 27 March by Michael Evans was carried under the headline 'The final turkey shoot'. But Evans never chose to condemn the slaughter. The nearest he approached criticism was this comment: 'It was the final "turkey shoot" of the war and in retrospect unwarranted. Further carnage would have been politically unsupportable and terrible publicity. President Bush knew it.' Thus it was unwarranted – not because of the damage to the Iraqis but to President Bush.

Pictures of the carnage appeared on television only on 1 March, significantly after the end of the massacres. Very few bodies, if any, were shown – just lots of burnt-out vehicles. Kate Adie, for the BBC, reported that the Iraqis had 'decided to make a fight of it'. The scene was both 'devastating and pathetic'. Christopher Morris, of Sky Television, described the scene as 'like a nightmare from Dante's Inferno'. Freelance photographer Kenneth Jarecke was in an American pool and his picture of a burnt-out head of an Iraqi soldier slumped over a truck was one of the most appalling images of the war. It appeared once in the UK – in the *Observer* on 10 March – the massacres having been halted. Only the *Chicago Tribune* in the mainstream press in the United States carried it. Five years later the BBC showed a picture of that same horrific, burnt-out head during a four-part series commemorating the 'war'. Predictably, voices from the massive global movement opposed to the war were nowhere heard in the series.

11 The press and the contradictions of new militarism

The attempt to resolve the contradictions of new militarism with a quickie, spectacular, manufactured war was inevitably represented in all the mainstream media as a triumph. *The Times* hailed a 'brief and brilliant military campaign'. *Today* of 1 March said the liberation of Kuwait heralded 'a victory for the freedom of all mankind'.

The centrality of sexual politics to the manufacture of the Gulf 'war' became evident in many of the press comments on the victory.[1] The *Sun* (1 March) went so far as to describe President Bush as 'Superman' and credit him with not one but three victories. Under the headline 'By George you're great' the paper pronounced: 'America last night finally admitted to President Bush – you're no wimp – you're Superman. Three stunning victories have ensured that the lanky leader will go down in history as one of the greats. Wham! He gave the go-ahead for the most successful military campaign since World War Two. Bam! His stand against naked aggression and Soviet meddling proved him to be the toughest leader since President Roosevelt. Thank you,

---

1   Feminist critics of militarism have identified the way in which a cultural process occurred in the US which, following the traumas of the Vietnam War, served to restore traditional notions of masculinity and military heroism. Boose, Linda (1993): *Gendering war talk*; Princeton University Press, Princeton NJ argues: 'As America's military interventionism resurged in the 1980s, filmgoers concurrently began witnessing the reascendancy – with a vengeance – of a masculine ethos so narcissistic in its need for self-display that it progressively eroded most of the space hitherto even available for female representation.' p 73. Quoted in Zalewski, Marysia (1995): 'Well, what is the feminist perspective on Bosnia?', *International Affairs*; London; 71. 2 pp 339-356. Zalewski comments: 'Relatively few men who have been in the military are ever involved in combat, yet it continues to have ideological potency, in large measure because it is wielded as a criterion to divide the "men from the boys" and more recently the men from the women.' p 350.

See also Enloe, Cynthia (1994): *The morning after: sexual politics at the end of the Cold War*; University of California Press; Berkeley, CA.

man! He has handed back America's pride after decades of being haunted by its worst defeat in Vietnam.' And significantly for the *Sun*, the 'war' had helped the President prove his virility: 'Today, Bush's countrymen agree with his wife, Barbara, who said: "I could never understand why people called George a wimp. He's all man – believe me."'

The theme of 'war' as man's sport is continued in the main headline describing Stormin' Norman and spanning pages four and five: 'Man of the match'. (The *Star* had 'Man of the shootin' match'.) New militarist 'warfare' is transmuted into Hollywood-style glitter: Schwarzkopf is described as 'superstar Norman of Arabia. Soon there will be Norman the book followed by Norman the movie ...' The 'Images of War' centre-spread carries nine pictures supposedly summoning up the conflict – none shows any dead.

The *Los Angeles Times* of 28 February followed identical mediacentric lines. Barry Bearak, under the headline 'Feeling on top of the world', wrote: 'And what of George Bush? Certainly the tag "wimp" has been swept over by the desert sand. Now the President is spoken of as something of a John Wayne with an Ivy League diploma.' And he captured the sporting metaphor in his celebration of the new militarism: 'This week the images being imprinted in the American psyche seem largely ones of a gutsy, resourceful nation. America is no longer the aging slugger who can't get the bat around on a fast ball. It is a lithe warrior and a cunning strategist and a heroic liberator.'

A typical follow-up in the press was to taunt those who had predicted a long, drawn-out conflict. The *Mail*'s 'Phoney profits of doom' feature of 1 March was typical. Denis Healey, former Labour minister, Marjorie Thompson, CND chair, Edward Heath, former Prime Minister, 'Anthony Wedgwood Benn' (as it persists in calling Tony Benn), Bruce Kent, former CND chair, Senator Edward Kennedy were among those said to end up 'with egg on their faces'. The *Star* predictably personalised the victory. 'We kicked his arsenal,' it headlined. (1 March) Yet victory was a mere illusion. Kuwait had been 'liberated' but at what cost?[2] And Saddam Hussein, whose head so much of the Western elite and media had supposedly sought since early August 1990, survived.

---

2   See Feuilherade, Peter (1991): 'Hammered by the Gulf crisis'; *Middle East International*; London; 25 September. p 14. World Bank report suggests that in Jordan unemployment rose in 1991 by more than 25 per cent with a return of migrant workers from the Gulf; Yemen also hit by return of some 750,000 migrant workers and their dependents. Over 15 per cent of the workforce is unemployed in the Maghreb countries, Egypt and Iran while the rate in Jordan and Yemen exceeds 25 per cent. Report from the Arab League and Arab Monetary Fund, the Arab Fund for Economic and Social Development and OAPEC said Arab nations had sustained an aggregate loss of $620bn because of the Gulf crisis. Kuwait lost $160bn and Iraq $190 billion in destroyed infrastructure. Arab nations were said to have spent $84bn on Operation Desert Shield and Desert Storm, the bulk by Saudi Arabia, Kuwait and the UAE. See also Seward, Valerie (1992): *The Middle East after the Gulf War*; HMSO; Wilton Park, West Sussex, After two disastrous wars Iraq has debts and reparation claims amounting to over $900 billion. Its total theoretical oil revenues are estimated at £1,850 billion. Thus one half of its total oil income was already mortgaged.

The waning of the Hitler hype

In many respects, Saddam Hussein's survival was useful for the US/UK elite.

- With the collapse of the Soviet Union, the Iraqi President served as a useful 'enemy' to help legitimise the new militarist elite's political and economic privileges. Following the massacres, Pentagon strategists confirmed moves to switch its focus to planning for wars with Third World enemies. The *Guardian* reported (18 February 1992) that leaked classified documents suggested that military chiefs had been told by the Pentagon to request forces 'sufficient to fight large regional wars against Iraq and North Korea, or against both at the same time'.

- It legitimised the Western elites' continuing sales of weapons to the Middle East after the massacres even though publicly calls were made to cut down the arms trade to the region.[3] President Bush created a Center for Defense Trade to stimulate arms sales while offering government guarantees of up to $1bn in loans for the purchase of US arms. Arms sales actually rose from $12bn in 1989 to almost $40bn in 1991. (Chomsky 1993: 104-105) Stork (1995: 16) records how the Middle East accounted for more than 72 per cent of the total US arms transfers to the Third World between 1990 and 1993 – up from 61 per cent over the previous four years.

- Iraq also proved to be a focus for the US elite's attempts to make the United Nations a mere instrument for the implemetation of its imperial policies.

But his survival also represented, on one level, a serious embarrassment for the US-led coalition. The new militarist strategy was built on the demonisation of Saddam Hussein – to simplify the conflict and make it more credible and acceptable to the doubting masses. Yet, despite all the public rhetoric, the Kurds and Shi'ites have never been favoured as potential leaders of Iraq. Prominent sections of the Western elite even want Saddam Hussein to maintain power. And so the Hitler hype faded away.

Significantly, two years later the Nazi analogy, no longer tied to Saddam, was to be fixed for a few months on to the Serbs of the former Yugoslavia. Images of Bosnian concentration camps, carried throughout the mainstream Western press, reinforced this rhetoric. But when the Serbian leader, Slobodan Milosevic, sought to win over the Bosnian Serbs to support the Contact Group's peace proposals for Bosnia the Nazi jibes suddenly stopped. With the collapse of the Soviet Union and the demise of anti-Red/commie rhetoric, Second World War rhetoric, which was used so relentlessly against Saddam Hussein in the 1990-1991 period has clearly become a potent, ideological 'weapon' for the Western elites. (Phillips 1992)

---

3   Tyler, Patrick (1992): 'Pentagon pleads case for 'regional war' firepower'; the *Guardian/New York Times*; 18 February. 'The classified documents show that the department has told military chiefs to request forces and weapons sufficient to fight large regional wars against Iraq and North Korea, or against both at the same time.'

Myth of the end of war: the secret war continues

The US secret war against the people of Iraq entered a new phase after the massacres. As Phyllis Bennis (1992: 124) argues, the ceasefire (called for in United Nations' Resolution 687) was a non-ceasefire, drawn up after typical US 'diplomacy' in the UN against sceptical countries: 'unspecified yet classic threats to Ecuador, and irresistible offers of cheap oil to impoverished Zimbabwe'. Bennis concludes: 'The pressure worked. The resolution passed.' The maintenance of crippling sanctions on Iraq was a continuation of 'warfare' by other means. And there was a strong element of hypocrisy about this policy, largely ignored in the press: sanctions had been considered inadequate to dislodge Saddam Hussein in 1990. Yet they were felt a suitable 'weapon' after March 1991.

With the country facing estimated reconstruction costs of up to $200 billion, demands that Iraq pay reparations for the destruction of Kuwait could only further victimise the Iraqi people with whom the coalition supposedly 'had no quarrel' (as *The Times* stressed once again in its editorial of 1 March, echoing the rhetoric of President Bush). The *New Statesman and Society* commented on 1 March 1991: 'Making the people pay for the crimes of their leaders – particularly when, as with Iraq, they are as much the victims of their leaders as anyone – is morally indefensible and practically insensible ... At the root of US support for reparations is the same desire to inflict an unequivocal and humiliating defeat upon Iraq that led it to begin the bombing before sanctions had been given sufficient time to work ...'

That kind of viewpoint was hardly heard in the mainstream press. And, bar a few exceptional features, the press in both the UK and US fell silent about the appalling fate of the Iraqi people in the aftermath of the massacres.[4] For instance, a report by researchers at Harvard University and the London School of Economics in May 1997 suggested that more than 500,000 children had died in Iraq since the 'war' directly as a result of the sanctions. Significantly, the sanctions policy aided the Iraqi regime. As Adbul-Haq, editor of the *Arab Review* in London, commented: 'He [Saddam] is stronger than he ever was. People are weakened by the sanctions and afraid to do anything. Instead, they are blaming the West, not Saddam.'[5]

The Great Media Myths: Part One: Halting the horror

So much of the history of the Middle East crisis and massacres years later still remains a mystery – inevitably so given the secrecy surrounding top-level decision making. Why did President Bush call a halt to the war when he did? Why didn't the American troops head for Baghdad and take over the capital? How many Iraqis died? We will never know. Yet from the soil of new militarist secrecy, important media myths and fictions can flower.

---

4   See Pilger, John (1992): 'The brainwashing of Britain': the *Guardian*; 14 September.
5   See O'Kane, Maggie (1997): 'Report condemns sanctions on Iraq', the *Guardian*, 18 May.

One myth that came to dominate coverage immediately after the halting of the massacres focused on the mediacentrism of the conflict: the President had halted the slaughter because of fears that pictures of scenes such as on the Basra Highway of Hell would turn people against the 'war'. This was most forcibly argued by Nik Gowing, diplomatic editor of ITN. He wrote (1991: 8): 'Fearful of a "second Vietnam" deep in Iraq and live on television, Bush halted the allied advance into Iraq. It made political not military sense. Fear of what television might witness meant that a significant proportion of Saddam Hussein's army in Kuwait escaped and re-grouped to fight another day – against the Kurds and Shi'as.'

In fact, pictures of the highway slaughter only appeared days after the cease-fire. They could not have influenced the Bush administration. But the media myth serves to promote a notion of 'democratic accountability' to both the press and political elite. Accordingly, the press, acting as the mouthpiece of the 'public will' independent of the state and mirror of an unproblematic reality, articulates the widespread concerns over the slaughter and pressuris-es the elite to change its policy. Nothing like this occurred. The reasons for the halting of the US-led coalition forces' advance remain obscure – but democratic concerns could not interfere with the elite's Desert Storm script.

The Great Media Myths: Part two: Caring for the Kurds

The coverage surrounding the Kurds after the halting of the massacres con-structed one of the greatest media myths – to compare, for instance, with the great William Howard Russell and Watergate media myths.[6] During the mas-sacres the press had become the overt propaganda arm of the state. The vast majority of journalists accepted the compromises and constraints involved. But the press bases much of its activities on the myth of 'freedom', of autonomy from the state. And so it became vital in the aftermath of the massacres to reassert the traditional role of the media as independent watchdogs on the state.

---

6   Knightley, Phillip (1982): *The first casualty: The war correspondent as hero, propagandist and myth-maker*; Quartet; London. Excellent critical examination of the Russell myth. Says that Russell chronicled the failings of the army in the Crimea but failed to expose and understand the causes. While he criticised the lot of the ordinary soldier he never attacked the officers 'to whose social class he belonged himself'. And Knightley continues (p 17): 'Above all, Russell made the mistake, common to many a war correspondent, of consider-ing himself part of the military establishment.' Indeed, when he returned from Crimea Russell was embraced by the establishment as one of them. He dined with the Queen. But the Russell reports came at a crucial time in the evolution of the press industry in Britain. The campaign against press taxes had just won its crucial victory and the way was set for the destruction of the radical press and the emergence of an elitist newspapers in the 'free' market place of opinion. (see Curran, James and Seaton, Jean (1991: 25-30): *Power with-out responsibility - The press and broadcasting in Britain*; Fourth edition; Routledge; London) Around Russell's reports in *The Times*, critical of Lord Raglan and the war effort, could emerge the myth of the fourth estate, separate from and critical of the state. *The Times* played only a minor role in the fall of the government. It was one small factor amongst very many others. An important section of the British elite was determined on Aberdeen's fall, irrespective of any views expressed in *The Times*. But the myth emerged of the adversary press constantly in conflict with the state and the military. Snoddy, Raymond (1992): *The good, the bad and the unacceptable: The hard news about the British press*;

The Kurdish rebellion provided the ideal opportunity for the resurrection of this crucial myth. The press represented itself as acting on behalf of a caring nation, even global community in defence of the 'tragically fated' Kurds and in the face intransigent and uncaring leadership. The mediacentrism of new militarist society was here serving (not through any great conspiracy but through the workings of complex ideological, political, economic processes) to mask the ruthless, imperial thrust of the secret state.

Gowing wrote: '[Six weeks after the end of the 'war'] television further forced the hands of Western politicians. Governments could not ignore the horror of the Kurdish catastrophe which unfolded hourly on their TV screens. The pictures were politically uncomfortable and strategically inconvenient. But no government could dare avoid them. Led by John Major, the British Government had to jettison policy papers drawn up in the bureaucratic comfort of Whitehall. On an RAF jet flying to Luxembourg Britain's Prime Minister was forced to sketch out – on the back of an envelope – a concept for "humanitarian enclaves". As television showed the deepening catastrophe, George Bush had no option but to follow the British initiative. The US troops which he promised would never send back into Iraq's civil war, were sent back.' (op cit: 9)

Here then is an extraordinarily clear exposition of the myth. TV (and Gowing could also have included the press who were following the same agenda), voicing the views of the compassionate, global community, was forcing governments to change policy and move towards more humanitarian ends. Martin Woollacott, for instance, in the *Guardian* of 20 August 1992, reported that the creation of the Kurdish safe haven was a job 'of which the whole world approved'.[7] Shaw (1996: 122) also argues that the media forced the government's hand on Kurdistan. He writes: 'With the exception of the broadsheets, the press jumped on television's bandwagon at a late stage. Its advocacy was nevertheless important to the campaign's political impact: its chorus was the final straw, the signal to Major that it could not be ignored ... Since Major's *volte-face* played an important part in

---

Faber and Faber; London reiterates the dominant William Howard Russell myth. pp 43-46. 'His reports from the Crimea were the single most important factor in the resignation of Lord Aberdeen's Cabinet and its replacement by one led by Lord Palmerston.' p 43.

Schudson, Michael (1992): 'Watergate: A study in mythology', *Columbia Journalism Review*; New York; May/June pp 28-33. Exposes persuasively the many media myths surrounding Watergate. In particular he argues that the press was just one small factor in bringing down President Nixon amongst many others – the FBI investigators, federal prosecutors, grand jury and congressional committees. The press as a whole did not uncover the scandal; moreover, the scandal did not lead to any great spurt of investigative reporting. 'By the Reagan years the investigative binge seemed over.' And the 'Watergate myth of an independent and irresponsible media is as much an invention of Richard Nixon as the invention of Woodward and Bernstein [the *Washington Post* reporters who uncovered the scandal]'. p 29. In times of crisis, the media could always serve as a useful scapegoat for the elite – as was seen during the Middle East crisis of 1990-1991.

7 Woollacott's reports from Kurdistan in March/April in the *Guardian* certainly 'helped put the human catastrophe of the Kurdish people at the top of the political agenda' (See Morgan, Jean (1991): 'A warning to the world'; *UK Press Gazette*; London; 8 April p 1.)

Bush's, not only British television and broadsheets but even some tabloids can be said to have made a significant contribution to the change in Western policy on Kurdistan.' In the States the same myth was constantly drawn. Daniel Schorr (1991: 22) commented: 'Within a two week period the president had been forced, under the impact of what Americans were seeing on television, to reconsider his hasty withdrawal of troops from Iraq...It is rare in American history, which is most often manipulated to support a policy, creates an unofficial plebiscite that forces a change of policy.'

The original mystification

As the massacres appeared in danger of failing to topple Saddam Hussein, President Bush called on 15 February, shortly after the bombing of the Ameriyya shelter, for the Iraqi people themselves to remove the tyrant. This call, it could be argued, amounted to a gross interference in the internal affairs of a sovereign state – but the dominant view represented it as heralding the revolts in Kurdistan and amongst the Shi'as in the southern marshes around Basra. In March, a number of cities fell to rebels – Basra in the south and Kirkuk and Sulaymaniyah in Kurdistan. But by 3 April, Iraqi forces were reported to have forced back the rebels, the regime having preserved its forces to use, in an archetypal militarist strategy, against internal threats. Once the flight of thousands of Kurds towards Turkey and Iran began the Western media gave the retreat blanket coverage.

In fact, the origins are shrouded in mystery. The press suggested the Kurdish rebellion was a sudden resurgence of the revolt which had been going on, with varying degrees of intensity, since the formation of the Iraqi state in the early 1920s. President Bush's call along with the disarray in the Iraqi army supposedly gave the Kurds (and the Shi'as in the south) just the chance they had been waiting for. Following the defeat of the rebellion the masses fled. Kamron Dilsoz, of the British Kurdish Media Bureau in London, hotly disputes this analysis of the origins of the Kurdish revolt and subsequent flight. He argues that Bush's call had little impact on the Kurdish revolt – this had been intensifying since 1988 and hardly needed outside interference to spark it off. And the mass flight began after a rebel strategy badly misfired. In the March/April period rebel leaders showed films of the 1988 Halabja bombing to mass meetings in Kurdish villages in an attempt to rouse up new hatred of the regime. Instead, the films caused an epidemic of panic and so the surge for the safety of the hills started.

Bulloch and Morris (1992: 144) support this view. They write: ''Those who watched (the films) were stunned into silence or wept uncontrollably. Afterwards the nationalists asked themselves whether it had been right to show the film to Kurdish civilians at such a time and whether the shock of seeing for themselves the events at Halabja contributed to the subsequent panic-stricken flight into the mountains in the face of the Iraqi counter-offensive.' In the lead-up to the massacres the Kurdish issue was marginalised in the press. Saddam Hussein was Iraq, after all, and so the dominant frame

took little account of the ethnic complexity of the country. Indeed, paradoxically, most of those Iraqis the allies slaughtered were probably Shi'as and
Kurds – the very groups whose revolts the allies were later to attempt to
exploit. (Pilger 1991c)

Now that Saddam Hussein had been transformed into the global threat and
monster, the Kurds fighting him could be represented as noble and tragic in
their suffering. Lederman highlights the political dimensions of the Kurdish
coverage. 'Unsurprisingly, coverage of the Shi'ite battles – and the Shi'ites'
defeat – was relatively short because a Shi'ite victory was not seen to be in
American interests or in support of American values. The fate of the Kurds
was another matter. Only the Kurds were able to project the image of victim
– not alone of Saddam Hussein but also of American policy that supported
the cause of wars of national salvation only verbally and superficially. As a
result, the plight of the Kurds was given far more extensive coverage than
that given the Shi'ites and far more coverage than had been given the
Kurdish civilians attacked in 1988 by the Iraqi army using poison gas.'
(Lederman 1992: 320)

The romantic presentation of the Kurdish plight (which fitted so neatly into
dominant, one-dimensional goodie versus baddie representational frames)
shrouded the the CIA's covert involvement in the Kurds' history, past and
present, which was always marginalised in the press.[8] As Heikal (1992: 320)
commented on the Kurds and Shi'as: 'If the two uprisings had been truly
motivated by the desire for radical changes in the structure of Iraq, they
might have succeeded; as it was, many of those involved were merely trying
to exploit a chaotic situation for reasons of greed and revenge.' Moreover,
while the media represented Prime Minister John Major (rather quaintly) as
dreaming up the enclave idea on the spur of the moment different political
pressures probably had far more impact. In particular, the Turkish leadership
feared the mass of Kurds fleeing over their borders would add support to the
growing revolt of Turkish Kurds spearheaded by the Marxist-oriented Partia
Karkaris Kurdistan (PKK), coverage of this group either non-existent or marginalised in the press. Given their support during the massacres, the Turks
probably felt they had reason to expect some favours from the US. In fact,
Turkish President Turgut Ozal first suggested the haven for the Kurds in
northern Iraq on 7 April. (Abrahams (ed) 1994: 40) Major's proposal came
only the following day. In the south, Saudi concern over Iranian, Shi'ite
advances into Iraq probably doomed that revolt to defeat. (ibid: 318)

In contrast to the press's representation of the allied intervention as altruis-
tic and in the interests of the global community, the reality was far different.

8   See Agee, Phil (1976): *Covert Action: what next?* Agee Hosenball Defence Committeee;
    London. Details CIA support for Kurds 1972-1975 along with Shah in war with Iraq. Once
    Shah arranged deal with Iraq on border dispute CIA support immediately collapsed. p 8.
    CIA support for Kurds in 1991 detailed in Bulloch, John and Morris, Harvey (1992): *No
    friends but the mountains: The tragic history of the Kurds*; Viking; London. p 31. See also
    Blum, William (1986): *The CIA: A forgotten history – US intervention since World War
    Two*; Zed Books; London p 278.

As Bill Frelick (1992: 27) comments: 'Far from being a breakthrough for human rights and humanitarian assistance to displaced persons, the allied intervention on behalf of the Kurds of Iraq instead affirmed the power politics and hypocrisies that have long characterised the actions of states with respect to refugees and other powerless victims of official terror.' The creation of the enclave in the north of Iraq also served as a significant precedent for intervention by the US and UK elites (cynically exploiting the UN behind all the idealistic 'new world order' rhetoric) into the affairs of foreign enemy states. Two years later, as the low intensity war continued against Iraq, America (with some allied support) tried to impose a similar enclave (though it was defined as an 'exclusion zone') in the south. The media significantly did not hype these acts as heroic warfare. 'Warfare' in new militarist societies is a very specific, mediacentric, spectacular phenomenon. When the conditions are not right then conflicts are pursued in secret, or given low-key coverage and called 'peacekeeping' or 'monitoring an exclusion zone'.

The disaster?

Coverage of the 'war' in the mainstream press in the months following the ceasefire was profoundly ambivalent. On the one hand, the coalition's military leaders were represented unproblematically as heroes of the victory and when most of them later went on to write their memoirs of the conflict they became instant best-sellers. Yet Saddam Hussein, formerly the 'monstrous global threat', remained stubbornly in power. Within months of the end of the massacres even mainstream journalists were describing the US policy in the Middle East as a 'disaster'. Simon Tisdall, for instance, in the *Guardian* of 17 August 1992 suggested that Panama and Iraq were President Bush's two main foreign policy 'disasters'. Valerie Seward, in an HMSO publication, even said of Saddam Hussein: 'He seems to have snatched a kind of victory from the jaws of defeat.' (Seward 1992: 6; see also Sciolini 1992) The conflict supposedly heralded the 'new world order'. But two years later the globe was ablaze with conflicts none of which the US/UK showed any ability or real will to resolve. In the *New York Times* of 29 September 1992, Anthony Lewis wondered: 'So what happened to the New World Order?'; in the *Guardian* of 20 August 1992, Martin Wollacott was asking 'The New World what?'

Even the 'Vietnam syndrome' was discovered not to have been finally kicked. As the American secret state wobbled over its policy towards the crumbling of the Yugoslav federation in 1992 (a messy conflict not of the US's choosing and so difficult to stage manage as a new militarist media spectacle) prominent US politicians were bewailing the persistence of the 'syndrome'. For instance, Richard Schifter, senior State Department official in the Reagan and early Bush administrations, called for military strikes against the Serbs but said the country was still paralysed by the 'Vietnam syndrome'. The *New York Times*, of 29 September 1992, reported him as saying: 'It is the Vietnam syndrome – the idea that you don't get involved in any application of military force unless it is overwhelming and the purpose is to win a victory.'

Somalia and Bosnia: the mediacentric, new militarist dimensions

In contrast, the US intervention in Somalia in December 1992 was an attempt to legitimise new militarism under the cloak of 'peacekeeping' and 'humanitarianism'. Gilkes (1993) significantly stresses the Pentagon's need to protect the military budget as a crucial factor behind the intervention. It proved a total disaster. It neither provided a short-term solution to the famine and political crisis in the country, nor even attempted to resolve the underlying, long-term problems. (Africa Rights 1993; 1993a)

A US-brokered agreement was signed (following secret negotiations) between the PLO and Israel on 13 September 1993 allowing Palestinians 'limited autonomy' in the Gaza Strip and Jordon on the West Bank. But only an uneasy peace followed. (Said 1995) And in the war-torn former Yugoslavia, the mediacentric dimension proved crucial. New militarist interventions, as we have seen, are always *chosen* by the state on the presumption that they will be quick, relatively risk-free, and controllable as media spectacles. Bosnia answered none of these requirements. (Keeble 1993) Given America's inability to control the ground in the former Yugoslavia, it was impossible to pool journalists as in Saudi Arabia in 1991 or keep unwanted, maverick reporters out. Hence, the major powers were, until late 1995 and the signing of the (somewhat fragile) Dayton peace agreement, reluctant to commit ground troops. Only occasionally were risk-free attacks from the air on Serbian targets dared. Instead, most of the Western interventions in the Bosnian war were archetypally new militarist – through covert channels.[9]

New militarism now: contradictions

During the last days of the Bush administration and the start of the Clinton administration, the US resumed bombing of Iraq. On 13 January 1993, more than 100 aircraft attacked targets in southern Iraq. Kellner argues: 'Once again the mainstream media in the United States failed to question the official US rationale for the bombing and once again served as a conduit for US propaganda and disinformation.' (Kellner 1993; see also 1995) Then in June 1993 US planes again attacked targets in Baghdad after stories emerged in the mainstream media (fed by US intelligence and thus almost impossible to verify independently) that Iraq had plotted to assassinate former US President George Bush during a trip to Kuwait in April. Both of these attacks were rapid, risk-free interventions from the air. They were archetypally new militarist: more symbolic than strategically necessary. They served to maintain Saddam Hussein as the necessary bogeyman for Western military/industrial elites though now he was transformed from 'global threat' to a kind of naughty schoolboy deserving a 'spanking' and 'a lesson'. (Keeble 1994)

---

9 For instance, see Cornwell, Rupert (1996): 'US "secretly agreed Iran arms for Bosnia"', the *Independent*, London; 6 April and Leigh, David and Vulliamy, Ed (1997): *Sleaze: The corruption of Parliament*; Fourth Estate; London, pp 108-129 on Conservative support for Serbia.

The *Sun* headline of 14 January ran 'Spank you and goodnight', while the story introed: 'More than 100 allied jets...gave tyrant Saddam Hussein a spanking.' Norman Fairclough (1995: 95) comments: 'This is a metaphysical application of an authoritarian discourse of family discipline which is a prominent element in representations of the attack – Saddam as the naughty child punished by his exasperated parents.' The *Guardian* editorial, headlined 'More a smack than a strike', described the attack as 'an act of punishment against a very bad boy who thumbed his nose several times too often'. But in its editorial the *Sun* echoed so many of the expressions which were so dominant in the propaganda during the 1990-1991 crisis. Under the headline 'Wipe out the mad menace' it commented: 'At long last, Allied warplanes have bombed the hell out of Saddam Hussein. The Iraqi madman has pushed the West too far. He has played a dangerous game and now he must pay the price.' The reference to the 'West' is blatantly propagandistic since the West, in fact, was deeply divided over the attack. And while the USA, Britain and France were claiming to be enforcing a United Nations resolution, neither the 'no-fly' zone they were imposing on Southern Iraq nor the attack in the north had been endorsed by the UN. The *Sun* editorial ended in typical gung-ho style: 'The tragedy is that we did not finish him off last time. Go get him boys!' Yet for those sections of the Western elites who still backed Hussein, such attacks hardly did his regime any damage. If anything, they achieved the opposite.

In September 1996, another typical 'Saddam scare' erupted after Iraqi troops were reported to have invaded Kurdistan in support of the KDP Kurdish faction headed by Massoud Barzani against the Iranian-backed PUK faction headed by Jalal al-Talabani. Targets in southern Iraq were attacked by US missiles, supposedly to 'punish Saddam' (as the press stressed) for 'his' advance in the north. Then, in the following month, the PUK faction regained its lost strongholds and the crisis suddenly disappeared from the media. Behind all the simplistic, hyper-personalised anti-Saddam rhetoric, US strategists were following a well-established policy: promoting a divided Kurdistan. Significantly, this remained also the favoured policy of US ally Turkey – always anxious to hinder moves towards Kurdish unity on its doorstep – and the Iraqi elite. Moreover, shortly after the Baghdad-backed assault on Sulaymaniyah in Iraqi Kurdistan, news of a disastrous attempt by the CIA to build an indigenous Kurdish force to overthrow Saddam received prominent coverage in the UK and US press. Reports suggested that President Clinton had authorised $20m for the covert action. Was this a CIA faction leaking the details to embarrass the weaker anti-Saddam faction within the agency?

Propaganda, silencing and myth

Ultimately it is impossible to answer in certainty since the state's responses to the Iraqi crisis (as to so many others) have always been enveloped in secrecy. But through all the fog of the conflicts examined in this work, one factor has beeen clearly identified: the press serves a crucial propaganda, silencing function in new militarist, mediacentric societies. And it achieves this not through any elite conspiracy but through an ideology of news reporting that incorporates a set of routines, constraint, expectations – and myths. As Reese and Buckalew (1995: 41) conclude in their study of the 1991 conflict: 'The most pervasive. powerful and difficult to counter illusion [of real warfare] emerged from the routine, structural workings of the media system.' And they add pointedly: 'The interlocking and reinforcing triangle of government, news media and corporate needs works together to further a culture supportive of military adventures such as those in the Gulf.'

It is a culture that needs to be challenged if more unnecessary massacres are to be avoided.

Bibliography

Abu-Lughood, Ibrahim (1992): 'The politics of linkage: The Arab-Israeli conflict in the Gulf War', *Beyond the Storm: A Gulf crisis reader*; (eds) Bennis, Phyllis, and Moushabeck, Michel; Canongate; Edinburgh pp 183-190

Aburish, Said K. (1994): *The rise, corruption and coming fall of the House of Saud*; Bloomsbury; London

Abrahams, Eddie (ed) (1994): *The new warlords: From the Gulf War to the recolonisation of the Middle East*; Larkin Publications; London

Adair, Gilbert (1991): 'Saddam meets Dr Strangelove', the *Guardian*; 29 January

Adams, James (1987): *Secret armies: The full story of SAS, Delta Force and Spetsnaz*; Hutchinson; London

(1994): *The new spies: Exploring the frontiers of espionage*; Hutchinson; London

Adams, Valerie (1986): *The media and the Falklands campaign*; Macmillan; London

Adams W.C. (1982): (ed) *Television coverage of international affairs*; Alblex; Norwood, New Jersey

Africa Rights (1993): *Operation Restore Hope: A preliminary assessment*; London; May

(1993a): *Human rights abuses by the United Nations forces*; London; July

Agee, Philip (1991): 'Gulf War launches "new world order"', *Open Eye*, No 1; London pp 16-23

Aksoy, Asu and Robins, Kevin (1991): 'Exterminating angels: technology in the Gulf', *Media Development*; London; October pp 26-29

Allen, Thomas B; Berry Clifton F. and Polmar, Norman (1991): *War in the Gulf: From the invasion of Kuwait to the day of victory and beyond*; Turner Publishing Inc; Atlanta, Georgia

Andersen, Robin (1991): 'The press, the public and the new world order', *Media Development*; London; October pp 20-26

(1992): 'USIA – propaganda as public diplomacy', *Covert Action Information Bulletin*; Washington; Winter pp 40-44

(1992a): 'Oliver North and the news', *Journalism and popular culture*; (eds) Dahlgren, Peter and Sparks, Colin; Sage; London/Newbury Park/New Delhi pp 171-189

Anderson, Ewan W. and Rashidian, Khalil (1991): *Iraq and the continuing Middle East crisis*; Pinter Publishers; London

Anderson, Steve (1990): 'Who calls the shots?', *Listener*, London, 22 November

(1991): 'Hi mate, where's the fighting?' *British Journalism Review*; London; Vol 2 No. 3; Spring pp 12-16

Andrew, Christopher (1995): *For the President's eyes only: Secret intelligence and the American presidency from Washington to Bush*; HarperCollins; London

Anthony, Andrew (1991): 'We interrupt', *City Limits*; London; 24-31 January p 7

Arkin, William; Durrant, Damian and Cherni, Marianne (1991): *On impact: Modern warfare and the environment – a case study of the Gulf War*; Greenpeace; Washington DC

Arnett, Peter (1993): *Live from the battlefield: From Vietnam to Baghdad – 35 years in the world's war zones*; Bloomsbury; London

Arrighi, Giovanni (1994): *The long twentieth century*; Verso; London

Article 19 (1989): *Freedom of expression in the UK*; London

Atkinson, Rick (1994): *Crusade: The untold story of the Gulf War*; HarperCollins; London

Aubrey, Crispin (ed) (1982): *Nukespeak: The media and the bomb*; Comedia; London

Azzam, Maha (1991): 'The Gulf crisis: Perceptions in the Muslim world', *International Affairs*; London; 67.3 pp 479-485

Badsey, Stephen (1992): 'The media war', *The Gulf war assessed*; (eds) Pimlott, John and Badsey, Stephen; Arms and Armour Press; London pp 219-245

Bagdikian, Ben H. (1992; orig 1983): *The media monopoly*; Beacon Press; Boston, Massachusetts

Baker, Chris (1991): 'The new age of imperialism', *Socialist Action*; London; Spring 1991 pp 3-8

Barnaby, Frank (1984): *Future war*; Michael Joseph; London

Barnet, Anthony (1982): 'Iron Britannia'; *New Left Review* No.134; London; July/August (occupied whole issue pp 5-96)

Barnet, Richard (1988): 'The costs and perils of intervention', *Low-intensity warfare: How the USA fights wars without declaring them*; (eds) Klare, Michael and Kornbluh, Peter; Methuen; London pp 207-222

Baudrillard, Jean (1976): *L'exchange symbolique et la mort*; Gallimard, Paris (1988): Selected writings; Polity Press; Cambridge

Bauman, Zygmunt (1990): 'Effacing the surface – on the social management of moral proximity', *Theory Culture and Society*; London; No 7 pp 5-38

Belgrano Action Group (1988): *The unnecessary war: Proceedings of the Belgrano enquiry, November 7/8 1986*; Spokesman; Nottingham

Bell, Martin (1995): *In harm's way: reflections of a war zone thug*; Hamish Hamilton; London

Bennett, James C (1988): 'Censorship by the Reagan Administration', *Index on Censorship*; London; August pp 28-32

Bennett, Lance (1990): 'Towards a theory of press-state relations in the United States', *Journal of Communication*, Philadelphia, Spring pp 103-127

Bennis, Phyllis (1992): 'False consensus: George Bush's United Nations'; *Beyond the Storm: A Gulf crisis reader*; (eds) Bennis and Moushabeck pp 112-128

Benson, Nicholas (1993): *Rat's tales: The Staffordshire Regiment at war in the Gulf*; Brassey's; London

Berghahn, V.R. (1981): *Militarism: The history of an international debate 1861-1979*; Berg Publishers; Leamington Spa, Warwickshire

Best, Geoffrey (1980): *Humanity in warfare*; Weidenfeld and Nicholson; London de la Billière, Sir Peter (1995): *Looking for trouble: SAS to Gulf Command*; HarperCollins; London

Black, Ian and Morris, Benny (1991): *Israel's secret wars: A history of Israel's intelligence services*; Futura/Hamish Hamilton; London

Bleifuss, Joel (1990): 'The first stone', *In these times*; 26 September

Bloch, Jonathan and Fitzgerald, Patrick (1983): *British intelligence and covert action*; Junction Books; London

Bolton, Roger (1990): *Death on the Rock and other stories*; W.H. Allen, London

Bonefeld, Werner (1993): *The recomposition of the British state during the 1980s*; Dartmouth; Aldershot, Hampshire

Boorstin, Daniel (1962): *The image*; Weidenfeld and Nicolson; London

Le Borgne, Claude (1992): *Un discret massacre: L'Orient, la guerre et après*; Francois Bourin; Paris

Boot, William (1991): 'The press stands alone', *Columbia Journalism Review*; New York; March/April pp 23-24

Bower, Tom (1988): *Maxwell: The outsider*; Mandarin, London

(1992): *Robert Maxwell: a very British experience*; The Sixth James Cameron Memorial Lecture; City University Graduate Centre for Journalism, London

(1995): *The perfect English spy: Sir Dick White and the secret war 1935-1990*; Heinemann; London

Boyd-Barrett, Oliver and Thussu, Daya (1992): *Contra-flow in global news: International and regional news exchange mechanisms*; John Libbey; London

Bramley, Corporal Vincent (1991): *Excursion to hell*; Bloomsbury, London

Brown, Ben and Shukman, David (1991): *By all necessary means: Inside the Gulf War*; BBC Books; London

Bulloch, John and Morris, Harvey (1991): *Saddam's War*; Faber and Faber, London

(1992): *No friends but the mountains: The tragic history of the Kurds*; Viking, London

Bunyon, Tony (1977): *The history and practice of the political police in Britain*; Quartet; London

Cainkar, Louise (1991): 'How Paul Lewis covers post-war Iraq', *Lies of our Times*; New York; July/August pp 3-5

(1992): 'Desert Sin: A post-war journey through Iraq', *Beyond the Storm: A Gulf crisis reader*; (eds) Bennis and Moushabeck pp 335-355

Campaign Against the Arms Trade (1989): *Death on delivery: The impact of the Arms Trade on the Third World*; London

(1991) *Arming Saddam: The supply of British military equipment to Iraq 1979-1990*; briefing document; London

Chibnall, Steve ((1977): *Law and order news*; Tavistock; London

Chilton, Paul (1982): 'Nuclear language, culture and propaganda', *Nukespeak: The media and the bomb*; (ed) Aubrey, Crispin; Comedia; London pp 94-112

(1983): 'Newspeak: it's the real thing', *Nineteen Eighty Four in 1984: Autonomy, control and communication*; (eds) Aubrey, Crispin and Chilton, Paul; Comedia, London pp 33-44

(1985): *Nukespeak today: Language and the nuclear arms debate*, (ed); Frances Pinter; Cambridge

Chomsky, Noam (1986): 'For thugs and loony tunes look to Washington', *New Statesman*, London; 6 April pp 17-18

(1988): *The culture of terrorism*; Pluto Press; London

(1989): *Necessary illusions: thought control in democratic societies*; Pluto; London

(1991): *Deterring democracy*; Verso; London

(1991a): *Pirates and emperors*; Black Rose Books; Montreal/New York

(1991b): 'Media control: The spectacular achievements of propaganda'; *Open Magazine*; New Jersey (constituted whole of issue)

(1992): 'The media and the war: what war?', *Triumph of the image: The media's war in the Persian Gulf – a global perspective*; (eds) Mowlana, Hamid; Gerbner, George; and Schiller, Herbert I; Westview Press; Boulder, Colorado pp 51-66

(1993): *Year 501: The conquest continues*; Verso; London

Cirino, Robert (1971): *Don't blame the people: How the news media use bias, distortion and censorship to manipulate public opinion*; Vintage Books; New York

Clark, Ramsay et al (1992): *War crimes: A report on United States war crimes against Iraq*; Maisonneuve Press; Washington DC

Cockburn, Alexander (1991): 'The TV war'; *New Statesman and Society*; London; 8 March p 14

(1991a): 'Dumb bombs', *New Statesman and Society*; London; 14 June p 17

Cockburn, Alexander and Cockburn, Leslie (1992): *Dangerous liaison – The inside story of the US-Israeli covert relationship*; Bodley Head; London

Cockburn, Alexander and Cohen, Andrew (1991): 'The unnecessary war', *The Gulf between us: The Gulf War and beyond*; (ed) Brittain, Victoria; Virago Press; London pp 1-26

Cohen, Julie (1991): 'Who will unwrap the October surprise?', *Columbia Journalism Review*; New York; September/October pp 32-34

Cohen, Roger and Gotti, Claudio (1991): *In the eye of the Storm: The life of General H. Norman Schwarzkopf*; Bloomsbury; London

Colhoun, Jack (1992): 'How Bush backed Iraq', *Merip*; Washington DC; May/June pp 35-37

Collins, John M. (1991): *America's small wars*; Brassey's (US); Washington/London

Combs, James (1993): 'From the Great War to the Gulf War: popular entertainment and the legitimation of warfare', *The media and the Persian Gulf War*; (ed) Denton, Robert; Praeger; Westport CT pp 257-284

Copeland, Miles (1989): *The game player*; Aurum Press; London

Crozier, Brian (1994): *Free agent: The unseen war 1941-1991*; HarperCollins; London

Cummings, Bruce (1992): *War and television*; Verso; London

Curran, James; Douglas, Angus and Whannel, Garry (1980); 'The political economy of the human interest story', *Newspapers and democracy; International essays on a changing medium*; (ed) Smith, Anthony; MIT Press, Cambridge, Massachusetts pp 288-316

Curran, James and Sparks, Colin (1991): 'Press and popular culture', *Media, Culture and Society*; London; Vol 13. No 2; April pp 224-228

Curran, James and Seaton, Jean (1991): *Power without responsibility: The press and broadcasting in Britain*; Routledge; London; fourth edition

Currey, Cecil (1991): 'Vietnam: Lessons learned', *America, France and Vietnam: Cultural history and ideas of conflict*; (eds) Helling, Phil and Roper, Jon; Avebury; Aldershot pp 71-90

Curtis, Mark (1995): 'A "great adventure": overthrowing the government of Iran', *Lobster*; Hull; December pp 1-5

Dalyell, Tam (1987): *Misrule: How Mrs Thatcher has misled Parliament – From the sinking of the Belgrano to the Wright affair*; Hamish Hamilton; London

Darwish, Adel and Alexander, Gregory (1991): *Unholy Babylon: The secret history of Saddam's War*; Victor Gollancz; London

Deacon, Richard (1990): *The French secret service*; Grafton Books; London

Debord, Guy (1991): *Comments on the society of the spectacle*; Pirate Press; Sheffield

Demac, D (1984): *Keeping America uninformed: Government secrecy in the 1980s*; Pilgrim Press, New York

Derbyshire, J. Denis and Derbyshire, Ian (1988): *Politics in Britain: From Callaghan to Thatcher*; Chambers; London (orig 1986: Sandpiper Publishing)

Dickson, Barney (1991): 'From emperor to policeman: Britain and the Gulf war'; *The Gulf War and the New World Order*; (eds) Bresheeth, Haim and Yuval-Davis, Nira; Zed Books: London pp 40-48

Dickson, Sandra H. (1994): 'Understanding media bias: The press and the US invasion of Panama', *Journalism Quarterly*; Vol 71 No 4; Washington pp 809-819

Dillon, G.M. (1989): *The Falklands, politics and war*; Macmillan; Basingstoke, Hampshire

Dionne, E.J. (1992): 'The illusion of technique: The impact of polls on reporters and democracy', *Media polls in American politics*; (eds) Mann, Thomas E and Orren, Gary R; Brookings Institute; Washington pp 150-167

Dockrill, Michael (1988): *British defence since 1945*; Blackwell; Oxford

Dorman, William (1991): 'The media and the Gulf: a closer look' (proceedings of the conference held 3-4 May at Graduate School of Journalism, University of California, Berkeley) pp 15-16

Dorman, William and Manzour, Farhang (1987): *The US press and Iran: Foreign policy and the journalism of deference*; University of California Press; Berkeley

Dorril, Stephen (1993): *The silent conspiracy: Inside the Intelligence Services in the 1990s*; Heinemann; London

Dorril, Stephen and Ramsay, Robin (1991): *Smear! Wilson and the secret state*; Fourth Estate; London

Draper, Theodore (1992): 'The Gulf War reconsidered', *New York Review of Books*; 16 January pp 46-52 and 'The true history of the Gulf War'; NY Review of Books; 30 January.pp 38-44

Drucker, Peter F. (1993): *Post-capitalist society*; Butterworth-Heinemann; Oxford

Dumbrell, John (1990): *The making of US foreign policy*; Manchester University Press; Manchester/New York

Easlea, Brian (1983): *Fathering the unthinkable: Masculinity and the nuclear arms race*; Pluto Press; London

Easthope, Anthony (1986): *What a man's gotta do: The masculine myth in popular culture*; Paladin Grafton Books, London

Edmunds, Martin (1988): *Armed services and society*; Leicester University Press; Leicester

Ehteshami, Anoushiravam (1987): 'Isreal, nuclear weapons and the Middle East', *On the brink: nuclear proliferation and the Third World*; (eds) Worsley, Peter and Hadjor, Kofi Buenor; Third World Communications; London pp 142-158

European Research Group (1992): *The media in Western Europe*; Sage; London

Fairclough, Norman (1995): *Media discourse*; Edward Arnold; London/New York

Falk, Richard (1991): 'How the West mobilised for war', *Beyond the Gulf War*; (ed) Gittings, John; Catholic Institute for International Relations; London pp 12-22

Farago, Ladislas (1967): *The broken seal: The dramatic story of Operation Magic and the Pearl Harbour disaster*; Mayflower; London

Farouk-Sluglett, Marion and Sluglett, Peter (1990): *Iraq since 1958: From revolution to dictatorship*; I. B. Tauris and Co; London/New York

Featherstone, Donald (1993): *Victorian colonial warfare: Africa*; Blandford; London (1993a): *Victorian colonial warfare: India*; Blandford; London

Fialka, John (1992): *The hotel warriors: Covering the Gulf*; The Media Studies Project/Woodrow Wilson Center; Washington

Fisk, Robert (1997): 'With Sten guns and sovereigns British and US saved Iran's throne for the Shah', the *Independent*; London, 16 March

Fiske, John (1992): 'Popularity and the politics of information', *Journalism and popular culture*; (eds) Dahlgren, Peter and Sparks; Colin. pp 45-63

Flanders, Laurie (1992) 'Restructuring reality: media mind games and the war', *Beyond the Storm: A Gulf crisis reader*; (eds) Bennis, Phyllis and Moushabeck, Michel; Canongate; Edinburgh. pp 160-172

Foot, Paul (1991): 'Strenuous liberty: a nervous revival', *British Journalism Review*; London; Vol 2 No 4 pp 5-8

Fore, William (1991): 'The shadow war in the Gulf'; in *Media Development*, London, October pp 51-53

Frank, Andre Gunder (1992): 'A Third World War: A political economy of the Persian Gulf War and the New World Order', *Triumph of the image: The media's war in the Persian Gulf – a global perspective*; (eds) Mowlana, Hamid; Gerbner, George and Schiller, Herbert I; pp 3-21

Freedman, Robert (1991): *Middle East from the Iran-Contra Affair to the Intifada*; Syracuse University Press; Syracuse

Freemantle, Brian (1983): *CIA: The 'honourable' company*; Michael Joseph/ Rainbird; London

Frelick, Bill (1992): 'The false promise of Operation Provide Comfort: Protecting refugees of protecting state power', *Merip*; Washington DC; May/June pp 22-27

Friedman, Alan (1993): *Spider's web: Bush, Saddam, Thatcher and the Decade of Deceit*; Faber and Faber; London

Friedman, Norman (1991): *Desert victory*; United States Naval Institute; Annapolis, Maryland

Fukuyama, Francis (1989): 'The end of history?', *National Interest*; Washington; Summer pp 3-18

Fund for Free Expression (1991): 'Freedom to do as they're told', *Index on Censorship*; London; Vol 20. No. 4/5; April/May p 37

Galbraith, John Kenneth (1977): *The age of uncertainty*; BBC Publications; London

Gall, Sandy (1984): *Don't worry about the money now*; New English Library; London

Gamble, Andrew (1988): *The free economy and the strong state: The politics of Thatcherism*; Macmillan Education; Basingstoke, Hampshire

Gannett Foundation (1991): *The media at war: The press and the Persian Gulf conflict*; The Freedom Forum; Columbia University; New York City

Gearty, Conor (1991): *Terror*; Faber; London

Gellhorn, Martha (1990): 'The invasion of Panama', *Granta*; Harmondsworth, Middlesex; Summer pp 205-229

Geraghty, Tony (1980): *Who dares wins: The story of the SAS 1950-1980*; Fontana; London

Gerbner, George (1992): 'Persian Gulf War: the movie', *Triumph of the image: The media's war in the Persian Gulf – a global perspective*; (eds) Mowlana, Gerbner, Schiller, pp 243-265

Giddens, Anthony (1985): *The nation state and violence*; Polity Press; Cambridge

Gilkes, Patrick (1993): 'From peacekeeping to peace enforcement: The Somali precedent', *Middle East Report*; Washington DC; November-December; pp 21-24

Gillies, Nigel (1991): 'Operating Desert Storm media centre', *Despatches* (the journal of the Territorial Army Pool of Public Information Officers); London; No 2; Autumn pp 12-16

Glasgow University Media Group (1985): *War and peace news*; Open University Press; Milton Keynes

(1991): *The British media and the Gulf War*; research working paper; Glasgow

Glavanis, Pandeli M (1991): 'Oil and the new helots of Arabia', *The Gulf war and the new world order*; (eds) Bresheeth, Haim and Yuval-Davis, Nira; Zed Press; London pp 181-190

Goldman, Francisco (1990): 'What price Panama: A visit to a barrio destroyed by US forces', *Harpers Magazine*; New York; September pp 71-78

Goose, Stephen D (1988): 'Low intensity warfare: The warriors and their weapons', *Low intensity warfare: how the USA fights wars without declaring them*; (eds) Klare, Michael T. and Kornbluh, Peter; Methuen; London pp 80-111

Gordon, Paul and Rosenberg, David (1989): *Daily racism: The press and black people in Britain*; Runnymede Trust, London

Gowing, Nik (1991): 'Dictating the global agenda', *Spectrum*; Independent Television Commission; London; Summer pp 7-9

Greaves, William (1991): 'The war that almost wasn't fought'; *The Times*, 1 January

Greenberg, Susan and Smith, Graham (1982): *Rejoice: Media freedom and the Falklands*; Campaign for Press and Broadcasting Freedom; London

Greenslade, Roy (1992): *Maxwell's fall: The appalling legacy of a corrupt man*; Simon and Schuster; London

(1995): 'If only it were true', the *Guardian*; August 21

Gripsrud, Jostein (1992): 'The aesthetics and politics of melodrama', *Journalism and Popular Culture* op cit pp 84-95

Guiterrez-Villalobos, Sonia, Hertog, James K. and Rush, Ramma R. (1994): 'Press support for the US administration during the Panama invasion: analysis of strategic and tactical critique in the domestic press', *Journalism Quarterly*; Washington; Vol 71 No. 3 pp 618-627

Gunn, Simon (1989): Revolution of the Right; Pluto/with the Transnational Institute; London

Hall, Stuart (1995): 'The whites of their eyes: Racist ideologies and the media', *Gender, race and class: a text-reader*; (eds) Dines, Gail and Humez, Jean M; Sage; Thousand Oaks/London/New Delhi pp 18-22

Halliday, Fred (1981): 'US intrigue in the Gulf'; *New Statesman*; London; 1 May p 5

(1983) 'Sources of the New Cold War', *State and societies*; (eds) Held, David; Anderson, James; Gieben, Bram; Hall, Stuart; Harris, Laurence; Lewis, Paul;

Parker, Noel and Turok, Ben; Martin Robertson/Open University; Oxford pp 540-549

(1986): *The making of the Second Cold War*; Verso, London

(1987) 'News management and counter insurgency: the case of Oman', *The media in British politics*; (eds) Seaton, Jean and Pimlott, Ben; Routledge, London pp 180-200

(1989): *Cold War,Third World: an essay on Soviet-American relations*; Radius; London

(1991): 'The Gulf war and its aftermath – first reflections'; *International Affairs*; London; 67.2 pp 223-234

Hallin, Daniel C (1986): *The 'uncensored war'*; Oxford University Press; Oxford

Hanlin, Bruce (1992): 'Owners, editors and journalists', *Ethical issues in journalism and the media*; (eds) Belsey, Andrew and Chadwick, Ruth; Routledge, London pp 33-48

Hanson, Christopher (Boot, William) (1991): 'The pool', *The media and the Gulf War; (ed) Smith, Hedrick;* Seven Locks Press; Washington DC pp 128-135

Harkins, Hugh (1995): *Tornado: Air defence variant protecting Britain's skies*; The Pentland Press; Durham

Harris, Laurence (1984): 'State and economy in the Second World War', *State and society in contemporary Britain: a critical introduction*; (eds) McLennan, George; Held, David and Hall, Stuart; Polity Press; Cambridge pp 50-76

Harris, Paul (1992): *Somebody else's war: Frontline reports from the Balkan Wars*; Spa Books; Stevenage, Herts

Harris, Robert (1983): *Gotcha! The media, government and the Falklands crisis*; Faber, London

Heibert, Ray Eldon (1995): 'Mass media as weapons of modern warfare', *Impact of mass media: current issues*; (ed) Heibert, Ray Eldon; Longman US; New York pp 327-334

Heikal, Mohamed (1992): *Illusions of triumph: An Arab view of the Gulf War*; HarperCollins; London

Held, David (1984): 'Power and legitimacy in contemporary Britain', *State and society in contemporary Britain: a critical introduction* (op cit) pp 299-369

Henderson, Simon (1991): *Instant Empire: Saddam Hussein's ambition for Iraq*; Mercury House; San Francisco

Hellinger, Daniel and Judd, Dennis (1991): *The democratic facade*; Cole Publishing Company; Pacific Grove, California

Henderson, Simon (1991): *Instant Empire: Saddam Hussein's ambition for Iraq*; Mercury House, San Francisco

Henwood, Doug (1992): 'The US ecomony – the enemy within', *Covert Action Information Bulletin*; Washington; Summer pp 45-49

Herman, Edward and Chomsky, Noam (1994): *Manufacturing consent: The political economy of the mass media*; Vintage; London (orig. 1988: Pantheon Books; New York)

Hersh, Seymour (1991): *The Samson Option: Israel, America and the Bomb*; Faber and Faber; London

Hertsgaard, Mark (1988): *On bended knee: The press and the Reagan presidency*; Farrar Straus Giroux; New York

Hiro, Dilip (1992): *Desert Shield to Desert Storm: The Second Gulf War*; Paladin; London

Hodgson, Godfrey (1991): 'Resident experts to flying deskmen', *British Journalism Review*; Vol 2 No.4; London pp 9-13

(1991a): *Truth, journalism and the Gulf*; City University; London

Hollingsworth, Mark (1986): *The press and political dissent*; Pluto, London

Hooper, Alan (1982): *The military and the media*; Gower; London

Horkheimer, Max and Adorno, Theodore (1973): *The dialectic of enlightenment*; Allan Lane; London.

Human Rights Watch/Middle East (1995): *Iraq's crime of genocide: The Anfal campaign against the Kurds*; Yale University Press; New Haven/London

Hunter, Jane (1991): 'Dismantling the war on Libya', *Covert Action Information Bulletin*; Washington DC; Summer pp 47-51

Hunter, Robin (1995): *True stories of the SAS*; Virgin; London

Hussain, Asaf (1988): *Political terrorism and the state in the Middle East*; Mansell Publishing; London/New York

Hutton, Will (1996 orig, 1995): *The state we're in*; Vintage; London

Index on Censorship (1988): bi-monthly monitoring censorship globally; issue September 1988 Vo 17 No 8 was focused on the UK

'Insight' (1980): *Siege!*; Hamlyn; London

al-Jabbar, Faleh Abd (1992): 'Why the uprisings failed', *Merip*; Washington DC; May/June pp 2-14

Jahanpour, Farhang (1991): 'A new order for the Middle East?' *The World Today*; London; May pp 74-77

James, Joy (1990): 'US policy in Panama'; *Race and Class*; London pp 17-32

Jeffords, Susan (1989): *The remasculination of America: Gender and the Vietnam War*; Indiana University Press; Bloomington and Indianapolis

Johnston, Anne (1993): 'Media coverage of women in the Gulf War', *The media and the Persian Gulf War*; (ed) Denton, Robert; Praeger; Westport CT pp 197-212

Jowett, Garth and O'Donnell, Victoria (1992): *Propaganda and persuasion*; Sage; London; second edition

Kabani, Rana (1991): 'The Gulf of Misunderstanding', *Independent on Sunday* 10 February

(1994 orig 1986): *Imperial fictions: Europe's myths of the Orient*; Pandora; London

Kagay, Michael R. (1992): 'Variability without fault: Why even well-designed polls can disagree', *Media polls in American politics*; (eds) Mann, Thomas E. and Orren Gary R.; Brookings Institute; Washington DC

Kaku, Michio (1992): 'Nuclear threats and the New World Order', *Covert Action Information Bulletin*; Washington; Summer pp 22-28

Kaldor, Mary (1982): *The baroque arsenal*; Andre Deutsch; London

(1990): *The imaginary war*; Verso; London

(1991): (ed) 'After the Cold War', *Europe from below*; Verso; London.

Karsh, Efraim and Rautsi, Inari (1991): 'Why Saddam Hussein invaded Kuwait', *Survival*; London; January/February pp 18-30

Kay, Richard (1992): *Soldier warrior*; Penumbra; London

Keane, John (1991): *The media and democracy*; Polity Press; Cambridge

Keeble, Richard (1986): 'Portraying the peace movement', *Bending reality*; (eds) Curran, James et al; Pluto; London pp 47-57

(1991): 'How the media took us to war', *Changes*; London; 2-15 February p 7

(1993): 'All myth, rhetoric and spectacle in Iraq and Somalia', Gemini News Service, London; 19 January

(1994): *The newspapers handbook*; Routledge; London

(1994): 'From butcher to bad boy', Gemini News Service, London; 11 January

(1997): 'Saddam the survivor', Gemini News Service, London, 14 January

Keegan, John (1993): *A history of warfare*; Random House; London

Kegley, Charles W. Jr and Wittkopf, Eugene R. (1987) *American foreign policy: pattern and process*; Macmillan Educational; Basingstoke, Hampshire

Kellner, Douglas (1990): *Television and the crisis of democracy*; Westview Press; Boulder/San Francisco/Oxford

(1992): *The Persian Gulf TV war*; Westview Press; Boulder/San Francisco/Oxford

(1993): 'Gulf War II the media offensive', *Lies of our Times*; New York; May pp 17-19

(1995): 'The US media and the 1993 war against Iraq', *The US media and the Middle East: Image and perception*; (ed) Kamalipour, Yahya R; Greenwood Press; Westport, Connecticut

Kelly, Michael (1993): *Martyr's day: Chronicle of a small war*; Macmillan; London

Kemp, Anthony (1995): *The SAS: Savage wars of peace*; Signet; London

Kennedy, Paul (1986): 'A.J.P.Taylor and profound causes in history', *Warfare, diplomacy and politics: Essays in honour of A.J.P.Taylor*; (ed) Wrigley, Chris; Hamish Hamilton; London. pp 14-29

Kerr, Philip (1990): *Book of lies*; Viking; London

Khanum, Saeed (1991): 'Inside Iraq'; *New Statesman and Society*; London 24 May pp 12-16

Klare, Michael (1980): 'Militarism: the issues today', *Problems in contemporary militarism*; (eds) Eide, Asbjorn and Thee, Marek; Croom Helm; London pp 36-46

Klare, Michael and Kornbluh, Peter (1988): *Low-intensity warfare: How the USA fights wars without declaring them*; Methuen; London

Kleinwachter, Wolfgang (1991): 'National security versus right to know', *Media Development*; London; October pp 5-6

Knightley, Phillip (1982): *The first casualty: The war correspondent as hero, propagandist and myth maker*; Quartet Books; London

(1986): *The second oldest profession: The spy as bureaucrat, patriot, fantasist and whore*; Andre Deutsch; London

(1991) 'Here is the patriotically censored news', *Index on Censorship*; London; No 4/5 pp 4-5

(1991a): 'Lies, damned lies and military briefings'; *New Statesman and Society*; London; 8 February pp 26-27

Kovel, Joel (1983): *Against the state of nuclear terror*; Pan; London

Kurtz, Howard (1994): *Media circus: The trouble with America's newspapers*; Times Books/Random House; New York

Lambakis, Stephen (1995): 'Space control in Desert Storm and beyond'; *Orbis*; Philadelphia; Vol 39. No 3; summer pp 417-437

Laurens, Henry (1992): '*Pourquoi Ryad préfère la parapluie américain*', *Le Monde diplomatique*; Paris; August. pp 8-9

Laurie, Peter (1980): *Beneath the City Streets*; Penguin, London

Layne, Christopher (1991): 'Why the Gulf War was not in the national interest', *Atlantic Monthly*, Boston, Massachusetts, July pp 615-681

Lederman, Jim (1992): *Battle lines: The American media and the Intifada*; Henry Holt and Company; New York

Leigh, David (1988): *The Wilson plot: The intelligence services and the discrediting of a prime minister*; Heinemann; London

Levinson, Nan (1991): 'Snappy visuals, hard facts and obscured issues', *Index on Censorship*; London; No. 4/5 pp 27-29

Lewis, Justin (1997): 'What counts in cultural studies', *Media Culture and Society*; London; Vol 19. No 1; pp 83-97

Lewis, Justin, Morgan, Michael and Jhally, Sut (1991): *The Gulf War: A study of the media, public opinion and public knowledge*; University of Massachusetts Centre for the Study of Communication

Lewis, Peter (1984): *A people's war*; Thames Methuen; London

Luckham, Robin (1983): 'Of arms and culture', *Current Research on Peace and Violence IV*; Tampere, Finland pp 1-63

Luttwak, Edward (1991): 'Victory through air power', *Commentary*, New York; Vol 92 No. 2; August pp 27-30

Lott, Tim (1990): 'Lie of the land and land of the lie', the *Guardian*; 14-15 July

MacArthur, Brian (ed) (1991): *Despatches from the Gulf War*; Bloomsbury; London (1991a): *Deadline Sunday: a life in the week of the Sunday Times*; Hodder and Stoughton; London

Macarthur, John R. (1993): *Second front: Censorship and propaganda in the Gulf War*; University of California Press; Berkeley and Los Angeles; second edition

Macedo, Donaldo (1994): *Literacies of power: What Americans are not allowed to know*; Westview Press; Boulder, San Francisco

McCormick, Thomas J. (1989): *America's half century: United States foreign policy in the Cold War*; John Hopkins University Press; Baltimore

McDaniel, Ann and Fineman, Howard (1991): 'The President's "spin" patrol', *The media and the Gulf war*; (ed) Smith, Hedrick; Seven Locks Press; Washington DC pp 154-157

McDonald, Trevor (1993): *Fortunate circumstances*; Weidenfeld and Nicolson; London

MacKenzie, John (1984): *Propaganda and empire: The manipulation of British public opinion 1880-1960*; Manchester University Press; Manchester

McMahon, Jeff (1984): *Reagan and the world: Imperial policy in the New Cold War*; Pluto Press; London

'McNab, Andy' (pseudonym of SAS member) (1994): *Bravo Two Zero*; Corgi; London

McNair, Brian (1988): *Images of the enemy*; Routledge; London (1995): *An introduction to political communication*; Routledge; London

McQuail, Denis (1977): *Analysis of newspaper content; Royal Commission on the Press*; Research Series Four; HMSO; London (1987): *Mass communication theory: An introduction*; Sage; London (1992): *Media performance: Mass communication and the public interest*; Sage; London

Makiya, Kanan (Al-Khalil, Samir) (1993): *Cruelty and silence: War, tyranny, uprising and the Arab World*; Penguin Books, London

Malek, Abbas and Leidig, Lisa (1991): 'US press coverage of the Gulf War', *Media Development*; London; October pp 15-19

Mann, Michael (1988): *States, wars and capitalism*; Blackwell; Oxford

Marshall, Jonathan, Scott, Peter Dale, and Hunter, Jane (1987): *The Iran-Contra connection*; South End Press; Boston

Martin, David and Walcott, John (1988): *Best laid plans – The inside story of America's war against terrorism*; Harper and Row; New York

Mason, R.A. (1991): 'The air war in the Gulf', *Survival*; London; May/June pp 211-229

Mercer, Derrik (ed) (1987): *The fog of war*; Heinemann; London

Middle East Watch (1991): *Needless deaths in the Gulf War: Civilian casualties during the air campaign and violations of the laws of war*; Human Rights Watch; New York

Miles, Sara (1987): 'The real war: post-Vietnam low intensity conflict', *Unwinding the Vietnam war: From war into peace*; (ed) Willams, Reece; The Real Comet Press; Seattle pp 316-331

Miliband, Ralph (1988; orig 1982): *Capitalist democracy in Britain*; Oxford University Press; Oxford/New York

Miller, Marc (1991): 'Patriotic blindness and anti-truth weapons', *Index on Censorship*; London; No. 10 pp 32-34

Moughrabi, Fouad (1993): 'Domesticating the body politic', *Merip*; Washington; January-February pp 38-40

Morgan, Kenneth (1990): *The people's peace 1945-1989*; Oxford University Press; Oxford

Morley, Richard (1991): 'The lost history of the Falklands War', *Open Eye*; Issue 1; London pp 4-11

Morrison, David E. (1992): *Television and the Gulf War*; John Libbey; London

Morrison, David and Tumber, Howard (1988): *Journalists at war: The dynamics of news reporting in the Falklands conflict*; Sage, London

Mowlana, Hamid (1992): 'Roots of war: The long road to intervention', *The media war in the Persian Gulf - a global perspective*; (eds) Mowlana, Gerbner, Schiller; pp 30-50

Moyers, Bill (1986): *The secret government: The constitution in crisis*; Seven Locks Press; Washington

Muir, Kate (1992): *Arms and the woman*; Sinclair/Stevenson; London

Mungham, Geoff (1986): 'Grenada: News blackout in the Caribbean', *The fog of war*; (ed) Mercer, Derrik; Heinemann; London pp 291-310

Murphy, David (1991): *The Stalker affair and the press*; Unwin Hyman; London

Neff, Donald (1992): 'Israel's dependence on the US: the full extent of the special relationship', *Middle East International*; London; 1 May pp 16-17

(1992a): 'America's unconditional hand-outs to Israel; *Middle East International*; London; 9 October p 3

Nelson, Keith and Olin, Spencer C (1979): *Why war? Ideology, theory and history*; University of California Press; Berkeley

Newsinger, John (1989): 'A forgotten war: British intervention in Indonesia', *Race and Class* 30.4; London pp 51-66

(1995): 'The myth of the SAS', *Lobster*; Hull; No 30 December pp 32-36

Niva, Steve (1992): 'The battle is joined', *Beyond the Storm* (op cit) pp 55-74

Nonneman, Gerd (1986): *Iraq, the Gulf States and the war*; Exeter Middle East Politics Series; Exeter; No 1

Northmore, David (1990): *Freedom of information handbook*; Bloomsbury; London

Norton, Anne (1991): 'Gender, sexuality and the Iraq of our imagination', *Merip*; Washington, No 173 Vol 21 No 6

Norton-Taylor, Richard (1991): 'Pressure behind the scenes', *Index on Censorship*; London; 4/5 pp 13-14

O'Kane, Maggie (1995): 'Bloodless words, bloody war', the *Guardian Weekend*; London; 16 December

Pagonis, Lt Gen. William G. (1992) (with Cruikshank, Jeffrey L.): *Moving mountains: Lessons in leadership and logistics from the Gulf War*; Harvard Business School Press; Boston

Parenti, Michael (1986): *Inventing reality: The politics of the mass media*; St Martin's Press; New York

Paxman, Jeremy (1990): *Friends in high places: Who rules Britain?*; Michael Joseph; London

Pelletierre, Stephen; Johnson, Douglas and Rosenberger, Leif (1990): *Iraqi power and US security in the Middle East*; Strategic Studies Institute; US Army War College (US Government Printing Office)

Perry, Mark (1992): *Eclipse: The last days of the CIA*; William Morrow and Company; New York

Peters E. (1985): *Torture*; Oxford; Blackwell

Peters, John and Nichol, John (1992): *Tornado Down*; Michael Joseph; London (with Pearson, William)

Phillips, Joan (1992): 'The invention of a holocaust'; *Living Marxism*; London; September pp 8-11

Pilger, John (1986): *Heroes*: Pan; London

(1991): 'The Great British Silence: behind the sanitised media-speak are dead bodies', *Free Press; Journal of Campaign for Press and Broadcasting Freedom*; London; January/February p 1

(1991a): 'Sins of Omission', *New Statesman and Society*; London; 8 February p 8

(1991b): 'A one-sided bloodfest'; *News Statesman and Society*; 8 March. pp 8-9

(1991c): 'Who killed the Kurds?'; *New Statesman and Society*; London; 12 April pp 6-7

(1991d): 'The poor world pays: Why isn't the UN assisting countries hit by the war?' *New Statesman and Society*; London; 19 April pp 10-11

(1992): *Distant voices*; Vintage; London

(1992a): 'Shredding crocodile tears', *New Statesman and Society*; London; 20 March p 10

Platt, Steve (1991): 'Casualties of war', *New Statesman and Society*; London; February 22 pp 12-13

Ponting, Clive (1989): 'Defence decision making and public opinion – a view from the inside', *Public opinion and nuclear weapons*; (eds) Marsh, Catherine and Fraser, Colin; Macmillan; London pp 171-191

(1990): *Secrecy in Britain*; Blackwell; Oxford

(1990a): *1940: Myth and reality*; Cardinal; London

Powell, Colin (1995): *Soldier's way*; Hutchinson; London (with Joseph Persico)

Power, Carla (1991): 'Writing off Islam', *Index on Censorship*; London; April/May pp 10-11

Prades, John (1986): *President's secret wars: CIA and Pentagon covert operations from World War II through Iranscan*; William Morrow; New York

Prange, Gordon W. (1991): *Pearl Harbour: The verdict of history*; Penguin; Harmonsworth

Prince, Stephen (1993): 'Celluloid heroes and smart bombs: Hollywood at war in the Middle East', *The media and the Persian Gulf War*; (ed) Denton pp 235-256

Quigley, John (1992): *The ruses for war – American interventionism since World War II*; Prometheus; New York

Ranelagh, John (1992): *CIA: A history*; BBC Books; London

Ray, Ellen and Schaap, William H. (1991): 'Disinformation and covert action', *Covert Action Information Bulletin*; Washington; No 37, Summer 9-13

Reese, Stephen D and Buckalew, Bob (1995): 'The militarisation of local television: The routine framing of the Persian Gulf War', in *Critical Studies in Mass Communication*; Annendale, VA; Vol 12 No. 1; March pp 40-59

Reginald, R. and Elliot, Dr Jeffrey M. (1985): *Tempest in a teacup*; Borgo Press; San Bernardino, California

Reich, Bernard (1987): (ed) *The powers in the Middle East: the ultimate strategic area*; Praeger; New York

Renton, Alex (1991): 'RAF was fighting war on two fronts in Gulf campaign'; the *Independent*; 24 May

Reynolds, Charles (1989): *The politics of war: A study of violence in inter-state relations*; Harvester Wheatsheaf; London

Roberts, John (1995): *Visions and mirages: The Middle East in a new era*; Mainstream Publishing; Edinburgh/London

Robins, Kevin and Levidow, Les (1991): 'The eye of the Storm', *Screen*; London; Vol 32 No 3; Autumn pp 324-328

Robinson, Stephen (1996): 'Gulf war bombs "were not smart" ', the *Telegraph*; London; July 10

Rochlin, Gene and Demchak, Chris C. (1991): 'The Gulf war: Technological organisation and organisational implications', *Survival*; Vol 33 No 3; London; May/June pp 260-273

Rogers, Paul (1991): 'The myth of the clean war', *Covert Action Information Bulletin*; Washington; No 37; Summer pp 26-30

(1992): 'Bushbacking: Britain goes to war', *Beyond the Storm* (op cit) pp 268-279

(1994): 'A note on British deployment of nuclear weapons in crises – with particular reference to the Falklands and Gulf Wars and the purpose of Trident', *Lobster*; Hull; December pp 4-7

Rose, John (1986): *Israel: the hijack state: America's watchdog in the Middle East*; Bookmarks; London

Rose, Stephen (1986): 'Spend, spend, spend – on military only', *New Statesman*, London, 3 January pp 11-12

Rose, Steven and Baravi, Abraham (1988): 'The meaning of Halabja: Chemical warfare in Kurdistan', *Race and Class*; London; 30.1 pp 74-77

Rosenblum, Mort (1993): *Who stole the news: Why we can't keep up with what happens in the world and what we can do about it*; John Wiley and Sons; New York

Rosen, Jay (1991): 'From slogan to spectacle: How the media and the left lost the war', *Tikkun*; Oakland, California; May/June p 23

Rosenfeld, Nancy Watt (1991): 'Buried alive', *Lies Of Our Times*; New York; October

Rusbridger, James (1989): *The intelligence game: Illusions and delusions of international espionage*; Bodley Head; London

Rusbridger, James and Nove, Eric (1991): *Betrayed at Pearl Harbour: How Churchill lured Roosevelt into war*; Michael O'Mara; London

'Ryan, Chris' (1995): *The one that got away*; Century; London

Ryle, Martin (1981): *The politics of nuclear disarmament*; Pluto Press; London

Sakur, Stephen (1991): 'The charred bodies at Mutla Ridge'; *London Review of Books*; London; 4 April. Reproduced in *Despatches from the Gulf War*; (ed) McArthur, Brian; Bloomsbury; London pp 261-267

Sadria, Mojtaba (1992): 'United States, Japan and the Gulf War', *Monthly Review*, Vol 43 April pp 1-16

Said, Edward (1981): *Covering Islam: How the media and experts determine how we see the rest of the world*; Routledge, London

(1992): 'Thoughts on a war: Ignorant armies clash by night', *Beyond the Storm* op cit pp 1-6

(1995): *Peace and its discontents: Gaza-Jericho 1993-1995*; Vintage; London

Salinger, Pierre and Laurent, Eric (1991): *Secret dossier: The hidden agenda behind the Gulf war*: Penguin; Harmondsworth, Middlesex

Sampson, Anthony (1992): 'The anatomy of Britain in 1992', the *Independent on Sunday*; 29 March

Schiller, Herbert I. (1992): 'Manipulating hearts and minds', *Triumph of the image: The media's war in the Persian Gulf – a global perspective*; (eds) Mowlana, Gerbner and Schiller pp 22-29

Schorr, Daniel (1991): 'Ten days that shook the White House'; *Columbia Journalism Review*; New York; July/August pp 21-23

Schostak, John (1993): *Dirty marks: The education of self, media and popular culture*; Pluto; London

Schlesinger, Philip (1991): 'The media politics of siege management', *Media, state and nation: Political violence and collective identities*; Sage; London pp 29-59

Schwarzkopf, General Norman H. (1992): *It doesn't take a hero*; Bantam Press; London/New York

Sciolini, Elaine (1992): 'US report shows Saddam rebuilding power in Iraq', *New York Times*/the *Guardian*; 17 June

Scott, John (1991): *Who rules Britain?*; Basil Blackwell; Oxford

Scott, Peter Dale (1991) 'US needs Kuwaiti petrodollars – not just oil', *San Francisco Chronicle*, 2 January

Seager, Joni (1992): 'Torching the earth', *New Internationalist*; Oxford; October pp 24-26

Searle, Chris (1989): *Your daily dose: racism and the Sun*; Campaign for Press and Broadcasting Freedom; London.

Sebba, Anne (1994): *Battling for news: The rise of the woman reporter*; Hodder and Stoughton; London

Segaller, Stephen (1986): *Invisible armies: Terrorism in the 1990s*; Michael Joseph; London

Servaes, Jan (1991): 'Was Grenada a testcase for the "disinformation war"?' *Media Development*, London, October pp 41-44

Seymour-Ure, Colin (1991): *The political impact of the mass media*; Constable; London

Shaw, Martin (1987): 'Rise and fall of the military-democratic state 1940-1985', *The sociology of war and peace*, (eds) Shaw, Martin and Creighton, Colin; Pluto, London pp 143-158

(1991): *Post military society*; Polity Press; Cambridge

(1996): *Civil society and media in global crises: representing distant violence*; Pinter; London/New York

Shaw, Martin and Carr-Hill, Roy (1991): *Mass media and attitudes to the Gulf War in Britain*; paper presented to EPOP conference, Oxford; 28 September

Sherwood, Ben (1992): 'That first Patriot scored a hit – on a cloud', *International Herald Tribune*; 25 September

Simons, Geoff (1992): '"Honest" Perot's Irangate secret'; *Socialist*; London; 17 July

Simpson, John (1991): *From the House of War*; Arrow; London

Sloyan, Patrick (1991): 'The silver bullet in Desert Storm', the *Guardian*; 23 May

Smith, Dan and Smith, Ron (1983): *The economics of militarism*; Pluto; London

Smith, Jean Edward (1992) *George Bush's war*; Henry Holt; New York

Smith, Joan (1985): *Clouds of deceit: The deadly legacy of Britain's bomb tests*; Faber and Faber; London

Smith, Robert Freeman (1994): *The Caribbean world and the United States: Mixing rum and Coca-Cola*; Twayne Publishers; New York

Sparks, Colin (1992): 'Popular journalism: Theories and practice', *Journalism and popular culture* (op cit) pp 24-44

Spaven, Malcolm (1986): 'A piece of the action: The use of US bases in Britain', *Mad Dogs: The US raids on Libya*; (eds) Thompson, Edward and Kaldor Mary; Pluto; London pp 16-34

(1991): 'Too close to the ground'; the *Guardian*; 27 January

State Research (1980): 'How the SAS ended the Prince's Gate siege'; *Bulletin No 18*; London; June/July

Steiner, George (1971): 'In Bluebeard's Castle', the *Listener*; London; 15 April pp 472-479

Stockwell, John (1991): *The Praetorian Guard: The US role in the New World Order*; South End Press; Boston

Stork, Joe (1986): 'Oil, arms and the Gulf War'; *Khamsin*; London pp 19-26

(1995): 'The Middle East arms bazaar after the Gulf War'; *Middle East Review*; Washington DC; November/December pp 14-19

Stork, Joe and Flanders, Laura (1993): 'Power structure and the American media', *Merip*; Washington DC; January/February pp 2-7

Stork, Joe and Lesch, Ann (1990): 'Why war: Background to the crisis', *Merip*; Washington DC; Issue No 167; November/December pp 11-18

Sultan, Khaled Bin (1995): *Desert warrior: A personal view of the Gulf War by the Joint Forces Commander* (with Seale, Patrick); HarperCollins; London

Sumaida, Hussein (1991): *Circle of fear* (with Jerome, Carole); St Edmundsbury Press; St Edmunds, Suffolk

Sutton, Antony C. (1976): *Wall Street and the rise of Hitler*; Bloomfield Books; Sudbury, Suffolk

Tanzer, Michael (1992): 'Oil and the Gulf crisis', *Beyond the Storm: A Gulf crisis reader* (op cit) pp 263-267

Tarock, Adam (1996): 'US-Iran relations: heading for confrontation', *Third World Quarterly*; Egham, Surrey pp 149-167

Taylor, John (1991): *War photography: Realism in the British press*; Routledge; London

Taylor, Philip (1992): *War and the media: Propaganda and persuasion in the Gulf War*; Manchester University Press; Manchester

Taylor, Robert (1970): 'The Campaign for Nuclear Disarmament', *The age of affluence 1951-1964*; (eds) Bogdanor, Vernon and Skidelsky, Robert; Macmillan; Basingstoke/London pp 221-253

Thee, Marek (1980): 'Militarism and militarisation in contemporary international relations', *Problems of contemporary militarism*; (eds) Elde, Asbjorn and Thee, Marek; pp 15-35

Thomas, Hugh (1967): *The Suez affair*; Weidenfeld and Nicolson; London

Thomas, Rosamund M. (1991): *Espionage and secrecy: The Official Secrets Acts 1911-1989*; Routledge; London

Thompson, Edward (1980): 'The secret state', *Writing by candlelight*; Merlin Press; London pp 149-180

(1980): *Protest and survive* (Edited with Smith, Dan); Penguin; London

(1982) 'Notes on exterminism – the last stage of civilisation', *Exterminism and the Cold War*; Verso; London pp 151-163

Thomson, Alex (1992): *Smokescreen: The media, the censors the Gulf*; Laburnham Books; Tunbridge Wells

Timmerman, Kenneth R. (1992): *The death lobby: How the West armed Iraq*; Fourth Estate; London

Toffler, Alvin and Toffler, Heidi (1995): *War and anti-war: Making sense of today's global chaos*; Warner Books; London

Traber, Michael and Davies, Ann (1991); 'Ethics of war reporting', *Media Development*; London, October pp 7-9

Trainor, Lt Gen Bernard E. (1991) 'The military and the media: a troublesome embrace', *The media and the Gulf War*; (ed) Smith, Hedrick. pp 69-80

Treverton, Gregory F. (1987): *Covert action: The CIA and the limits of American intervention in the post-war world*; I.B. Tauris and Co Ltd; London

Tunstall, Jeremy and Palmer, Michael (1991): *Media moguls*; Routledge; London

Tuchman, G. (1978): *Making the news: A study in the construction of reality*; Free Press; New York

Underwood, John and Hulls, Brian (1990): 'Farzad Bazoft: The lessons and the questions', *British Journalism Review*; London, Vol 1 No 3 pp 11-14

Urban, Mark (1996): *UK Eyes Alpha: The inside story of British intelligence*; Faber and Faber; London

Van Alstyne, Richard W. (1974): *The rising American empire*; Norton; New York

Van Evera (1991): 'American intervention in the Third World'; *Security Studies*; London; Autumn. pp 1-24

Vaux, Kenneth L. (1992): *Ethics and the Gulf War: Religion, rhetoric and righteousness*; Westview Press; Boulder, San Francisco

Verrier, Anthony (1983): *Through the looking glass: British foreign policy in the age of illusions*; Jonathan Cape; London

Vidal, Gore (1991): 'The National Security State', *A view from the diners club*; Andre Deutsch; London pp 174-180

Vilanilam, J.V. (1989): *Reporting a revolution*; Sage; Trivandrum

Wallace, William (1970): 'World without tears'; *The age of affluence 1951-1964*; (eds) Bogdanor, Vernon and Skidelsky, Robert pp 192-220

Weeks, John and Gunson, Phil (1991): *Panama: Made in the USA*; Latin American Bureau; London

Weiner, Tim (1996): 'Smart arms in Gulf War are found overrated', *International Herald Tribune*; July 10

Wells, Donald A. (1967): *The war myth*; Pegasus; New York

Williams, Granville (1994): *Britain's media: How they are related*; Campaign for Press and Broadcasting Freedom; London

Williams, Raymond (1962): *Britain in the Sixties: communications*; Penguin; Harmondsworth; Middlesex

Williams, Kevin (1987): 'Vietnam: The first living room war', *The fog of war*; (ed) Mercer, Derrik; Heinemann, London pp 213-260

(1993) 'The light at the end of the tunnel: The mass media, public opinion and the Vietnam War', *Getting the message: News, truth and power*; (ed) Eldridge, John; Routledge; London 305-328

Williams, Reece (1987): (ed) *Unwinding the Vietnam War: From war to peace*; Real Comet Press; Seattle

Wills, Garry (1988): *Reagan's America: Innocents at home*; Heinemann; London

Witherow, John (1989): 'On HMS Invincible for *The Times*', *Untold stories from the Falklands War*; (eds) Bilton, Michael and Kosminsky, Peter; Andre Deutsch, London pp 266-273

Woodward, Bob (1987): *Veil: The secret wars of the CIA*; Simon Schuster; London

(1991): *The commanders*; Simon and Schuster; New York/London

Woodward, Gary C. (1993): 'The rules of the game: The military and the press in the Gulf War', *The media and the Persian Gulf War*; (ed) Denton pp 1-26

Worcester, Robert (1991): *British public opinion – A guide to the history and methodology of public opinion polling*; Basil Blackwell; Oxford

Wright Mills C. (1956): *The power elite*; Oxford University Press; Oxford

Wybrow, Robert (1991): 'The Gulf crisis: a political perspective', *International Journal of Public Opinion Research*; London; Vol 3 No 3

Yallop, David (1994): *To the ends of the earth: The hunt for the Jackal*; Corgi; London

Yant, Martin (1991): *Desert mirage: The true story of the Gulf War*; Prometheus; Buffalo, New York

Young, Hugo (1989): *One of us*; Macmillan; London

Young, Marilyn (1991): 'This is not Vietnam', *Merip*; Massachussetts; July/August pp 21-25

Yousif, Sami (1992): 'The Iraqi US war: A conspiracy theory', *The Gulf War and the new world order* (op cit) pp 51-66

Zakheim, D.S (1991): 'Rating weapons systems in the Gulf War', *Policy Review*; London; Summer

Index